Functional Interfaces in Java

Fundamentals and Examples

Ralph Lecessi

Apress®

Functional Interfaces in Java: Fundamentals and Examples

Ralph Lecessi
Kendall Park, NJ, USA

ISBN-13 (pbk): 978-1-4842-4277-3   ISBN-13 (electronic): 978-1-4842-4278-0
https://doi.org/10.1007/978-1-4842-4278-0

Library of Congress Control Number: 2019932794

Managing Director, Apress Media LLC: Welmoed Spahr
Acquisitions Editor: Steve Anglin
Development Editor: Matthew Moodie
Coordinating Editor: Mark Powers

Cover designed by eStudioCalamar

Cover image designed by Freepik (www.freepik.com)

Distributed to the book trade worldwide by Springer Science+Business Media New York, 233 Spring Street, 6th Floor, New York, NY 10013. Phone 1-800-SPRINGER, fax (201) 348-4505, e-mail orders-ny@springer-sbm.com, or visit www.springeronline.com. Apress Media, LLC is a California LLC and the sole member (owner) is Springer Science + Business Media Finance Inc (SSBM Finance Inc). SSBM Finance Inc is a **Delaware** corporation.

For information on translations, please e-mail editorial@apress.com; for reprint, paperback, or audio rights, please email bookpermissions@springernature.com.

Apress titles may be purchased in bulk for academic, corporate, or promotional use. eBook versions and licenses are also available for most titles. For more information, reference our Print and eBook Bulk Sales web page at http://www.apress.com/bulk-sales.

Any source code or other supplementary material referenced by the author in this book is available to readers on GitHub via the book's product page, located at www.apress.com/9781484242773. For more detailed information, please visit http://www.apress.com/source-code.

Printed on acid-free paper

Table of Contents

About the Author

Ralph Lecessi is a software engineer with over 30 years' professional programming experience in the aerospace, telecommunications, and payment industries at companies including Lockheed Martin, Alcatel-Lucent, AT&T, and Northrop Grumman. He is currently lead embedded software developer at TranSendIT, Inc in Mount Laurel, New Jersey.

Ralph is also the author of *JAVA™ - The Beginnings*—a text on basic Java programming that includes many examples and diagrams.

Ralph is an adjunct professor of programming at Middlesex County College, where he teaches basic and object-oriented programming in Java. He lives in South Brunswick, New Jersey, with his wife and two children.

About the Technical Reviewer

Manuel Jordan Elera is an autodidactic developer and researcher who enjoys learning new technologies for his own experiments and creating new integrations. Manuel won the 2010 Springy Award Community Champion and Spring Champion 2013. In his little free time, he reads the Bible and composes music on his guitar. Manuel is known as dr_pompeii. He has tech-reviewed numerous books for Apress, including *Pro Spring, Fourth Edition* (2014); *Practical Spring LDAP* (2013); *Pro JPA 2, Second Edition* (2013); and *Pro Spring Security* (2013). Read his 13 detailed tutorials about many Spring technologies, contact him through his blog at www.manueljordanelera.blogspot.com, and follow him on his Twitter account, @dr_pompeii.

Foreword

Functional Interfaces in Java shows how to organize and simplify Java programs through the use of functional interfaces.

Chapters 1 and 2 introduce functional interfaces and discuss their implementation using lambda expressions.

Chapters 3 through 7 discuss the functional interfaces present in the `java.util.function` package.

Chapters 8 through 15 show how to use functional interfaces to perform various programming tasks.

The appendix discusses method references and how they can be used in the implementation of functional interfaces.

The text presents each topic with detailed descriptions and many examples. Each chapter also contains a project through which I will guide you step by step to the solution. Each chapter also contains short homework problems which reinforce the subject matter and longer assignments which utilize the current topic to solve a real-world problem.

Knowledge of basic Java programming is needed to understand the examples in this text. If you need a primer on basic Java, I recommend *JAVA™- The Beginnings*.

Here are some notes regarding the programming style used in this book:

1) The rules of encapsulation have been relaxed (most class fields have been given package access) to make the examples easier to read.

2) Method references are not used in the chapter portion of this text. Lambda expressions have been used instead to present a consistent implementation of functional interfaces. Method references are discussed in the appendix.

All examples have been tested in Java 9, Java 10, and Java 11 unless otherwise noted.

I hope you enjoy reading *Functional Interfaces in Java* as much as I have enjoyed writing it.

—Ralph Lecessi

CHAPTER 1

Functional Interfaces

Section 1.1: Interfaces in Java

In Java, an *interface* specifies one or more methods. The interface is a contract which must be honored by all implementing classes. The interface defined in Listing 1-1 specifies methods method1 and method2.

Listing 1-1. I1.java

```java
interface I1
{
    void method1();
    String method2(String x);
}
```

Any class that implements an interface must provide implementations for all the methods declared in the interface (or the class must be declared as abstract). Since the class defined in Listing 1-2 provides implementations for both method1 and method2, objects of class C1 can be instantiated.

Listing 1-2. C1.java

```java
class C1 implements I1
{
    @Override
    public void method1() {}
    @Override
    public String method2(String x) { return x; }
}
```

© Ralph Lecessi 2019
R. Lecessi, *Functional Interfaces in Java*, https://doi.org/10.1007/978-1-4842-4278-0_1

Section 1.2: Enhancements to Interfaces in Java 8 and Java 9

In Java 8, interfaces were allowed to have static and default methods. A static method has a single instance associated with the interface. A *static* method can be called without creation of an object. A *default* method is an implementation provided by the interface that does not have to be overridden by an implementing class. Default methods help in the compilation of legacy code.

The program in Listing 1-3 defines interface I2 that declares field s which contains the string "I2". If a constant is common to all classes which implement an interface, it should be defined as a field in the interface. The interface also defines a static and a default method.

Since method1 is static, it can be called directly from interface I2, without creating an object. When called, it prints "I2", which is the value of field s. Since class C2 overrides method2, the call to method2 from objC2 executes the C2 implementation, which returns the string argument and prints "Hello". Since class C3 does not override method2, the call to method2 from objC3 executes the default implementation provided in interface I2, which concatenates the string argument to field s and prints "I2World".

Listing 1-3. I2.java

```java
interface I2
{
    String s = "I2";
    static void method1()
    {
        System.out.println(s);
    }

    default String method2(String x)
    {
        return s + x;
    }
}
```

```java
class C2 implements I2
{
    @Override
    public String method2(String x) { return x; }
}

class C3 implements I2 {}

class TestI2
{
    public static void main(String[] args)
    {
        I2.method1();
        I2 objC2 = new C2();
        I2 objC3 = new C3();
        System.out.println(objC2.method2("Hello"));
        System.out.println(objC3.method2("World"));
    }
}
```

PROGRAM OUTPUT:

```
I2
Hello
I2World
```

In Java 9, interfaces were allowed to have private methods. Private methods are useful to call from default methods. The program in Listing 1-4 concatenates a random integer between 0 and 99 to the string "Hello". Interface I3 contains private method getNumber which generates the integer. This method is called by default method M1.

Listing 1-4. I3.java

```java
import java.util.Random;
interface I3
{
    private int getNumber() { return (new Random()).nextInt(100); }
    default String M1(String s)
```

```
    {
        return s + getNumber();
    }
}

class C4 implements I3
{
}

class TestI3
{
    public static void main(String[] args)
    {
        I3 objC4 = new C4();
        System.out.println(objC4.M1("Hello"));
    }
}
```

PROGRAM OUTPUT:

Hello21

In Java 9, interfaces can also have private static methods. Since the static methods of an interface can be called without creation of an implementing object, these methods can only be called by public static methods defined in the interface.

Interface I4 in the following program defines public static method getName which calls private static method getPrefix to add the prefix "Mr." or "Ms." based on gender. The getName method can be called from the main method of class TestI4. The getPrefix method can be called only from inside method getName.

Listing 1-5. I4.java

```
interface I4
{
    private static String getPrefix(String p)
    {
        return p.equals("male")? "Mr. " : "Ms. ";
    }
    public static String getName(String n, String p)
```

4

```
    {
        return getPrefix(p) + n;
    }
}

class TestI4
{
    public static void main(String[] args)
    {
        System.out.println(I4.getName("Smith", "female"));
        System.out.println(I4.getName("Jones", "male"));
    }
}
```

PROGRAM OUTPUT:

```
Ms. Smith
Mr. Jones
```

Section 1.3: Functional Interfaces Defined

A *functional interface* is an interface with a single abstract method, called its *functional method.* The code in Listing 1-6 defines functional interface StringProcessor, which specifies functional method process that takes a string argument and returns a string. The @FunctionalInterface annotation instructs the compiler to verify that the interface has only one abstract method.

Listing 1-6. StringProcessor.java

```
@FunctionalInterface
interface StringProcessor
{
        String process(String x);
}
```

If StringProcessor contained more than one abstract method, the @FunctionalInterface annotation would cause a compilation error to be generated. The code in Listing 1-7 demonstrates.

Listing 1-7. StringProcessor.java (Incorrect)

```
@FunctionalInterface    ERROR: Not a functional interface.
                        Contains more than one abstract
                        method.
interface StringProcessor
{
    String process(String x);
    String process2(String x);
}
```

Functional interfaces are ideal for defining a single problem or operation. In Java 8, the API was enhanced to utilize functional interfaces. Many of the functional interfaces can contain static and default methods, making them extendable by the user.

Section 1.4: Implementing Functional Interfaces with Pre-Java 8 Constructs

A functional interface can be implemented by defining a named class that provides the functional method. The class in Listing 1-8 implements functional interface `StringProcessor` by providing an implementation of functional method `process`.

Listing 1-8. NamedStringProcessor.java

```
class NamedStringProcessor implements StringProcessor
{
    @Override
    public String process(String s) { return s; }
}
```

A functional interface can also be implemented by an anonymous class that provides the functional method. The following code defines an anonymous class that implements `StringProcessor`. The anonymous implementation is referenced by variable `anonSP`.

```
StringProcessor anonSP = new StringProcessor() {
    @Override
    public String process(String x)
    {
        return x.toUpperCase();
    }
};
```

The program in Listing 1-9 provides both named class and anonymous class implementations for functional interface StringProcessor.

Listing 1-9. TestStringProcessor.java

```
public class TestStringProcessor
{
    public static void main(String[] args)
    {
        NamedStringProcessor namedSP = new NamedStringProcessor();

        StringProcessor anonSP = new StringProcessor() {
            @Override
            public String process(String x)
            {
                return x.toUpperCase();
            }
        };
        System.out.println(namedSP.process("hello"));
        System.out.println(anonSP.process("hello"));
    }
}
```

PROGRAM OUTPUT:

```
Hello
HELLO
```

Section 1.5: Providing Default Methods in Functional Interfaces

A functional interface can provide default methods. An implementing class can use the default methods or provide its own versions.

Suppose a program needs to print different receipts based on item, price, discount, and tax. Listing 1-10 defines the Receipt class that contains the corresponding fields.

Listing 1-10. Receipt.java

```java
class Receipt
{
    String item;
    double price;
    double discount;
    double tax;
    public Receipt(String i, double a, double d, double s)
    {
        item     = i;
        price    = a;
        discount = d;
        tax      = s;
    }
    public Receipt(Receipt r)
    {
        item     = r.item;
        price    = r.price;
        discount = r.discount;
        tax      = r.tax;
    }
}
```

In order to define a framework for receipt printing, a functional interface with a functional method that accepts a Receipt argument can be utilized. Listing 1-11 defines functional interface ReceiptPrinter whose functional method print accepts a Receipt. ReceiptPrinter also provides a default method that calculates the total amount based on price, discount, and tax, but allows implementing classes to override the calculation. The default method calls private method getDiscounterPrice which applies the discount to the price.

Listing 1-11. ReceiptPrinter.java

```
@FunctionalInterface
interface ReceiptPrinter
{
    void print(Receipt receipt);

    private double getDiscountedPrice(Receipt receipt)
    {
        return receipt.price
            - (receipt.price * receipt.discount);
    }

    default double computeTotal(Receipt receipt)
    {
        double discountedPrice = getDiscountedPrice(receipt);

        return discountedPrice + (discountedPrice * receipt.tax);
    }
}
```

The following ReceiptPrinter implementation prints each Receipt field on a separate line followed by the total. It uses the default total calculation.

```
ReceiptPrinter simpleReceiptPrinter = new ReceiptPrinter() {
    @Override
    public void print(Receipt receipt)
    {
        System.out.println("\nItem :\t" + receipt.item);
        System.out.println("Price:\t"   + receipt.price);
        System.out.println("Disc:\t"    + receipt.discount);
        System.out.println("Tax:\t"     + receipt.tax);
        System.out.println("Total:\t"   + computeTotal(receipt));
    }
};
```

9

The following ReceiptPrinter implementation is for merchants who are exempt from tax. It provides its own implementation of the total calculation which does not include tax.

```
ReceiptPrinter exemptReceiptPrinter = new ReceiptPrinter() {
    @Override
    public void print(Receipt receipt)
    {
        System.out.println("\nItem :\t" + receipt.item);
        System.out.println("Price:\t"   + receipt.price);
        System.out.println("Disc:\t"    + receipt.discount);
        System.out.println("Total:\t"   + computeTotal(receipt));
    }
    @Override
    public double computeTotal(Receipt receipt)
    {
        return receipt.price - (receipt.price * receipt.discount);
    }
};
```

The simpleReceiptPrinter and ExemptReceiptPrinter implementations can be used to print the same receipt. The following code prints one copy of the receipt whose total is based on tax and a second copy of the receipt whose total is not based on tax:

```
Receipt receipt = new Receipt("shirt", 20.00, 0.05, 0.07);
simpleReceiptPrinter.print(receipt);
exemptReceiptPrinter.print(receipt);
```

OUTPUT:

```
Item :    shirt
Amount:   20.0
Disc:     0.05
Tax:      0.07
Total:    20.33

Item :    shirt
Amount:   20.0
Disc:     0.05
Total:    19.0
```

Section 1.6: Providing Static Methods in Functional Interfaces

A functional interface can also have static methods. Static methods are useful to define helper methods that are not meant to be overridden by implementing classes.

Listing 1-12 enhances the StringProcessor interface by adding helper methods to check if a string is uppercase or lowercase.

Listing 1-12. StringProcessor.java (Version 2)

```java
@FunctionalInterface
interface StringProcessor
{
    String process(String s);

    static boolean isLowerCase(String s)
    {
        boolean result = true;
        for (int i = 0; i < s.length() && result; ++i)
            result &= Character.isLowerCase(s.charAt(i));
        return result;
    }

    static boolean isUpperCase(String s)
    {
        boolean result = true;
        for (int i = 0; i < s.length() && result; ++i)
            result &= Character.isUpperCase(s.charAt(i));
        return result;
    }
}
```

In the following example, one StringProcessor implementation is provided whose functional method converts a string to lowercase, and another implementation is provided that converts a string to uppercase:

```
StringProcessor toLowerCase = new StringProcessor() {
    @Override
    public String process(String s)
    {
        return s.toLowerCase();
    }
};

StringProcessor toUpperCase = new StringProcessor() {
    @Override
    public String process(String s)
    {
        return s.toUpperCase();
    }
};
```

The static methods can be used to verify the case of the processed string.

```
String s = toLowerCase.process("FUNCTIONALINTERFACES");
System.out.println(s);
System.out.println("Lower case: " + StringProcessor.isLowerCase(s));
System.out.println("Upper case: " + StringProcessor.isUpperCase(s));

String t = toUpperCase.process(s);
System.out.println("\n" + t);
System.out.println("Lower case: " + StringProcessor.isLowerCase(t));
System.out.println("Upper case: " + StringProcessor.isUpperCase(t));
```

OUTPUT:

```
functionalinterfaces
Lower case: true
Upper case: false

FUNCTIONALINTERFACES
Lower case: false
Upper case: true
```

Section 1.7: Generic Functional Interfaces

Many of the functional interfaces defined in the Java API are generic for one or more types. Suppose a program needs methods that take two arguments of a type and returns a result of the same type, but both the type and the operation performed can vary. A functional interface can be defined that is generic for type X and has a functional method that accepts two arguments of type X and returns a value of type X.

Listing 1-13. TwoArgsProcessor.java

```java
@FunctionalInterface
interface TwoArgsProcessor<X> {
    X process(X arg1, X arg2);
}
```

The program simply needs to provide different implementations of TwoArgsProcessor and call the process method of each. The program in Listing 1-14 declares a TwoArgsProcessor<Integer> implementation that multiplies two Integers. It also declares a TwoArgsProcessor<Double> implementation that adds two Doubles. Lastly, it declares a TwoArgsProcessor<String> implementation that compares two strings and returns the largest.

Listing 1-14. TestTwoArgsProcessor.java

```java
class TestTwoArgsProcessor {
    public static void main(String[] args)
    {
        TwoArgsProcessor<Integer> multiplyInts
            = new TwoArgsProcessor<>() {
                @Override
                public Integer process(Integer arg1, Integer arg2)
                {
                    return arg1 * arg2;
                }
            };
```

```
        TwoArgsProcessor<Double> addDoubles
            = new TwoArgsProcessor<>() {
                @Override
                public Double process(Double arg1, Double arg2)
                {
                    return arg1 + arg2;
                }
            };

        TwoArgsProcessor<String> compareStrings
            = new TwoArgsProcessor<>() {
                @Override
                public String process(String arg1, String arg2)
                {
                    return arg1.compareTo(arg2) > 0? arg1: arg2;
                }
            };

        System.out.println(multiplyInts.process(2,3));
        System.out.println(addDoubles.process(4.1,5.2));
        System.out.println(compareStrings.process("ace","age"));
    }
}
```

PROGRAM OUTPUT:

6
9.3
age

Section 1.7.1: Generic Functional Interfaces with Type Restrictions

Generic functional interfaces can be restricted to certain types. The class in Listing 1-15 extends the Receipt class to include county tax.

Listing 1-15. CountyReceipt.java

```java
public class CountyReceipt extends Receipt
{
    double countyTax;
    public CountyReceipt(Receipt r, double c)
    {
        super(r);
        countyTax = c;
    }
}
```

As a result, the version of `ReceiptPrinter` given in Listing 1-11 is no longer adequate. It should be rewritten as in Listing 1-16 to be generic for classes that extend `Receipt`.

Listing 1-16. ReceiptPrinter.java (Version 2)

```java
@FunctionalInterface
public interface ReceiptPrinter<X extends Receipt>
{
    void print(X receipt);

    private double getDiscountedPrice(X receipt)
    {
        return receipt.price
            - (receipt.price * receipt.discount);
    }

    default double computeTotal(X receipt)
    {
        double discountedPrice = getDiscountedPrice(receipt);

        return discountedPrice + (discountedPrice * receipt.tax);
    }
}
```

simpleReceiptPrint also needs to be rewritten as an implementation of ReceiptPrinter<Receipt>.

```
ReceiptPrinter<Receipt> simpleReceiptPrinter
    = new ReceiptPrinter<> () {
        @Override
        public void print(Receipt receipt)
        {
            System.out.println("\nItem :\t" + receipt.item);
            System.out.println("Price:\t"   + receipt.price);
            System.out.println("Disc:\t"    + receipt.discount);
            System.out.println("Tax:\t"     + receipt.tax);
            System.out.println("Total:\t"   + computeTotal(receipt));
        }
};
```

The following code provides an implementation of ReceiptPrinter<CountyReceipt> that includes the county tax. The total calculation is overridden to include county tax.

```
ReceiptPrinter<CountyReceipt> countyReceiptPrinter
    = new ReceiptPrinter<> () {
        @Override
        public void print(CountyReceipt receipt)
        {
            System.out.println("\nItem :\t" + receipt.item);
            System.out.println("Price:\t"   + receipt.price);
            System.out.println("Disc:\t"    + receipt.discount);
            System.out.println("Tax:\t"     + receipt.tax);
            System.out.println("CnTax:\t"   + receipt.countyTax);
            System.out.println("Total:\t"   + computeTotal(receipt));
        }

        @Override
        public double computeTotal(CountyReceipt receipt)
        {
            double discountedPrice = receipt.price
                            - (receipt.price * receipt.discount);
```

```
        return discountedPrice
            + (discountedPrice * receipt.tax)
            + (discountedPrice * receipt.countyTax);
    }
};
```

The following code uses the two implementations defined previously to print two receipts from the same transaction. Only the second receipt contains county tax.

```
Receipt receipt = new Receipt("shirt", 20.00, 0.05, 0.07);
simpleReceiptPrinter.print(receipt);

CountyReceipt countyReceipt = new CountyReceipt(receipt, 0.04);
countyReceiptPrinter.print(countyReceipt);
```

OUTPUT:

```
Item :   shirt
Price:   20.0
Disc:    0.05
Tax:     0.07
Total:   20.33

Item :   shirt
Price:   20.0
Disc:    0.05
Tax:     0.07
CnTax:   0.04
Total:   21.09
```

Section 1.8: Specializing a Generic Functional Interface

If the generic functional interface of a particular type is used frequently, it is convenient to specialize it for that type. Many examples exist in the Java API. Specialization is accomplished by extending or implementing the generic functional interface of one type. The resulting interface or class is not generic for that type.

Functional interface `TwoArgsProcessor` can be specialized for type Integer by defining a new functional interface that only processes Integers.

```
@FunctionalInterface
public interface TwoIntsProcessor
    extends TwoArgsProcessor<Integer>
{
}
```

`TwoArgsProcessor` can also be specialized by creating an abstract class that processes Integers.

```
abstract class TwoIntsProcessorAbstract
    implements TwoArgsProcessor<Integer>
{
}
```

The program in Listing 1-17 demonstrates that the functional interface `TwoIntsProcessor` is implemented by `multiplyInts` and subtractInts and abstract class `TwoIntsProcessorAbstract` is extended by `divideInts`.

Listing 1-17. TwoIntsProcessor.java

```
@FunctionalInterface
public interface TwoIntsProcessor
    extends TwoArgsProcessor<Integer>
{
}

abstract class TwoIntsProcessorAbstract
    implements TwoArgsProcessor<Integer>
{
}
class TestTwoIntsProcessor {
    public static void main(String[] args)
```

```
    {
        TwoIntsProcessor multiplyInts = new TwoIntsProcessor() {
            @Override public Integer process(Integer arg1,
                                                Integer arg2)
            {
                return arg1 * arg2;
            }
        };

        TwoIntsProcessor subtractInts = new TwoIntsProcessor() {
            @Override public Integer process(Integer arg1,
                                                Integer arg2)
            {
                return arg1 - arg2;
            }
        };

        TwoIntsProcessorAbstract divideInts
            = new TwoIntsProcessorAbstract() {
            @Override public Integer process(Integer arg1,
                                                Integer arg2)
            {
                return arg1 / arg2;
            }
        };

        System.out.println(multiplyInts.process(2,3));
        System.out.println(subtractInts.process(5,2));
        System.out.println(divideInts.process(10,2));
    }
}
```

PROGRAM OUTPUT:

6
3
5

PROJECT 1: Playful Pets

Problem Statement

The Playful Pets pet store wants a program to search for pets currently in the store. The information stored for each pet is name, animal, breed, color, and price. When performing a search, the program should list the first pet that matches the criterion and then list all the pets that match the criterion. The most common search criteria are search by breed and search by price. Use the program to search for poodles and to search for pets for $800 or less.

Solution

A Pet class which stores information pertaining to each pet can be written. The Pet class can contain a list of pets. It should define an equals method to compare two pets' animal and breed.

Listing 1-18. Pet.java

```java
import java.util.*;
public class Pet
{
    String name;
    String animal;
    String breed;
    String color;
    double price;
    static List<Pet> pets = new ArrayList<>();
    public Pet(String n, String a, String b, String c, double p)
    {
        name   = n;
        animal = a;
        breed  = b;
        color  = c;
        price  = p;
    }
    @Override
    public String toString()
```

```
    {
        return name + ":" + " a " + color + " " + breed
            + " " + animal + " for $" + price;
    }
    @Override
    public boolean equals(Object o)
    {
        Pet p = (Pet)o;
        return animal.equals(p.animal) && breed.equals(p.breed);
    }
}
```

A functional interface whose functional method matches a search criterion can be written. PetMatcher's match method returns a list of pets. PetMatcher should also have a default method called first that uses the Pet class's equals method to find the first match, therefore matching by animal and breed.

```
@FunctionalInterface
interface PetMatcher
{
    List<Pet> match(Pet pet);
    default Pet first(Pet pet)
    {
        int index = Pet.pets.indexOf(pet);
        return index > -1? Pet.pets.get(index) : null;
    }
}
```

An implementation of PetMatcher that searches by animal and breed can be provided. This implementation will use the default implementation of the first method.

```
PetMatcher breedMatcher = new PetMatcher() {
    @Override
    public List<Pet> match(Pet pet)
    {
        List<Pet> matches = new ArrayList<>();
```

```
        for (Pet p : Pet.pets)
            if (p.equals(pet))
                matches.add(p);
        return matches;
    }
};
```

An implementation of PetMatcher that searches by price can also be provided. This implementation defines its own implementation of the first method.

```
PetMatcher priceMatcher = new PetMatcher() {
    @Override
    public List<Pet> match(Pet pet)
    {
        List<Pet> matches = new ArrayList<>();
        for (Pet p : Pet.pets)
            if (p.price <= pet.price)
                matches.add(p);
        return matches;
    }
    @Override
    public Pet first(Pet pet)
    {
        int index = -1;
        for(Pet p : Pet.pets)
            if (p.price <= pet.price)
                return p;
        return null;
    }
};
```

The complete program is shown and demonstrated as follows. The breedMatcher implementation is used to find the poodles in the store. This returns the first poodle, Scruffy, followed by a list containing Scruffy and Max. Then, the priceMatcher implementation is used to find pets available in the store for $800 or less. This returns the first match, Meow the cat, followed by a list containing Meow the cat, Max the poodle, and Slider the snake.

Listing 1-19. PlayfulPets.java

```java
import java.util.*;

@FunctionalInterface
interface PetMatcher
{
    List<Pet> match(Pet pet);
    default Pet first(Pet pet)
    {
        int index = Pet.pets.indexOf(pet);
        return index > -1? Pet.pets.get(index) : null;
    }
}

class PlayfulPets
{
    private static void matchPet(String criteria,
                                 PetMatcher matcher, Pet pet)
    {
        System.out.println("\n" + criteria + ":");
        System.out.println("First: " + matcher.first(pet));
        System.out.println("All matches:");
        List<Pet> matches = matcher.match(pet);
        for (Pet p : matches)
            System.out.println(p);
    }

    public static void main(String[] args)
    {
        Pet.pets.add(new Pet("Scruffy","dog","poodle",
                             "white",895.00));
        Pet.pets.add(new Pet("Meow","cat","siamese","white",740.25));
        Pet.pets.add(new Pet("Max","dog","poodle","black",540.50));
        Pet.pets.add(new Pet("Cuddles","dog","pug","black",1282.75));
        Pet.pets.add(new Pet("Slider","snake","garden",
                             "green",320.00));
```

```java
PetMatcher breedMatcher = new PetMatcher() {
    @Override
    public List<Pet> match(Pet pet)
    {
        List<Pet> matches = new ArrayList<>();
        for (Pet p : Pet.pets)
            if (p.equals(pet))
                matches.add(p);
        return matches;
    }
};

PetMatcher priceMatcher = new PetMatcher() {
    @Override
    public List<Pet> match(Pet pet)
    {
        List<Pet> matches = new ArrayList<>();
        for (Pet p : Pet.pets)
            if (p.price <= pet.price)
                matches.add(p);
        return matches;
    }
    @Override
    public Pet first(Pet pet)
    {
        int index = -1;
        for(Pet p : Pet.pets)
            if (p.price <= pet.price)
                return p;
        return null;
    }
};
```

```
matchPet("Poodles",breedMatcher,
        new Pet(null, "dog", "poodle", null, 0.0));
matchPet("Pets for $800 or less",priceMatcher,
        new Pet(null, null, null, null, 800.0));
    }
}
```

PROGRAM OUTPUT:

```
Poodles:
First: Scruffy: a white poodle dog for $895.0
All matches:
Scruffy: a white poodle dog for $895.0
Max: a black poodle dog for $540.5

Pets for $800 or less:
First: Meow: a white siamese cat for $740.25
All matches:
Meow: a white siamese cat for $740.25
Max: a black poodle dog for $540.5
Slider: a green garden snake for $320.0
```

Short Problems

1) Write a functional interface named InputStreamOpener whose
   functional method, named open, accepts a String argument
   and returns an InputStream. Write an implementation that
   opens a DataInputStream. Write a second implementation that
   opens an ObjectInputStream. Write a third implementation that
   opens a BufferedInputStream. Use anonymous classes for all
   implementation. Demonstrate the implementation in a main
   program.

2) Write a generic functional interface named Summer, and use it to
   compute the sum of two Integers, the sum of two Doubles, and the
   sum of two Longs.

25

3) Write a functional interface named `ListManipulator` that is generic for type T. Its functional method, named `manipulate`, accepts a `List<T>` and a T as arguments and returns `void`. `ListManipulator` has a default method named `create` that creates an `ArrayList<T>`. The default method takes no arguments and returns a `List<T>`.

Write three implementations of `ListManipulator`:

- `sListAdd` which implements `ListManipulator<String>` and whose functional method adds an element of type T to the end of the list

- `iListAdd` which implements `ListManipulator<Integer>` and whose functional method adds an element of type T to the end of the list

- `iListRmv` which implements `ListManipulator<Integer>` and whose functional method removes the first occurrence of an element of type T from the list

Implementations `iListAdd` and `iListRmv` override default method `create` with an implementation that sets the initial `ArrayList` capacity to 50 elements.

Demonstrate the three implementations in a main program.

Long Problems

1) Write a functional interface named `ToString` that is generic for type T. Its functional method, named convert, converts a T to a `String`.

Write two implementations of ToString:

- `l2s` which converts a List<String> by creating a comma-separated string

- `m2s` which converts a Map<String,Integer> by creating a comma-separated field for each map entry with a colon between the key and the value

Demonstrate the two implementations in a main program.

2) Write a functional interface named `Area,` and use it to compute the area of a circle, a rectangle, and an isosceles right triangle. Include a `numberOfSides` method that by default returns 4.

3) A typical used car's list value is its original price minus $1000 per year since its manufacturing minus $500 for every 10,000 miles driven. A used sports car's list value adds back a $250 vintage factor for every year since its manufacturing.

Write a functional interface named `ListValue` which computes the list value for both typical cars and sports cars.

CHAPTER 2

Lambda Expressions

If your applications require many implementations of functional interfaces, you would have to create many named classes or inline many anonymous class implementations. This would make your code excessively large and difficult to read. Fortunately, Java 8 has provided lambda expressions to represent functional interfaces using a very succinct syntax.

Section 2.1: Lambda Expressions Defined

A *lambda expression* is used to represent a statement. They were introduced in Java 8 to support functional programming. The basic form of a lambda expression is the following:

```
lambda_argument_list -> lambda_body
```

Section 2.2: Using Lambda Expressions to Represent Functional Interfaces

Lambda expressions are used to represent functional interfaces. The code specified in `lambda_body` provides the implementation of the functional method. The arguments to the functional method are specified in `lambda_argument_list`.

The functional interface `StringProcessor` defined in Section 3 of Chapter 1 has functional method process, which takes a string argument and returns a string.

```
@FunctionalInterface
interface StringProcessor
{
    String process(String x);
}
```

© Ralph Lecessi 2019
R. Lecessi, *Functional Interfaces in Java*, https://doi.org/10.1007/978-1-4842-4278-0_2

This can be represented by the following lambda expression:

```
x -> x
```

The argument provided in `lambda_argument_list`, namely, x, becomes the argument to functional method `process`. Since `Lambda_body` contains a single expression, it is said to be specified in *expression form*. The expression is evaluated and then returned as the `String` result of method `process`. In this example, the `Lambda_body` is explicitly specified as the String variable x. Since this is merely an expression, it does not end in a semicolon or contain the return keyword.

The following statement assigns the lambda expression to an object of a class that implements functional interface `StringProcessor`:

```
StringProcessor lambdaSP = x -> x;
```

When the functional method of the object is called, the lambda expression executes passing "Hello" into parameter x in `lambda_arg_list`. The expression x is evaluated and "Hello" is provided as the return value of the `process` method.

```
System.out.println(lambdaSP.process("Hello"));
```

OUTPUT:

```
Hello
```

If the functional method represented by a lambda has return type `void`, the body of the lambda must be an expression that results in a `void` type. Listing 2-1 defines functional interface `FIVoid` whose functional method `method1` has return type `void`.

Listing 2-1. FIVoid.java

```
@FunctionalInterface
interface FIVoid
{
    void method1(int i);
}
```

The body of any lambda expression that represents `FIVoid` must then be an expression that results in a `void` type. The following example uses a `System.out.println` statement, which has `void` return type, as the body of a lambda that represents functional interface `FIVoid`. Lambda argument x represents the i formal parameter of the `method1` in interface `FIVoid`.

```
FIVoid LambdaVoid = x -> System.out.println(x);
LambdaVoid.method1(5);
```

OUTPUT:

5

Section 2.3: The Scope of a Lambda Expression

The scope of a lambda coincides with the definition of the expression. Therefore, any variables that are in scope at the definition of a lambda expression are in scope for the functional method it represents. This include fields and final or effectively final local variables (non-final local variables whose value doesn't changed after initialization). In the program of Listing 2-2, the lambda expression is defined on lines 7 and 8, and both static field myField and effectively final local variable myLocal are in scope. Functional method method1 adds its argument, myField, and myLocal together and prints 14.

Listing 2-2. TestLambdaScope.java

```
 1: class TestLambdaScope
 2: {
 3:     private static int myField = 2;
 4:     public static void main(String[] args)
 5:     {
 6:         int myLocal = 7;
 7:         FIVoid lambdaVoid = x -> System.out.println(
 8:                                 x + myField + myLocal);
 9:
10:         lambdaVoid.method1(5);
11:     }
12: }
```

PROGRAM OUTPUT:

14

Local variables used in lambda expressions must be final or effectively final. If myLocal in the previous example were to be assigned a new value, then the lambda expression definition would generate an error.

```
int myLocal = 7;
myLocal++;

FIVoid lambdaVoid
    = x -> System.out.println(          ERROR: local variables used
                x + myField + myLocal);    in lambdas must be
                                           final or effectively
                                           final
```

Section 2.4: Lambda Argument List Variations

If lambda_arg_list contains a single argument and the type of the argument can be inferred, the argument may be specified without parentheses.

```
x -> x
```

A type may be provided for the argument, but then lambda_arg_list must be enclosed in parentheses.

```
(String x) -> x
```

The following example attempts to pass an instance of Z<A> to static method m2, but the compiler is unable to infer from lambda argument x that its type is A, and an error is generated.

```
class A { int i; }
@FunctionalInterface
interface Z<T>
{
    int m(T t);
}

class Inference
```

```
{
    static <T> void m2(Z<T> arg) {}
    public static void main(String[] args)
    {
        m2(x -> x.i); // ERROR
    }
}
```

Providing the type of lambda argument x fixes the problem.

```
m2( (A x) -> x.i); // OK
```

If `lambda_arg_list` contains several arguments, each must be separated by a comma, and the list must be enclosed by parentheses. The argument types do not need to be specified if they can be inferred by the compiler.

```
(x, y) -> x + y
```

In the following example, functional method `method1` takes a `String` and an `int` argument:

```
@FunctionalInterface
interface FI2
{
    String method1(String x, int y);
}
```

The compiler is able to infer the types of the two lambda arguments, so the types do not need to be provided.

```
FI2 fi2Lambda1 = (a, b) -> a + Integer.toString(b);
```

However, types may be provided if desired.

```
FI2 fi2Lambda2 = (String c, int d) -> c + Integer.toString(d+1);
```

```
System.out.println(fi2Lambda1.method1("Hello",1));
System.out.println(fi2Lambda2.method1("Hello",1));
```

OUTPUT:

```
Hello1
Hello2
```

If `lambda_arg_list` contains no arguments, it must be specified by an empty set of parentheses.

```
() -> 5
```

The functional interface defined in Listing 2-3 specifies functional method `method1` that takes no arguments.

Listing 2-3. FI3.java

```
@FunctionalInterface
interface FI3
{
    Integer method1();
}
```

The argument list for any lambda that represents `FI3` must consist of an empty set of parentheses. The following example represents `FI3` with a lambda expression that accepts no arguments and returns the `Integer` value 99:

```
FI3 fi3Lambda1 = () -> 99;
System.out.println(fi3Lambda1.method1());
```

OUTPUT:

99

Section 2.5: Lambda Bodies in Block Form

Enclosing the body of a lambda in curly braces places it in *block form*.

Expression Form:

```
FIVoid lambda1 = x -> System.out.println(x);
```

Block Form:

```
FIVoid lambda2 = x -> { System.out.println(x); };
```

In block form, the lambda body may consist of multiple statements, each ending in a semicolon. The following example uses a lambda expression in block form to represent functional interface FIVoid. The `lambda_body` contains two statements: the first statement increments lambda parameter x, and the second statement prints x. Note that each statement ends in a semicolon and that a semicolon must follow the curly brace that encloses the lambda expression.

```
FIVoid lambdaBlock = x -> {
    x++;
    System.out.println(x);
};

lambdaBlock.method1(5);
```

OUTPUT:

```
6
```

If a lambda expression in block form returns a value, a `return` statement must be provided. The following example uses a lambda expression in block form to represent functional interface `StringProcessor` from Chapter 1. The lambda expression contains a return statement that concatenates lambda parameter x with itself and returns the result as the `String` return value of the `process` method.

```
StringProcessor spBlock = x -> {
    System.out.print(x + " ");
    return x + x;
};

System.out.println(spBlock.process("Hello"));
```

OUTPUT:

```
Hello HelloHello
```

A lambda expression in block form is similar to a method body in that it may contain local variables. However, since the lambda is just a series of expressions and not a separate scope, local variable names must be unique in the current scope. The lambda expression in the following example declares local variable z. Since a variable named z already exists in the current scope, a compilation error occurs.

```
int z = 2;
FIVoid lambdaLocalBad = x -> {
    int z =4;                        ERROR: z already defined
    System.out.println(x + z);
};
```

The lambda expression must choose something else for the name of its local variable.

```
int z = 2;
FIVoid lambdaLocalGood = x -> {
    int y =4;                        // OK
    System.out.println(x + y);
};

lambdaLocalGood.method1(8);
```

OUTPUT:

12

A lambda expression may also contain if statements and loops. The lambda expression in the following example contains an if statement inside a for loop that increments local variable oddSum each time the loop counter is odd.

```
FIVoid lambdaOddSum = x -> {
    int oddSum = 0;
    for (int i = 0; i <= x; ++i) {
        if ( i%2 != 0)
            oddSum += i;
    }
    System.out.println(oddSum);
};

lambdaOddSum.method1(7);
```

OUTPUT:

16

A lambda expression may also contain exception handling. The lambda expression in the following example contains a `try/catch` block that protects its code from an `ArrayIndexOutOfBounds` exception. The exception is thrown and caught when `FIVoid` implementation `lambdaSubscript` is called with the value 5.

```
int[] array = {11,12,13,14,15};
FIVoid lambdaSubscript = x -> {
    try {
        int value = array[x];
        System.out.println(value);
    } catch (ArrayIndexOutOfBoundsException e) {
        System.out.println("Index " + x + " is out of bounds.");
    }
};

lambdaSubscript.method1(5);
lambdaSubscript.method1(4);
```

OUTPUT:

```
Index 5 is out of bounds.
15
```

Section 2.6: Limitations of Lambda Expressions

The code in a lambda expression becomes the functional method of the functional interface it implements. Therefore, lambdas cannot be used to override a functional interface's default method. If overriding the default method is required, a named or anonymous class must be used. For example, the following code attempts to use a lambda expression to implement the ReceiptPrinter functional interface and override default method computeTotal. The default method implementation inside the lambda generates a compilation error.

```
ReceiptPrinter exemptReceiptPrinter = x -> {
    System.out.println("\nItem :\t"  + x.item);
    System.out.println("Price:\t"    + x.price);
    System.out.println("Disc:\t"     + x.discount);
    System.out.println("Tax:\t"      + x.tax);
```

```
    public double computeTotal(Receipt receipt)// ERROR: illegal
                                            // start of expression
    {
        return receipt.price - (receipt.price * receipt.discount);
    }
};
```

Since the `simpleReceiptPrinter` implementation from Section 5 of Chapter 1 does not override default method `computeTotal`, it can be represented by a lambda expression.

```
ReceiptPrinter simpleReceiptPrinter = x -> {
    System.out.println("\nItem :\t"  + x.item);
    System.out.println("Price:\t"    + x.price);
    System.out.println("Disc:\t"     + x.discount);
    System.out.println("Tax:\t"      + x.tax);
};
```

Note that it is not possible to call `computeTotal` from inside the lambda expression. This is because the lambda expression is just simple code that has no idea it is part of an implementation of interface `ReceiptPrinter`, so calling an instance method is not possible.

```
ReceiptPrinter simpleReceiptPrinter = x -> {
System.out.println("\nItem :\t"  + x.item);
System.out.println("Price:\t"    + x.price);
System.out.println("Disc:\t"     + x.discount);
System.out.println("Total:\t"
        + computeTotal(x)); // ERROR: cannot find symbol
                            // method computeTotal(Receipt)
```

Instead, `computeTotal` can be explicitly called from outside the lambda expression.

```
Receipt receipt = new Receipt("shirt", 20.00, 0.05, 0.07);
simpleReceiptPrinter.print(receipt);
System.out.println("Total:\t"
                + simpleReceiptPrinter.computeTotal(receipt));
```

OUTPUT:

```
Item :   shirt
Price:   20.0
Disc:    0.05
Tax:     0.07
Total:   20.33
```

Lambda expressions can be used to represent implementations of functional interfaces that contain static methods as well. Functional interface `StringProcessor` from Section 6 of Chapter 1 contains static methods `isLowerCase` and `isUpperCase`. Implementations `toLowerCase` and `toUpperCase` can be implemented by lambda expressions.

```
StringProcessor toLowerCase = x -> x.toLowerCase();

String s = toLowerCase.process("FUNCTIONALINTERFACES");
System.out.println(s);
System.out.println("Lower case: " + StringProcessor.isLowerCase(s));
System.out.println("Upper case: " + StringProcessor.isUpperCase(s));

StringProcessor toUpperCase = x -> x.toUpperCase();

String t = toUpperCase.process(s);
System.out.println("\n" + t);
System.out.println("Lower case: " + StringProcessor.isLowerCase(t));
System.out.println("Upper case: " + StringProcessor.isUpperCase(t));
```

OUTPUT:

```
functionalinterfaces
Lower case: true
Upper case: false

FUNCTIONALINTERFACES
Lower case: false
Upper case: true
```

Lambda expressions cannot be used to represent abstract classes that specialize generic functional interfaces. If a lambda expression is used in the implementation of abstract class `TwoIntsProcessorAbstract` from Section 8 of Chapter 1, a compilation error will be generated.

```
TwoIntsProcessorAbstract divideInts = (x,y) -> x / y    ERROR:
TwoIntsProcessorAbstract is not a functional interface
```

PROJECT 2: Compute Square

Problem Statement

Write an application with a Swing graphical user interface (GUI) that displays two text fields and a button. A user enters a number in the first text field. When the user presses the button, the square of the number is displayed in the second text field. If the text in the first field is not a number, a message stating that the text is not a number is displayed.

Solution

An implementation of the `ActionListener` interface is registered with a `Swing` `JButton` in order to specify the action performed when the button is pressed.

```
public interface ActionListener extends EventListener
{
    void actionPerformed(ActionEvent event);
}
```

Although `ActionListener` is not annotated with `@FunctionalInterface`, it contains a single abstract method, and therefore its implementations can be represented by lambda expressions. In the following example, a lambda expression is used to provide the code that is executed by the `actionPerformed` method. The `lambda_arg_list` contains one argument x of type `ActionEvent`. When the user presses `myButton`, the string "Button Pressed" is displayed.

```
JButton myButton = new JButton("Press me");
myButton.addActionListener(
    x -> System.out.println("Button Pressed"));
```

In this program, the button needs an `ActionListener` that reads the string entered in a text field, converts it to an integer, and then displays the square of the integer in another text field. The listener also needs to detect if the entered text is not a number and to display an error message if so.

Since lambda expressions can contain exception handling, its code can be protected from the `NumberFormatException` that occurs when a non-numeric string is parsed as an integer, and the caught exception can be used to print an error message.

```java
submit = new JButton("Submit");
submit.addActionListener( x -> {
    try {
        int num = Integer.parseInt(number.getText());
        square.setText(Integer.toString(num*num));
    }
    catch (NumberFormatException e) {
        System.out.println(number.getText() + " is not a number");
    }
});
```

The complete program is shown and demonstrated as follows. When 10 is entered and the button is pressed, 100 appears in the second text field. When "s" is entered and the button is pressed, the `ActionListener` represented by the lambda expression catches a `NumberFormatException`, and an error message is displayed.

Listing 2-4. ComputeSquare.java

```java
import javax.swing.*;
import java.awt.*;
import java.awt.event.ActionListener;
class ComputeSquare extends JFrame
{
    JTextField number;
    JTextField square;
    JButton submit;
    JPanel panel;
    public ComputeSquare()
    {
```

```java
        number = new JTextField(10);
        square = new JTextField(10);
        submit = new JButton("Submit");

        submit.addActionListener( x -> {
            try {
                int num = Integer.parseInt(number.getText());
                square.setText(Integer.toString(num*num));
            }
            catch (NumberFormatException e) {
                System.out.println(number.getText()
                                    + " is not a number");
            }
        });

        panel = new JPanel();
        setSize(200,130);
        panel.add(number);
        panel.add(square);
        panel.add(submit);
        add(panel);
        setDefaultCloseOperation(JFrame.EXIT_ON_CLOSE);
        setVisible(true);
    }
    public static void main(String[] args)
    {
        new ComputeSquare();
    }
}
```

PROGRAM OUTPUT (events shown in **BOLD** and parentheses):

(type "10" in first text field)
(press Submit)
("100" appears in second text field)
(type "s" in first text field)
s is not a number

Short Problems

1) Rewrite the functional interface implementations from short problem 1 from Chapter 1 using lambda functions. Demonstrate in a main program.

2) Rewrite the functional interface implementations from short problem 2 from Chapter 1 using lambda functions. Demonstrate in a main program.

3) Remove the default method from functional interface `ListManipulator` in short problem 3 from Chapter 1. Then rewrite the implementations using lambda expressions.

Long Problems

1) Implement long homework problem 1 from Chapter 1 using lambda expressions.

2) Implement long homework problem 3 from Chapter 1 using lambda expressions.

3) Write a functional interface named `SumFromZero` whose functional method accepts a single argument and returns the sum of all numbers from zero up to and including the argument. Implement `SumFromZero` using a lambda expression.

CHAPTER 3

Predicates

Section 3.1: The java.util.function Package

In Java 8, the java.util.function package was added to the Java API. It contains many functional interfaces designed to assist with functional programming. These functional interfaces follow one of four basic models:

Table 3-1. *Basic Models for java.util.function Interfaces*

Model	Has Arguments	Returns a Value	Description
Predicate	yes	boolean	Tests argument and returns true or false.
Function	yes	yes	Maps one type to another.
Consumer	yes	no	Consumes input (returns nothing).
Supplier	no	yes	Generates output (using no input).

Many of the interfaces in the java.util.function package are generic, but in several cases specializations are available.

Section 3.2: The Predicate Interface

Predicate is a functional interface whose functional method, called test, evaluates a condition on an input variable of a generic type. The test method returns true if the condition is true, and false otherwise.

```
@FunctionalInterface
public interface Predicate<T>
{
    boolean test(T t);
```

© Ralph Lecessi 2019
R. Lecessi, *Functional Interfaces in Java*, https://doi.org/10.1007/978-1-4842-4278-0_3

```
    // some static and default methods
    ...
}
```

A Predicate of Integer type is declared as follows:

```
 Predicate<Integer> p1;
```

Predicate p1's test method will accept an Integer argument, and return true if its condition results in true.

Predicate p1 can be used to check if an integer is greater than 7. The following statement uses a lambda expression to represent this condition:

```
 p1 = x -> x > 7;
```

The lambda accepts a single argument x, and its expression results in true when x is greater than 7.

Since the Predicate interface's test method returns a boolean result, it can be used as the boolean expression of an if statement.

```
if ( p1.test(9))
    System.out.println("Predicate x > 7 is true for x==9.");
```

The program in Listing 3-1 demonstrates. The first boolean expression results in true, while the second boolean expression results in false.

Listing 3-1. TestTest.java

```
import java.util.function.*;
class TestTest
{
    public static void main(String[] args)
    {
        Predicate<Integer> p1 = x -> x > 7;

        if (p1.test(9))
            System.out.println("Predicate x > 7 is true for x==9.");
        else
            System.out.println("Predicate x > 7 is false for x==9.");
```

```
        if (p1.test(3))
            System.out.println("Predicate x > 7 is true for x==3.");
        else
            System.out.println("Predicate x > 7 is false for x==3.");
    }
}
```

PROGRAM OUTPUT:

```
Predicate x > 7 is true for x==9.
Predicate x > 7 is false for x==3.
```

Section 3.3: Passing a Predicate to a Method

When a predicate is passed to a method and the Predicate object's test method is called inside the method, whatever condition that was associated with the predicate will be executed. Therefore, if several Predicate objects are defined, the same logic can be applied to each condition by passing each predicate to a method.

The program in Listing 3-2 demonstrates. The first time the result method is called, Predicate p's test method checks if arg is equal to 5. The second time result is called, Predicate p's test method checks if arg is even.

Since the result method expects a Predicate<Integer> as its first argument, a lambda expression can be directly provided in the call to result without the use of a reference variable. This is done in the second call to result, where a lambda which tests for evenness is provided directly in the first argument of the result method.

Listing 3-2. PredicateMethods.java

```
import java.util.function.*;
class PredicateMethods
{
    public static void result(Predicate<Integer> p, Integer arg)
    {
        if (p.test(arg))
            System.out.println("The Predicate is true for " + arg);
        else
            System.out.println("The Predicate is false for " + arg);
```

```
    }
    public static void main(String[] args)
    {
        Predicate<Integer> p1 = x -> x == 5;

        result(p1,5);
        result(y -> y%2 == 0, 5);
    }
}
```

PROGRAM OUTPUT:

```
The Predicate is true for 5
The Predicate is false for 5
```

The result method in Listing 3-2 can only accept Predicate<Integer> objects. This method can be made generic by defining a type parameter in its header as shown in Listing 3-3. Then, the result method can accept Predicate objects of any type.

Listing 3-3. PredicateHelper.java

```
import java.util.function.*;
class PredicateHelper
{
    public static <X> void result(Predicate<X> p, X arg)
    {
        if (p.test(arg))
            System.out.println("The Predicate is true for " + arg);
        else
            System.out.println("The Predicate is false for " + arg);
    }
}
```

The program in Listing 3-4 demonstrates. Reference variables p1 and p2 specify the type of the Predicate object passed to the result method. The first time result is called, Integer is substituted for type parameter T. The second time result is called, String is substituted for type parameter T.

Listing 3-4. TestPredicateHelper.java

```java
import java.util.function.*;
import static PredicateHelper.result;
class TestPredicateHelper
{
    public static void main(String[] args)
    {
        Predicate<Integer> p1 = x -> x > 2;
        Predicate<String>  p2 = s -> s.charAt(0) == 'H';
        result(p1, 6);
        result(p2, "Hello");
    }
}
```

PROGRAM OUTPUT:

```
The Predicate is true for 6
The Predicate is true for Hello
```

If a reference variable is not provided, Java will attempt to infer the data type of the Predicate object. In the following example, Java is able to infer the Integer type because the int literal 6 is passed as parameter arg.

```java
result(x -> x > 2, 6);
```

In the following example, Java is able to infer the String type because the string literal "Hello" is passed as arg.

```java
result(s -> s.charAt(0) == 'H', "Hello");
```

In the following example, a compilation error occurs because the String type is inferred due to string literal "Hello" which cannot be compared relationally to the int literal 2.

```java
result(x -> x > 2, "Hello"); ERROR
```

49

Section 3.4: Chains of Functional Interfaces

Many of the functional interfaces in the `java.util.function` package have default methods that return new functional interface objects, whose methods can, in turn, be called down the method chain. Using this technique, long chains of functional interfaces can be used to perform series of calculations and to inline the logic of your program.

Section 3.5: Predicate Chaining Creates Complex Logical Expressions

Since the `Predicate` interface's default methods return new `Predicate` objects, chains of predicates can be used to create complex logical expressions. A predicate chain combines the logic performed by two consecutive predicates into a *composed predicate*. The composed predicate of the first two operations becomes the first operand of the second composed predicate, and so on. Functional method `test`, which should be the final link in the chain, is evaluated first, followed by each link of the chain in order.

Assuming p1, p2, p3, and p4 are Predicate<Integer> implementations, and `method2`, `method3`, and `method4` are one of the methods described later in this section, then the following predicate chain executes predicate p1 followed by p2, followed by p3, followed by p4 on the integer value 5, provided that none of the predicates have been short-circuited.

```
p1.method2(p2)    // p2 second
  .method3(p3)    // p3 third
  .method4(p4)    // p4 fourth
  .test(5);       // p1 first
```

Section 3.5.1: Chains Involving the OR Operation

Suppose a program needs to evaluate the logical expression x > 7 || x < 3. This can be accomplished by performing the OR operation on two predicates, one with condition x > 7 and another with condition x < 3. The `Predicate` interface's default `or` method does this by creating a composed predicate whose condition is the logical OR of the existing predicate's condition with the condition of its argument.

```
default Predicate<T> or(Predicate<? super T> other);
```

The resulting predicate is the logical OR of both conditions. A composed predicate which evaluates x > 7 || x < 3 is written as follows:

```
Predicate<Integer> p1 = x -> x > 7;
System.out.println(p1.or(x -> x < 3)
                      .test(9));
```

OUTPUT:

```
true
```

Since the logical OR operation is short-circuited, and condition x > 7 is true when x equals 9, the condition x < 3 is not evaluated and true is displayed.

The following example evaluates the same predicate without declaring a reference variable through the use of a typecast:

```
System.out.println(((Predicate<Integer>)(x -> x > 7))
                                        .or(x -> x < 3)
                                        .test(2));
```

OUTPUT:

```
true
```

The program in Listing 3-5 further demonstrates the use of the or method in predicate chains. The composed predicate in the first call to result is short-circuited because condition 9 > 7 is true. The predicates in the second and third calls are not short-circuited, and condition 9 < 3 is evaluated.

Listing 3-5. TestOr.java

```
import java.util.function.*;
import static PredicateHelper.result;
class TestOr
{
    public static void main(String[] args)
    {
        Predicate<Integer> p1 = x -> x > 7;
```

```
        result(p1.or(x -> x < 3), 9);
        result(p1.or(x -> x < 3), 2);
        result(p1.or(x -> x < 3), 5);
    }
}
```

PROGRAM OUTPUT:

```
The Predicate is true for 9
The Predicate is true for 2
The Predicate is false for 5
```

Section 3.5.2: Chains Involving the AND Operation

Suppose a program needs to evaluate the logical expression $x > 7$ && $x\%2 == 1$. The Predicate interface's default and method accomplishes this by creating a composed predicate whose condition is the logical AND of the existing predicate's condition with the condition of its argument.

```
default Predicate<T> and(Predicate<? super T> other);
```

The composed predicate which evaluates $x > 7$ && $x\%2 == 1$ is written as follows:

```
Predicate<Integer> p1 = x -> x > 7;
System.out.println(p1.and(x -> x%2 == 1) // 9 > 7 evaluated first,
                 .test(9));           // then AND'ed with 9%2 == 1
```

OUTPUT:

```
true
```

The System.out.println statement prints true because both conditions $9 > 7$ and $9\%2 == 1$ are true.

The program in Listing 3-6 further demonstrates the use of the and method in predicate chains. The composed predicates in the first two calls to result are short-circuited because their arguments are not greater than 7. The predicates in the third and fourth calls are not short-circuited because their arguments are greater than 7, so each argument must be tested for oddness.

Listing 3-6. TestAnd.java

```java
import java.util.function.*;
import static PredicateHelper.result;
class TestAnd
{
    public static void main(String[] args)
    {
        Predicate<Integer> p1 = x -> x > 7;

        result(p1.and(y -> y%2 ==1), 3);
        result(p1.and(y -> y%2 ==1), 4);
        result(p1.and(y -> y%2 ==1), 9);
        result(p1.and(y -> y%2 ==1), 10);
    }
}
```

PROGRAM OUTPUT:

```
The Predicate is false for 3
The Predicate is false for 4
The Predicate is true for 9
The Predicate is false for 10
```

Section 3.5.3: Chains Involving the ! Operation

The Predicate interface's default negate method reverses the result of the current predicate.

```java
default Predicate<T> negate();
```

In the following example, the condition of the current predicate, 9 > 7, is true. The negate method returns a new predicate with the opposite result, and false is displayed.

```java
Predicate<Integer> p1 = x -> x > 7;
System.out.println(p1.negate()
                     .test(9));
```

53

OUTPUT:

```
false
```

In a chain of predicates, the position of negate matters. For example:

```
Predicate<Integer> p1 = x -> x > 7;

System.out.println(p1.and(x -> x%2 == 1)
                     .negate()
                     .test(8) );

System.out.println(p1.negate()
                     .and(x -> x%2 == 1)
                     .test(8) );
```

OUTPUT:

```
true
false
```

In the first `println` statement, the composed predicate of `p1` with the `and` predicate is negated. This results in the expression `!( (x > 7) && (x%2 == 1) )`, which results in `true` when x is 8.

In the second `println` statement, only `Predicate p1` is negated. This results in the expression `( !(x > 7) && (x%2 == 1) )`, which results in `false` when x is 8.

Section 3.5.4: Using `Predicate.isEqual`

The `Predicate` interface's static `isEqual` method uses the `equals` method of the `Predicate` object's type parameter to check if the argument to the `test` method is equal to a value.

```
static <T> Predicate<T> isEqual(Object targetRef);
```

In the following example, the `isEqual` method uses the `equals` method of the `Integer` class to create a `Predicate<Integer>` that checks if an integer is equal to 3. Since `Predicate p2's test` method is called with the value 3, the string "The Predicate is true" is printed.

```
Predicate<Integer> p2 = Predicate.isEqual(3);
if (p2.test(3))
    System.out.println("The Predicate is true");
```

OUTPUT:

```
The Predicate is true
```

In the following example, `Predicate p1's` or method creates a composed predicate containing the logical OR of the existing condition, `x > 7`, and the condition of its argument, `Integer.equals(3)`. Since the condition `Integer.equals(3)` is true, the string "true" is displayed.

```
Predicate<Integer> p1 = x -> x > 7;
System.out.println (p1.or(Predicate.isEqual(3))
                                   .test(3));
```

OUTPUT:

```
true
```

Section 3.5.5: Using Predicate.not [JAVA 11]

The `Predicate` interface's static not method reverses the result of the calculation performed by its predicate argument. While the negate method changes the result of an existing predicate, the not method changes the result of a predicate argument.

```
static <T> Predicate<T> not(Predicate<T> target);     [JAVA 11]
```

In the following example, the and method creates a composed predicate containing the logical AND of the condition `x > 7` and the NOT of the condition `x%2 == 1`. Since 8 > 7 is true and `!(8%2 == 1)` is true, the string "true" is displayed.

```
Predicate<Integer> p1 = x -> x > 7;
System.out.println(p1.and(Predicate.not(x -> x%2 == 1))
                    .test(8) );
```

OUTPUT:

```
true
```

Section 3.6: Overriding `Predicate` Default Methods

Suppose a program needs to check if a string starts with the character "a" and is greater than four characters in length. The following example accomplishes this using two Predicate<String> objects:

```
Predicate<String> lengthGr4 = x -> x.length() > 4;
Predicate<String> charOisA = x -> x.charAt(0) == 'a';

System.out.println(lengthGr4.and(charOisA)
                            .test("alpha"));
```

OUTPUT:

```
true
```

The Predicates in the previous example will, however, throw a NullPointerException if the string tested is null.

```
try {
    System.out.println(lengthGr4.and(charOisA)
                                .test(null));
}
catch (NullPointerException e) {
    System.out.println("NullPointerException");
}
```

OUTPUT:

```
NullPointerException
```

The predicates can be made safe for null strings if the and method were to first check if the string is null before calling the test method of the Predicate objects. A named or anonymous class must be provided which overrides the default and method in addition to the test method (note that a lambda expression cannot be used in this case, since a default method is being overridden).

```
Predicate<String> nullProtectedLengthGr4 = new Predicate<String> () {
    @Override
    public boolean test(String x)
    {
```

```
        return x.length() > 4;
    }
    @Override
    public Predicate<String> and(Predicate<? super String> p)
    {
        return x -> x == null? false: test(x) && p.test(x);
    }
};
```

Now, if the string tested is null, the and method returns false for the composed Predicate without calling either test method.

```
System.out.println(nullProtectedLengthGr4.and(charOisA)
                                        .test("alpha"));
```

```
System.out.println(nullProtectedLengthGr4.and(charOisA)
                                        .test(null));
```

OUTPUT:

```
true
false
```

Section 3.7: Specializations of Predicates

The Java API provides the non-generic IntPredicate, LongPredicate, and DoublePredicate interfaces which can be used to test Integers, Longs, and Doubles, respectively. These interfaces provide specialized versions of the generic Predicate interface, since they specify test, or, and, and negate methods that behave the same way as Predicate.

```
@FunctionalInterface
public interface IntPredicate
{
    boolean test(int value);
    // other default methods
    ...
}
```

```
@FunctionalInterface
public interface LongPredicate
{
    boolean test(long value);
    // other default methods
    ...
}

@FunctionalInterface
public interface DoublePredicate
{
    boolean test(double value);
    // other default methods
    ...
}
```

The isEqual method is not defined for predicate specializations since a lambda expression is easily created using the == operator and an autoboxed number.

The following example demonstrates predicate specializations. IntPredicate i tests if int literal 2 is greater than 5, which results in false. LongPredicate l tests if long literal 10 is either even or equal to 6, which results in true. DoublePredicate d tests if double literal 8.5 is both greater than 8.0 and less than 9.0, which results in true.

```
IntPredicate i = x -> x > 5;
LongPredicate l = y -> y%2 == 0;
DoublePredicate d = z -> z > 8.0;

System.out.println(i.test(2));
System.out.println(l.or(a -> a == 6L)
                    .test(10L));
System.out.println(d.and(b -> b < 9.0)
                    .test(8.5));
```

OUTPUT:

```
false
true
true
```

Section 3.8: Binary Predicates

It is often useful to create a single predicate of two different types. The `BiPredicate` interface specifies two type parameters.

```
@FunctionalInterface
public interface BiPredicate<T, U>
{
    boolean test(T t, U u);
    // other default methods
    ...
}
```

In the following example, a `BiPredicate` with type parameters `String` and `Integer` tests if a string equals "Manager" and an integer is greater than 100000. When its `test` method is called with arguments "Manager" and 150000, the string "true" is displayed.

```
BiPredicate<String, Integer> bi = (x, y) -> x.equals("Manager")
                                    && y > 100000;
String position = "Manager";
int salary = 150000;
System.out.println(bi.test(position,salary));
```

OUTPUT:

```
true
```

PROJECT 3: Discount Dave
Problem Statement

Discount Dave owns a car dealership that sells Hyundai Elantras, Toyota Priuses, and Honda Odysseys. Dave doesn't want his salespeople to try to sell cars to people with little chance of buying them, so he hired Cutting Edge Marketing Resources to research which customers are more likely to buy Hyundai Elantras, Toyota Priuses, and Honda Odysseys. The marketing company created a list of four questions that should be used by his sales team to qualify a customer for each car. The questions are based on a customer's gender, state of residence, age, and level of education. For example, the research showed that female customers who live in New Jersey or Pennsylvania, are between the ages 40 and 50, and have a bachelor's degree or higher are most likely to buy a Hyundai Elantra.

Table 3-2. *Cutting Edge's Qualification Questions for Discount Dave*

Car	Hyundai Elantra	Toyota Prius	Honda Odyssey
Question 1	Are you female?	Are you male?	Are you female?
Question 2	Do you live in New Jersey or Pennsylvania?	Do you live in New York?	Do you live in New Jersey?
Question 3	Are you between 40 and 50 years of age?	Are you between 20 and 30 years of age?	Are you older than 40 years of age?
Question 4	Do you have a bachelor's degree or higher?	Do you have a bachelor's degree?	Do you have a master's degree or PhD?

Dave has instructed his sales team to ask a customer their gender, state of residence, age, and level of education when they walk into the showroom. This information will then be used to qualify the customer for one of the cars as follows: if the answer to three or more of the questions in the qualifier is yes, then the customer is likely to buy the car, and the salesperson should attempt to sell it to them.

Three customers entered Dave's showroom today:

> Customer 1: a 43-year-old female from New York with a master's degree

> Customer 2: a 45-year-old male from New York with a bachelor's degree

> Customer 3: a 52-year-old female from New York with a PhD

Write a program which qualifies customers for each car based on the marketing research. Qualify all three customers for each car, and print a message stating which car for which they qualify.

Solution

A Customer class which stores each customer's gender, state of residence, age, and highest level of education can be written.

```
enum Education {ELEMENTARY, HIGHSCHOOL, BACHELORS, MASTERS, PHD }

class Customer
{
    String gender;
    String state;
    int age;
    Education ed;
    public Customer(String g, String st, int a, Education e)
    {
        gender = g;
        state = st;
        age = a;
        ed = e;
    }
    @Override
    public String toString()
    {
        return age + " year old " + gender + " from "
            + state + " with " + ed;
    }
}
```

The qualification questions for the cars can then be organized as an ArrayList of type Predicate<Customer>. The logic in the first column of Table 3-2 is implemented in the elantraQualifier. The logic in the second and third columns of Table 3-2 is implemented in the priusQualifier and the odysseyQualifier, respectively.

```
ArrayList< Predicate<Customer> > elantraQualifier
    = new ArrayList<>();

ElantraQualifier.add(c -> c.gender.equals("female"));
ElantraQualifier.add(c -> c.state.equals("New Jersey")
                || c.state.equals("Pennsylvania"));
ElantraQualifier.add(c -> c.age > 40 && c.age < 50);
ElantraQualifier.add(c -> c.ed.compareTo(Education.HIGHSCHOOL) > 0);
```

```
ArrayList< Predicate<Customer> > priusQualifier
    = new ArrayList<>();

priusQualifier.add(c -> c.gender.equals("male"));
priusQualifier.add(c -> c.state.equals("New York"));
priusQualifier.add(c -> c.age > 20 && c.age < 30);
priusQualifier.add(c -> c.ed.equals(Education.BACHELORS));

ArrayList< Predicate<Customer> > odysseyQualifier
    = new ArrayList<>();

odysseyQualifier.add(c -> c.gender.equals("female"));
odysseyQualifier.add(c -> c.state.equals("New Jersey"));
odysseyQualifier.add(c -> c.age > 40);
odysseyQualifier.add(c -> c.ed.compareTo(Education.BACHELORS) > 0);
```

A helper method that accepts Customer and ArrayList<Predicate<Customer> > arguments can be written. The method should loop through the Predicate objects in the ArrayList, calling the test method of each Predicate object using the supplied Customer. If three or more of the questions result in true, the method returns true.

```
private static boolean qualifyCustomer(
    Customer c,
    ArrayList< Predicate<Customer> > pList)
{
    int count = 0;
    for (Predicate<Customer> p : pList)
    {
        if (p.test(c))
        {
            count++;
            System.out.println("MATCH " + count);
        }
    }
    return count >= 3;
}
```

The complete program is shown and demonstrated as follows. The first customer qualifies for an Elantra since she is a female between 40 and 50 years of age with a bachelor's degree or higher. She doesn't qualify for a Prius since she only matches two criteria (New Yorker with a BS). She doesn't qualify for an Odyssey since she only matches two criteria (female older than 40). The second customer qualifies for a Prius since he is male from New York with a bachelor's degree. He doesn't qualify for an Elantra since he only matches two criteria (40 to 50 years old with a BS or higher). He doesn't qualify for an Odyssey since he only matches one criterion (between 40 and 50 years of age). The third customer qualifies for an Odyssey since she is a female older than 40 with a master's degree or higher. She doesn't qualify for an Elantra since she only matches two criteria (female with a BS or higher). She doesn't qualify for a Prius since she only matches one criterion (is a New Yorker).

Listing 3-7. DiscountDave.java

```java
import java.util.function.Predicate;
import java.util.ArrayList;
enum Education {ELEMENTARY, HIGHSCHOOL, BACHELORS, MASTERS, PHD }
class Customer
{
    String gender;
    String state;
    int age; Education ed;
    public Customer(String g, String st, int a, Education e)
    {
        gender = g;
        state = st;
        age = a;
        ed = e;
    }
    @Override
    public String toString()
    {
        return age + " year old " + gender + " from "
            + state + " with " + ed;
    }
}
```

```java
class DiscountDave
{
    private static boolean qualifyCustomer(
        Customer c,
        ArrayList< Predicate<Customer> > pList)
    {
        int count = 0;
        for (Predicate<Customer> p : pList)
        {
            if (p.test(c))
            {
                count++;
                System.out.println("MATCH " + count);
            }
        }
        return count >= 3;
    }

    public static void main(String[] args)
    {
        ArrayList< Predicate<Customer> > elantraQualifier
            = new ArrayList<>();

        elantraQualifier.add(c -> c.gender.equals("female"));
        elantraQualifier.add(c -> c.state.equals("New Jersey")
                                || c.state.equals("Pennsylvania"));
        elantraQualifier.add(c -> c.age > 40 && c.age < 50);
        elantraQualifier.add(
            c -> c.ed.compareTo(Education.HIGHSCHOOL) > 0);

        ArrayList< Predicate<Customer> > priusQualifier
            = new ArrayList<>();

        priusQualifier.add(c -> c.gender.equals("male"));
        priusQualifier.add(c -> c.state.equals("New York"));
        priusQualifier.add(c -> c.age > 20 && c.age < 30);
        priusQualifier.add(c -> c.ed.equals(Education.BACHELORS));
```

```
ArrayList< Predicate<Customer> > odysseyQualifier
    = new ArrayList<>();

odysseyQualifier.add(c -> c.gender.equals("female"));
odysseyQualifier.add(c -> c.state.equals("New Jersey"));
odysseyQualifier.add(c -> c.age > 40);
odysseyQualifier.add(
    c -> c.ed.compareTo(Education.BACHELORS) > 0);

Customer c1 = new Customer("female", "New York", 43,
                        Education.BACHELORS);
Customer c2 = new Customer("male", "New York", 45,
                        Education.BACHELORS);
Customer c3 = new Customer("female", "New York", 52,
                        Education.PHD);

System.out.println("Qualify customer: " + c1);
if (qualifyCustomer(c1,elantraQualifier))
    System.out.println("Sell customer a Hyundai Elantra");
if (qualifyCustomer(c1,priusQualifier))
    System.out.println("Sell customer a Toyota Prius");

if (qualifyCustomer(c1,odysseyQualifier))
    System.out.println("Sell customer a Honda Odyssey");

System.out.println("Qualify customer: " + c2);
if (qualifyCustomer(c2,elantraQualifier))
    System.out.println("Sell customer a Hyundai Elantra");
if (qualifyCustomer(c2,priusQualifier))
    System.out.println("Sell customer a Toyota Prius");
if (qualifyCustomer(c2,odysseyQualifier))
    System.out.println("Sell customer a Honda Odyssey");

System.out.println("Qualify customer: " + c3);
if (qualifyCustomer(c3,elantraQualifier))
    System.out.println("Sell customer a Hyundai Elantra");
if (qualifyCustomer(c3,priusQualifier))
    System.out.println("Sell customer priusQualifier");
```

```
      if (qualifyCustomer(c3,odysseyQualifier))
          System.out.println("Sell customer a Honda Odyssey");
   }
}
```

PROGRAM OUTPUT:

Qualify customer: 43 year old female from New York with BACHELORS
MATCH 1
MATCH 2
MATCH 3
Sell customer a Hyundai Elantra
MATCH 1
MATCH 2
MATCH 1
MATCH 2
Qualify customer: 45 year old male from New York with BACHELORS
MATCH 1
MATCH 2
MATCH 1
MATCH 2
MATCH 3
Sell customer a Toyota Prius
MATCH 1
Qualify customer: 52 year old female from New York with PHD
MATCH 1
MATCH 2
MATCH 1
MATCH 1
MATCH 2
MATCH 3
Sell customer a Honda Odyssey

Short Problems

1) Write a predicate that tests if a string contains only digits. Demonstrate in a main program.

2) Write a predicate that implements the following logical expression. Demonstrate in a main program.

   `NOT(x < 100 OR x is odd) AND x > 20`

3) Using the `BiPredicate interface`, implement the following logical expression and demonstrate in a main program:

   `NOT(x > 2 AND y < x)`

Long Problems

1) Using a single chain of predicates, determine if a five-letter word is a palindrome or not. A *palindrome* is a word that is spelled the same backward and forward. For example, "kayak" is a palindrome, while "apple" is not.

2) The Internal Revenue Service defines your dependent as someone who meets all of the following conditions with relation to you:

   – Is your son, daughter, stepchild, or foster child

   – Is under age 19 and younger than you, or is a student under 24 and younger than you, or is permanently disabled

   – Did not provide over half of his or her support

   – Did not file a joint tax return or filed a joint return only to claim a refund

   – Lived with you for more than half a year

   Using a single chain of predicates, determine if your child is a dependent or not.

3) A playing card consists of a face value (2–10, Jack, Queen, King, and Ace) and a suite (Hearts, Clubs, Spades, and Diamonds). A poker hand consists of five playing cards.

Write predicates to determine if a poker hand is any of the following:

- *A Straight*: the face values of the cards in the hand form a series of consecutive values.

- *A Flush*: the suites of the cards in the hand are the same.

- *A Full House*: three of the cards in the hand have the same face value, while the remaining cards match a different face value.

CHAPTER 4

Functions

Section 4.1: The Function Interface

Function is a functional interface with two type parameters T and R. Its functional method, called apply, takes an argument of type T and returns an object of type R. Functions are ideal for converting an object of type T to one of type R.

```
@FunctionalInterface
public interface Function<T, R>
{
    R apply(T t);
    ...
}
```

A Function of String, Integer type is declared as follows:

```
Function<String, Integer> f;
```

Function f's apply method will accept a String argument and return an Integer. The following statement represents this function using a lambda expression:

```
f = x -> Integer.parseInt(x);
```

The lambda expression accepts a single String argument x and returns the Integer that results from autoboxing the result of the Integer.parseInt method called on x.

Calling Function f's apply method with argument "100" assigns the value 100 to Integer variable i.

```
Integer i = f.apply("100");
System.out.println(i);
```

OUTPUT:

100

© Ralph Lecessi 2019
R. Lecessi, *Functional Interfaces in Java*, https://doi.org/10.1007/978-1-4842-4278-0_4

Section 4.2: Passing a Generic Function to a Method

To pass a generic function to a method, two type parameters must be specified in the method's header.

The following `transform` method specifies type parameters T and R. It takes an T and a Function<T, R> as arguments. It then calls Function f's apply method with the parameter of type T, and the resulting object of type R is returned.

```
private static <T,R> R transform(T t, Function<T, R> f)
{
    return f.apply(t);
}
```

The program in Listing 4-1 demonstrates. The first call to `transform` accepts a Function<String, Integer> and converts the String argument to an Integer using the Integer class's parseInt method. The second call to `transform` accepts a Function<Integer, String> and converts the Integer argument to a String using the Integer class's toString method.

Listing 4-1. Transformer.java

```
import java.util.function.Function;
class Transformer
{
    private static <T,R> R transform(T t, Function<T, R> f)
    {
        return f.apply(t);
    }

    public static void main(String[] args)
    {
        Function<String , Integer> fsi = x -> Integer.parseInt(x);
        Function<Integer, String>  fis = x -> Integer.toString(x);

        Integer i = transform("100", fsi);
        String  s = transform(200  , fis);
        System.out.println(i);
        System.out.println(s);
    }
}
```

PROGRAM OUTPUT:

100
200

Section 4.2.1: Passing a Function with Restricted or Known Type Parameters

Often, the type parameters of a function passed to a method are known or can be restricted to certain types. Suppose a program needs to parse a string as one of several numeric types. The program can pass a function to a parse method where the first type is String and the second type is constrained to a subclass of Number. Therefore, only one type parameter needs to be specified in the method's header.

```
private static <R extends Number> R parse(String x,
                                        Function<String, R> f)
{
    return f.apply(x);
}
```

The program can declare an ArrayList of type Function whose implementations call the parse methods of each numeric wrapper classes. The first type argument of the Function is String. Since the second argument should constrain the type to a Number or one of its subclasses, wildcarding can be used.

```
ArrayList< Function<String,? extends Number> > list
    = new ArrayList<>();

list.add(x -> Byte.parseByte(x));
list.add(x -> Short.parseShort(x));
list.add(x -> Integer.parseInt(x));
list.add(x -> Long.parseLong(x));
list.add(x -> Float.parseFloat(x));
list.add(x -> Double.parseDouble(x));
```

The program in Listing 4-2 demonstrates. It loops through the list and calls the parse method to transform an array of Strings to an array of numeric wrapper objects. The value returned from each of the wrapper class's parse methods is autoboxed, and the result is polymorphically assigned to an entry in the array of Numbers.

71

Listing 4-2. NumberParser.java

```java
import java.util.function.Function;
import java.util.ArrayList;
class NumberParser
{
    private static <R extends Number> R parse(String x,
                                              Function<String, R> f)
    {
        return f.apply(x);
    }
    public static void main(String[] args)
    {
        ArrayList< Function<String,? extends Number> > list
            = new ArrayList<>();
        list.add(x -> Byte.parseByte(x));
        list.add(x -> Short.parseShort(x));
        list.add(x -> Integer.parseInt(x));
        list.add(x -> Long.parseLong(x));
        list.add(x -> Float.parseFloat(x));
        list.add(x -> Double.parseDouble(x));
        String[] numbers = {"10", "20", "30", "40", "50", "60"};
        Number[] results = new Number[numbers.length];

        for (int i=0; i < numbers.length; ++i)
        {
            results[i] = parse(numbers[i], list.get(i));
            System.out.println(results[i]);
        }
    }
}
```

PROGRAM OUTPUT:

```
10
20
30
40
50.0
60.0
```

Section 4.3: Function Chaining

Similar to Predicate, the Function interface has default methods that return new functions, supporting chains of functions that can perform many conversions in series.

Section 4.3.1: Chains Involving the andThen Method

The Function interface's default andThen method applies an additional operation after the operation specified by the apply method completes. It can be used to create chains of functions.

```
default <V> Function<T,V> andThen(Function<? super R>, ? extends V> after);
```

A function which converts a String to a Boolean is defined as follows:

```
Function<String, Boolean> fsb = x -> Boolean.parseBoolean(x);
```

The following example creates a chain of functions by using the andThen method in conjunction with the apply method. The apply method converts the string "true" to Boolean value true, which is input to the function executed by the andThen method. This function converts Boolean value true to Integer value 1.

The transformations along the function chain are listed on the right in the comments.

```
System.out.println(
    fsb.andThen(x -> x==true? 1:0) // Function<Boolean, Integer>
      .apply("true"));             // Function<String, Boolean>
```

OUTPUT:

1

Section 4.3.2: Chains Involving the compose Method

The Function interface's default compose method applies a preliminary operation before the operation specified by the apply method is executed.

```
default <V> Function<V,R> compose(Function<? super V>, ? extends T> before);
```

Functions that convert from Boolean to Integer and from String to Boolean are defined as follows:

```
Function<Boolean, Integer> fbi = x -> x==true? 1:0;
Function<String, Boolean>  fsb = x -> Boolean.parseBoolean(x);
```

In the following example, the compose method uses Function fsb to convert string "true" to Boolean value true. Then, the apply method uses Function fbi to convert true to Integer value 1, which is displayed.

```
System.out.println(fbi.compose(fsb)     // Function<String, Boolean>
                    .apply("true")); // Function<Boolean, Integer>
```

OUTPUT:

```
1
```

Section 4.4: The Function.identity Method

The Function interface's static identity method creates a Function whose apply method returns its input parameter.

```
static default <T> Function<T,T> identity()
```

Several methods in the Java API expect mapping functions which will change the input. Passing the Function.identity method to one of these methods will cause the methods to process without changing the input.

The following example creates a Function which returns the string passed to the apply method. Therefore, the string "HELLO WORLD" is displayed.

```
Function<String,String> f = Function.identity();
System.out.println(f.apply("HELLO WORLD"));
```

OUTPUT:

```
HELLO WORLD
```

Section 4.5: Specializations of Functions Which Convert from Primitive Types

The Java API provides the IntFunction, LongFunction, and DoubleFunction interfaces which convert from int, long, and double primitive types, respectively. These interfaces are generic for a single type parameter which specifies the type of the object returned from the apply method.

```
@FunctionalInterface
public interface IntFunction<R> {
    R apply(int value);
}
```

```
@FunctionalInterface
public interface LongFunction<R> {
    R apply(long value);
}
```

```
@FunctionalInterface
public interface DoubleFunction<R> {
    R apply(long value);
}
```

The following example demonstrates. IntFunction fi converts int literal 5 to a String containing "5". DoubleFunction fd converts double literal 4.5 to Boolean value false, since 4.5 is less than 5.0. LongFunction fl converts long literal 20 to Integer value 20.

```
IntFunction<String> fi = x -> (new Integer(x)).toString();
DoubleFunction<Boolean> fd = x -> x > 5.0? true : false;
LongFunction<Integer> fl = x -> (int)x;

System.out.println(fi.apply(5));
System.out.println(fd.apply(4.5));
System.out.println(fl.apply(20L));
```

OUTPUT:

```
5
false
20
```

Section 4.6: Specializations of Functions Which Convert to Primitive Types

The Java API provides the ToIntFunction, ToLongFunction, and ToDoubleFunction interfaces which convert to int, long, and double primitive types, respectively. These interfaces are generic for a single type parameter which specifies the type of the argument to their functional methods.

```
@FunctionalInterface
public interface ToIntFunction<T> {
    int applyAsInt(T value);
}

@FunctionalInterface
public interface ToLongFunction<T> {
    long applyAsLong(T value);
}

@FunctionalInterface
public interface ToDoubleFunction<T> {
    double applyAsDouble(T value);
}
```

The following example demonstrates. ToIntFunction ti converts string literal "5" to int value 5. ToLongFunction tl converts double literal 5.1 to long value 5. ToDoubleFunction td converts int literal 7 to double value 7.0.

```
ToIntFunction<String> ti     = x -> Integer.parseInt(x);
ToLongFunction<Double> tl    = x -> x.longValue();
ToDoubleFunction<Integer> td = x -> (new Integer(x)).doubleValue();

System.out.println(ti.applyAsInt("5"));
System.out.println(tl.applyAsLong(5.1));
System.out.println(td.applyAsDouble(7));
```

OUTPUT:

5
5
7.0

Section 4.7: Non-generic Specializations of Functions

The Java API provides non-generic specializations of the Function interface which convert between int, long, and double primitive types. These include DoubleToIntFunction, DoubleToLongFunction, IntToDoubleFunction, IntToLongFunction, LongToDoubleFunction, and LongToIntFunction. The following example demonstrates:

```
DoubleToIntFunction  di = x -> (new Double(x)).intValue();
DoubleToLongFunction dl = x -> (new Double(x)).longValue();
IntToDoubleFunction  id = x -> (new Integer(x)).doubleValue();
IntToLongFunction    il = x -> (new Integer(x)).longValue();
LongToDoubleFunction ld = x -> (new Long(x)).doubleValue();
LongToIntFunction    li = x -> (new Long(x)).intValue();

System.out.println(di.applyAsInt(4.1));
System.out.println(dl.applyAsLong(5.2));
System.out.println(id.applyAsDouble(6));
System.out.println(il.applyAsLong(7));
System.out.println(ld.applyAsDouble(8));
System.out.println(li.applyAsInt(9));
```

OUTPUT:

```
4
5
6.0
7
8.0
9
```

Section 4.8: Binary Functions

Sometimes a conversion requires two input types. The BiFunction interface specifies two type parameters for input types in addition to the output type parameter. The apply method takes an argument of each input type.

```
@FunctionalInterface
public interface BiFunction<T,U,R> {
    R apply(T t, U u);
}
```

The following BiFunction uses an Integer and a Character to produce a string. The lambda expression has two parameters, x of type Integer and z of type Character. Parameter x determines if the result is even or odd, while parameter z determines the case of the String returned.

```
BiFunction<Integer,Character,String> bi = (x, z) -> {
    if (Character.isUpperCase(z))
        return (x%2)==0? "EVEN" : "ODD";
    return (x%2)==0? "even" : "odd";
};

System.out.println(bi.apply(4,'U'));
```

OUTPUT:

```
EVEN
```

Section 4.9: Creating Chains Using **BiFunctions**

The BiFunction interface's default andThen method applies an additional operation after the operation specified by the apply method completes.

```
default <V> BiFunction<T,U,V> andThen(Function<? super R>, ? extends V> after);
```

A function which converts the String to Double can be added to the result of the previous example using the andThen method, causing a Double to be printed instead of a String.

```
Function<String,Double> bi2 = x ->
    x.equalsIgnoreCase("even")? 3.0 : 4.0;

Double d = bi.andThen(bi2)  // Function<String,Double>
            .apply(4,'U'); // BiFunction<Integer,Character,String>

System.out.println(d);
```

OUTPUT:

```
3.0
```

Section 4.10: Specializations of BiFunctions Which Convert to Primitive Types

The Java API provides the ToIntBiFunction, ToLongBiFunction, and ToDoubleBiFunction interfaces which convert to int, long, and double primitive types, respectively. These interfaces are generic for two type parameters which specify the types of the arguments to their functional method.

```
@FunctionalInterface
public interface ToIntBiFunction<T,U> {
    int applyAsInt(T t, U u);
}

@FunctionalInterface
public interface ToLongBiFunction<T,U> {
    long applyAsLong(T t, U u);
}

@FunctionalInterface
public interface ToDoubleBiFunction<T,U> {
    double applyAsDouble(T t, U u);
}
```

The following example demonstrates. ToIntBiFunction tib converts string literal 5 and double literal 4.2 to int value 9. ToLongtBiFunction tlb converts double literal 5.1 and string literal "6" to long value 1. ToDoubltBiFunction tdb converts int literal 7 and long literal 8 to double value 15.0.

```
ToIntBiFunction<String, Double> tib = (x,z) ->
    Integer.parseInt(x) + (new Double(z)).intValue();
ToLongBiFunction<Double, String> tlb = (x,z) ->
    x.longValue() + Long.parseLong(z);
ToDoubleBiFunction<Integer, Long> tdb = (x,z) ->
    (new Integer(x)).doubleValue() + (new Long(z)).doubleValue();

System.out.println(tib.applyAsInt("5",4.2));
System.out.println(tlb.applyAsLong(5.1, "6"));
System.out.println(tdb.applyAsDouble(7, 8L));
```

OUTPUT:

```
9
11
15.0
```

PROJECT 4: Sales Promotions

Problem Statement

A retailer runs weekly sales promotions targeting certain customers. If a customer has been targeted for a promotion, a representative from the sales department will call him or her and discuss something of personal interest during the conversion. The retailer runs a football promotion on Sundays, a high-tech promotion on Tuesdays, and a bring-a-friend promotion on Fridays. On Sundays, a rep will call customers who enjoy football attempting to sell them football-related products while discussing the customer's favorite team. On Tuesdays, a rep will call customers with a grade point average (GPA) of 3.75 or higher to sell them non-fiction books while discussing the customer's favorite subject. On Fridays, a rep will call customers who have one or more friends on record to sell them any product and will ask permission to call their friend as well.

Solution

A `Customer` class containing fields for a customer's name, phone number, favorite sport, favorite team, grade point average, favorite subject, number of friends, and a list of his or her friends can be written.

```
class Customer
{
    String name;
    String phoneNum;
    String sport;
    String team;
    double gpa;
    String subject;
    int numFriends;
    String friends;
```

```java
public Customer(String n, String pn, String sp, String t,
                double g, String s, int nf, String f)
{
    name = n;
    phoneNum = pn;
    sport = sp;
    team = t;
    gpa = g;
    subject = s;
    numFriends = nf;
    friends = f;
}
}
```

The program should create a customer database consisting of several Customer objects.

```java
final static Customer[] customers = {
    new Customer("John Smith", "9084321212", "football",
                "Giants", 3.61, null, 0, null),
    new Customer("Indira Patel", "7325551234", "tennis",
                null, 3.92, "Java", 0, null),
    new Customer("Sarah Johnson", "2123231245", "football",
                "Eagles", 3.71, null, 1,
                "Jane Hernadez,2017765765"),
    new Customer("Javier Jones", "8568768765", "golf",
                null, 3.85, "Physics", 1,
                "Maria Regina,9086547654")
};
```

On Sundays, the sales rep will query the database for customers who enjoy football by matching the following Customer object:

```java
new Customer(null, null, "football", null, Double.MAX_VALUE,
            null, Integer.MAX_VALUE, null);
```

On Tuesdays, the sales rep will query the database for customers with grade point averages of 3.75 or higher by matching the following Customer object:

```
new Customer(null, null, null , null, 3.75 , null,
          Integer.MAX_VALUE, null);
```

On Fridays, the sales rep will query the database for customers with one or more friends on record by matching the following Customer object:

```
new Customer(null, null, null , null, Double.MAX_VALUE, null,
          1, null);
```

The query needs to generate a record that the sales rep will use during the phone call with the targeted customer containing the customer's name, phone number, and item of personal interest. The record should also keep track of the customer's position in the database. The records are different for each query, but the common fields can be grouped inside abstract class Record.

```
abstract class Record
{
    String name;
    String phoneNum;
    int index;
    public Record(String n, String pn, int i)
    {
        name = n;
        phoneNum = pn;
        index = i;
    }
    @Override
    public String toString() {
        return "name: " + name + " phone number: " + phoneNum;
    }
}

class SportRecord extends Record
{
    String team;
    public SportRecord(String n, String pn, int i, String t)
```

```
    {
        super(n, pn, i);
        team = t;
    }
    @Override
    public String toString() {
        return super.toString() + " favorite team is the " + team;
    }
}

class GpaRecord extends Record
{
    String subject;
    public GpaRecord(String n, String pn, int i, String s)
    {
        super(n, pn, i);
        subject = s;
    }
    @Override
    public String toString() {
        return super.toString() + " favorite subject is " + subject;
    }
}

class FriendsRecord extends Record
{
    String friends;
    public FriendsRecord(String n, String pn, int i, String f)
    {
        super(n, pn, i);
        friends = f;
    }
    @Override
    public String toString() {
        return super.toString() + " friends are " + friends;
    }
}
```

The football promotion query needs to transform a `Customer` object to a `SportRecord` using the current position in the customer database. A `BiFunction<Customer, Integer, SportRecord>` can accomplish this. Starting at the current position in the database, the `BiFunction` will return a `SportRecord` for the first customer whose sport matches "football." The `SportRecord` contains the customer's position in the database.

```
BiFunction<Customer,Integer,SportRecord> fsport = (x,z) -> {
    SportRecord sport = null;
    for (int i=z; i < customers.length && sport == null; ++ i)
        if (customers[i].sport.equals(x.sport))
            sport = new SportRecord(customers[i].name,
                customers[i].phoneNum, i, customers[i].team);
    return sport;
};
```

The high-tech promotion query needs to transform a `Customer` object to a `GpaRecord` using the current position in the customer database. A `BiFunction<Customer, Integer, GpaRecord>` can accomplish this. Starting at the current position in the database, the `BiFunction` will return a `GpaRecord` for the first customer with a GPA of 3.75 or higher. The `GpaRecord` contains the customer's position in the database.

```
BiFunction<Customer,Integer,GpaRecord> fgpa = (x,z) -> {
    GpaRecord gpa = null;
    for (int i=z; i < customers.length && gpa == null; ++ i)
        if (customers[i].gpa >= x.gpa)
            gpa = new GpaRecord(customers[i].name,
                customers[i].phoneNum, i, customers[i].subject);
    return gpa;
};
```

The bring-a-friend promotion query needs to transform a `Customer` object to a `FriendsRecord` using the current position in the customer database. A `BiFunction<Customer, Integer, FriendsRecord>` can accomplish this. Starting at the current position in the database, the `BiFunction` will return a `FriendsRecord` for the first customer with one or more friends on record. The `FriendsRecord` contains the customer's position in the database.

```
BiFunction<Customer,Integer,FriendsRecord> ffriends = (x,z) -> {
    FriendsRecord friends = null;
    for (int i=z; i < customers.length && friends == null; ++ i)
        if (customers[i].numFriends >= x.numFriends)
            friends = new FriendsRecord(customers[i].name,
                customers[i].phoneNum, i, customers[i].friends);
    return friends;
};
```

The BiFunctions can be stored in an ArrayList where the third BiFunction type parameter is wildcarded for Record and its subclasses.

```
ArrayList< BiFunction<Customer,Integer,? extends Record> > list
    = new ArrayList<>();
        list.add(fsport);
        list.add(fgpa);
        list.add(ffriends);
```

To perform the queries, a method that accepts the customer query and the BiFunction list as arguments can be written. The method will execute each BiFunction for all customers in the database using the customer query. The record generated by the BiFunction is printed for the sales rep. The index stored in the record is used to keep track of the current position in the database which is used in the next execution of the BiFunction.

```
private static void matchCustomers(Customer c,
    ArrayList< BiFunction<Customer,Integer, ? extends Record> > f)
{
    for (int j=0; j < f.size(); ++j)
    {
        Record record;
        int index = 0;
        do
        {
            record = f.get(j).apply(c,index);
            if (record != null)
            {
```

85

```
            System.out.println(record);
            index = record.index + 1;
        }
    } while (record != null);
    }
    System.out.println();
}
```

The program in Listing 4-3 demonstrates. The sales rep first runs the Sunday football promotion by passing a `Customer` object whose sport is football to method `matchCustomer`. The `fsport BiFunction` matches customer John Smith and outputs a `SportRecord` that tells the rep that John's favorite team is the Giants. The record also stores John's customer index, 0, so that the next iteration of `fsport` will begin at 1. The `fsport BiFunction` then matches customer Sarah Johnson and outputs a `SportsRecord` that tells the rep that Sarah's favorite team is the Eagles. The record also stores Sarah's customer index, 2, so that the next iteration of `fsport` will begin at 3. The `fgpa` and `ffriends BiFunctions` return no records because the matching `Customer` has the maximum values for GPA and number of friends.

Next, the sales rep runs the high-tech promotion by passing a `Customer` object whose GPA is 3.75 to method `matchCustomer`. The `fgpa BiFunction` matches customer Indira Patel and outputs a `GpaRecord` that tells the rep that Indira's favorite subject is Java. The record also stores Indira's customer index, 1, so that the next iteration of `fgpa` will begin at 2. The `fgpa BiFunction` then matches customer Javier Jones and outputs a `GpaRecord` that tells the rep that Javier's favorite subject is physics. The `fsport` and `ffriends BiFunctions` match no records because the matching `Customer` has a null sport and the maximum value for number of friends.

Finally, the sales rep runs the bring-a-friend promotion by passing a `Customer` object whose number of friends is 1. The `ffriends BiFunction` matches customer Sarah Johnson and outputs a `FriendsRecord` that tells the rep that Sarah has a friend named Jane Hernandez. The record also stores Sarah's customer index, 2, so that the next iteration of `ffriends` will begin at 3. The `ffriends BiFunction` then matches customer Javier Jones and outputs a `FriendsRecord` that tells the rep that Javier has a friend named Maria Regina. The `fsport` and `fgpa BiFunctions` match no records because the matching `Customer` has a null sport and the maximum value for GPA.

Listing 4-3. SalesPromotion.java

```java
import java.util.function.*;
import java.util.ArrayList;

class Customer
{
    String name;
    String phoneNum;
    String sport;
    String team;
    double gpa;
    String subject;
    int    numFriends;
    String friends;
    public Customer(String n, String pn, String sp, String t,
                    double g, String s, int nf, String f)
    {
        name = n;
        phoneNum = pn;
        sport = sp;
        team = t;
        gpa = g;
        subject = s;
        numFriends = nf;
        friends = f;
    }
}

abstract class Record
{
    String name;
    String phoneNum;
    int index;
    public Record(String n, String pn, int i)
    {
```

```java
        name = n;
        phoneNum = pn;
        index = i;
    }
    @Override
    public String toString() {
        return "name: " + name + " phone number: " + phoneNum;
    }
}

class SportRecord extends Record
{
    String team;
    public SportRecord(String n, String pn, int i, String t)
    {
        super(n, pn, i);
        team = t;
    }
    @Override
    public String toString() {
        return super.toString() + " favorite team is the " + team;
    }
}

class GpaRecord extends Record
{
    String subject;
    public GpaRecord(String n, String pn, int i, String s)
    {
        super(n, pn, i);
        subject = s;
    }
    @Override
    public String toString() {
        return super.toString() + " favorite subject is " + subject;
    }
}
```

```java
class FriendsRecord extends Record
{
    String friends;
    public FriendsRecord(String n, String pn, int i, String f)
    {
        super(n, pn, i);
        friends = f;
    }
    @Override
    public String toString() {
        return super.toString() + " friends are " + friends;
    }
}

class SalesPromotion
{
    final static Customer[] customers = {
            new Customer("John Smith", "9084321212", "football",
                    "Giants", 3.61, null, 0, null),
            new Customer("Indira Patel", "7325551234", "tennis",
                    null, 3.92, "Java", 0, null),
            new Customer("Sarah Johnson", "2123231245", "football",
                    "Eagles", 3.71, null, 1,
                    "Jane Hernadez,2017765765"),
            new Customer("Javier Jones", "8568768765", "golf",
                    null , 3.85, "Physics", 1,
                    "Maria Regina,9086547654")
        };

    private static void matchCustomers(Customer c,
      ArrayList< BiFunction<Customer,Integer, ? extends Record> > f)
    {
        for (int j=0; j < f.size(); ++j)
        {
            Record record;
```

```
        int index = 0;
        do
        {
            record = f.get(j).apply(c,index);
            if (record != null)
            {
                System.out.println(record);
                index = record.index + 1;
            }
        } while (record != null);
    }
    System.out.println();
}
public static void main(String[] args)
{
    BiFunction<Customer,Integer,SportRecord> fsport = (x,z) -> {
        SportRecord sport = null;

        for (int i=z;
            i < customers.length && sport == null;
            ++ i)
            if (customers[i].sport.equals(x.sport))
                sport = new SportRecord(customers[i].name,
                    customers[i].phoneNum, i, customers[i].team);
        return sport;
    };

    BiFunction<Customer,Integer,GpaRecord> fgpa = (x,z) -> {
        GpaRecord gpa = null;
         for (int i=z; i < customers.length && gpa == null; ++ i)
            if (customers[i].gpa >= x.gpa)
                gpa = new GpaRecord(customers[i].name,
                                    customers[i].phoneNum, i,
                                    customers[i].subject);
        return gpa;
    };
```

```
BiFunction<Customer,Integer,FriendsRecord> ffriends = (x,z) -> {
    FriendsRecord friends = null;
    for (int i=z;
        i < customers.length && friends == null;
        ++ i)
        if (customers[i].numFriends >= x.numFriends)
            friends = new FriendsRecord(customers[i].name,
                                        customers[i].phoneNum,
                                        i,
                                        customers[i].friends);
    return friends;
    };

    ArrayList< BiFunction<Customer,Integer,? extends Record> >
        list = new ArrayList<>();
        list.add(fsport);
        list.add(fgpa);
        list.add(ffriends);

        System.out.println(
        "SUNDAY FOOTBALL PROMOTION - Call the following customers:");
        matchCustomers(new Customer(null, null, "football", null,
            Double.MAX_VALUE, null, Integer.MAX_VALUE, null), list);

        System.out.println(
        "TUESDAY HIGH-TECH PROMOTION - Call the following customers:");
        matchCustomers(new Customer(null, null, null, null, 3.75,
                null, Integer.MAX_VALUE, null), list);

        System.out.println(
    "FRIDAY BRING A FRIEND PROMOTION - Call the following customers:");
        matchCustomers(new Customer(null, null, null, null,
            Double.MAX_VALUE, null, 1, null), list);
    }
}
```

PROGRAM OUTPUT:

SUNDAY FOOTBALL PROMOTION - Call the following customers:
name: John Smith phone number: 9084321212 favorite team is the Giants
name: Sarah Johnson phone number: 2123231245 favorite team is the Eagles

TUESDAY HIGH-TECH PROMOTION - Call the following customers:
name: Indira Patel phone number: 7325551234 favorite subject is Java
name: Javier Jones phone number: 8568768765 favorite subject is Physics

FRIDAY BRING A FRIEND PROMOTION - Call the following customers:
name: Sarah Johnson phone number: 2123231245 friends are Jane Hernadez,2017765765
name: Javier Jones phone number: 8568768765 friends are Maria Regina,9086547654

Short Problems

1) Given the following two classes,

```
class A                                class B
{                                      {
    Double d;                              Double a;
    String s;                              String b;
    Integer i;                             String c;
    public A(Double x, String y,           public B(Double x, String y,
            Integer z)                             String z)
    {                                      {
        d = x;                                 a = x;
        s = y;                                 b = y;
        i = z;                                 c = z;
    }                                      }
    public String toString()               public String toString()
    {                                      {
        return d + " " + s + " "               return a + " " + b + " "
            + i;                                   + c;
    }                                      }
}                                      }
```

write a function that converts from an A to a B and another function that converts from a B to an A. Demonstrate the functions in a main program.

2) Classes D and E are subclasses of class C. Write a method named execute that accepts a C, D, or E and a function which converts the object to an Integer containing the sub of the object's fields. The execute method returns the sum to a main method, which prints it.

3) Using a chain of functions, convert from an A to a B, then to a String which concatenates all the fields in B delimited by percent signs. Demonstrate in a main program.

Long Problems

1) A deck of cards consists of 52 playing cards, 1 for each of the 13 face values (2–10, Jack, Queen, King, and Ace) and each of the 4 suites (Hearts, Clubs, Spades, and Diamonds). Write a single loop that uses a function to create a deck of playing cards.

2) Modify the solution in homework problem #1 to use a function chain to shuffle the deck after creating each card. Shuffling produces a random series of cards in the deck. Note that each playing card in the deck must be unique (the combination of a face value and a suite cannot be repeated).

3) A map contains the following entries:

key: dog   **value**: wolf descendant

key: cat   **value**: feline with nine lives

key: rat   **value**: rodent with long tail

Use a function chain to switch the keys and values of each entry (**Hint**: first convert the map to a list, and then back to a map with the keys and values switched).

CHAPTER 5

Operators

When a Function object's input type is the same as its output type, an Operator interface can be used in place of a Function. Operator interfaces define a single type parameter.

Section 5.1: The UnaryOperator Interface

UnaryOperator is a functional interface with one type parameter such that UnaryOperator<T> inherits Function<T, T>. Like Function, a lambda expression that represents the apply method with a single argument must be provided. UnaryOperator supports andThen, compose, and identity as well. It is useful for implementing operations on a single operand.

```
@FunctionalInterface
public interface UnaryOperator<T>
extends Function<T,T> {
    static <T> UnaryOperator<T> identity();
}
```

The following example demonstrates. The UnaryOperator<String> concatenates String argument "My" with itself to output the String "MyMy". The UnaryOperator<Integer> increments Integer argument 4 to output Integer value 5. The UnaryOperator<Long> decrements Long argument 4 to output Long value 3. Note that prefix notation must be used with the increment and decrement operators for the changes to take effect in the output objects. The UnaryOperator<String> implemented by the static identity method outputs its String argument "My".

```
UnaryOperator<String>  concat = x -> x + x;
UnaryOperator<Integer> increment = x -> ++x;
UnaryOperator<Long>    decrement = x -> --x;
```

© Ralph Lecessi 2019

R. Lecessi, *Functional Interfaces in Java*, https://doi.org/10.1007/978-1-4842-4278-0_5

```
System.out.println(concat.apply("My"));
System.out.println(increment.apply(4));
System.out.println(decrement.apply(4L));

UnaryOperator<String> sident = UnaryOperator.identity();
System.out.println(sident.apply("My"));
```

OUTPUT:

```
MyMy
5
3
My
```

Section 5.2: Specializations of UnaryOperator

The Java API provides non-generic specializations of the UnaryOperator interface which perform a single operation on an int, long, or double primitive argument, respectively. These interfaces include IntUnaryOperator, DoubleUnaryOperator, and LongUnaryOperator.

```
@FunctionalInterface
public interface IntUnaryOperator {
    int applyAsInt(int operand);
    ...
}
```

```
@FunctionalInterface
public interface LongUnaryOperator {
    long applyAsLong(long operand);
    ...
}
```

```
@FunctionalInterface
public interface DoubleUnaryOperator {
    double applyAsDouble(double operand);
    ...
}
```

The following example demonstrates. IntUnaryOperator iuo adds 5 to int argument 4 to output the int value 9. LongUnaryOperator luo divides int argument 9 by 3 to output the int value 3. DoubleUnaryOperator duo multiplies double argument 4.1 by 2.1 to output the double value 8.61.

```
IntUnaryOperator    iuo = x -> x + 5;
LongUnaryOperator   luo = x -> x / 3L;
DoubleUnaryOperator duo = x -> x * 2.1;
System.out.println(iuo.applyAsInt(4));
System.out.println(luo.applyAsLong(9L));
System.out.println(duo.applyAsDouble(4.1));
```

OUTPUT:

```
9
3
8.61
```

Section 5.2.1: Chains Involving UnaryOperator Specializations

The UnaryOperator specializations provide andThen, compose, and identity methods that use UnaryOperator specializations as arguments and return types. The following example demonstrates. IntUnaryOperator iuo uses the andThen method to multiply 9, the result of the applyAsInt method, by 2 and outputs 18. LongUnaryOperator luo uses the compose method to multiply 4 by 6 and pass 24 to the applyAsLong method which outputs 8. The DoubleUnaryOperator duo uses the andThen method to apply the identity to 8.61, the result of the applyAsDouble method, which results in 8.61.

```
System.out.println(iuo.andThen(x -> x * 2)
                    .applyAsInt(4));
System.out.println(luo.compose(x -> x * 6)
                    .applyAsLong(4));
System.out.println(duo.andThen(DoubleUnaryOperator.identity())
                    .applyAsDouble(4.1));
```

OUTPUT:

```
18
8
8.61
```

Section 5.3: The BinaryOperator Interface

BinaryOperator is a functional interface with one type parameter such that
BinaryOperator<T> inherits BiFunction<T, T, T>. Like BiFunction, a lambda
expression that represents the apply method with two arguments must be provided.
BinaryOperator is useful for implementing operations on two operands.

```
@FunctionalInterface
public interface BinaryOperator<T>
extends BiFunction<T,T,T> {
    // some static methods
    ...
}
```

The following example demonstrates. The BinaryOperator<String> concatenates
String argument "AB" with String argument "CD" to output the String "ABCD". The
BinaryOperator<Integer> subtracts Integer argument 1 from Integer argument 4 to
output the Integer value 3. The BinaryOperator<Long> multiplies Long argument 4 by
Long argument 3 to output the Long value 12.

```
BinaryOperator<String>  concat   = (x,y) -> x + y;
BinaryOperator<Integer> subtract = (x,y) -> x - y;
BinaryOperator<Long>    multiply = (x,y) -> x * y;

System.out.println(concat.apply("AB", "CD"));
System.out.println(subtract.apply(4, 1));
System.out.println(multiply.apply(4L, 3L));
```

OUTPUT:

```
ABCD
3
12
```

Section 5.4: Non-generic Specializations of BinaryOperator

The Java API provides non-generic specializations of the BinaryOperator interface which perform a single operation on two int, long, and double primitive arguments, respectively. These interfaces include IntBinaryOperator, DoubleBinaryOperator, and LongBinaryOperator.

```
@FunctionalInterface
public interface IntBinaryOperator {
   int applyAsInt(int left,int right);
}
```

```
@FunctionalInterface
public interface LongBinaryOperator {
   long applyAsLong(long left, long right);
}
```

```
@FunctionalInterface
public interface DoubleBinaryOperator {
   double applyAsDouble(double left, double right);
}
```

The following example demonstrates. IntBinaryOperator ibo adds 5 to sum of int arguments 4 and 2 to output the int value 11. LongBinaryOperator lbo divides the sum of long arguments 9 and 3 by 3 to output the long value 4. DoubleBinaryOperator dbo multiples the product of double arguments 4.0 and 6.0 to output the double value 12.0.

```
IntBinaryOperator     ibo = (x,y) -> x + y + 5;
LongBinaryOperator    lbo = (x,y) -> (x + y)/ 3L;
DoubleBinaryOperator dbo = (x,y) -> x * y * 0.5;
```

```
System.out.println(ibo.applyAsInt(4,2));
System.out.println(lbo.applyAsLong(9L,3L));
System.out.println(dbo.applyAsDouble(4.0,6.0));
```

OUTPUT:

```
11
4
12.0
```

PROJECT 5: Calculator

Problem Statement

Write a calculator program that interacts with a user through the command line interface. The calculator should prompt the user to select one of the following operations:

Operation	Description
+	Addition
-	Subtraction
*	Multiplication
/	Division
POW	Raise a number to a power
LOG	$\log_{10}$ of a number
EXP	e raised to a number
SIN	The sine of a number in degrees
COS	The cosine of a number in degrees
TAN	The tangent of a number in degrees
QUI	Quit the program

If the operation selected does not match any of those listed here, the program should print an error message. If QUI is selected, the program terminates. Otherwise, the program should prompt the user for the first operand. If the operation is a binary operation, it should prompt the user for the second operand. Then, the program should perform the operation and print the result. Then the program should prompt the user to select another operation. The process continues until the user selects QUI.

Solution

All operations should be performed using `doubles`. `DoubleBinaryOperators` should be written for addition, subtraction, multiplication, division, and raising a number to a power.

```
DoubleBinaryOperator sum = (x,y) -> x + y;
DoubleBinaryOperator dif = (x,y) -> x - y;
```

```
DoubleBinaryOperator mul = (x,y) -> x * y;
DoubleBinaryOperator div = (x,y) -> x / y;
DoubleBinaryOperator pow = (x,y) -> Math.pow(x,y);
```

DoubleUnaryOperators should be written for absolute value, common logarithm, e raised to a number, sine, cosine, and tangent.

```
DoubleUnaryOperator abs = x -> Math.abs(x);
DoubleUnaryOperator log = x -> Math.log(x);
DoubleUnaryOperator exp = x -> Math.exp(x);
DoubleUnaryOperator sin = x -> Math.sin(Math.toRadians(x));
DoubleUnaryOperator cos = x -> Math.cos(Math.toRadians(x));
DoubleUnaryOperator tan = x -> Math.tan(Math.toRadians(x));
```

A method that prompts the user to enter an operand can be written. The method should return the value of the operand as a double.

```
public static double getOp()
{
    Scanner scan = new Scanner(System.in);
    System.out.print("Enter an operand:");
    return Double.parseDouble(scan.nextLine());
}
```

The program should switch on the selected operation, and call the applyAsDouble method of the corresponding operator. Each case in the switch statement calls the getOp method once or twice depending on how many operands the corresponding operation requires.

```
switch (op)
{
    case "+"    : System.out.println(
                        sum.applyAsDouble(getOp(),getOp()));
                  break;
    case "-"    : System.out.println(
                        dif.applyAsDouble(getOp(),getOp()));
                  break;
    case "*"    : System.out.println(
                        mul.applyAsDouble(getOp(),getOp()));
                  break;
```

```
    case "/"    : System.out.println(
                        div.applyAsDouble(getOp(),getOp()));
                break;
    case "POW"  : System.out.println(
                        pow.applyAsDouble(getOp(),getOp()));
                break;
    case "ABS"  : System.out.println(
                        abs.applyAsDouble(getOp()));
                break;
    case "LOG"  : System.out.println(
                        log.applyAsDouble(getOp()));
                break;
    case "EXP"  : System.out.println(
                        exp.applyAsDouble(getOp()));
                break;
    case "SIN"  : System.out.println(
                        sin.applyAsDouble(getOp()));
                break;
    case "COS"  : System.out.println(
                        cos.applyAsDouble(getOp()));
                break;
    case "TAN"  : System.out.println(
                        tan.applyAsDouble(getOp()));
                break;
    case "QUI"  : done = true;
                break;
    default:      System.out.println("Invalid operation");
}
```

The program in Listing 5-1 demonstrates. The user selects the "+" operation which has two operands. The user is prompted to enter both operands, and the program prints 9.1 which is the sum of operands 4.0 and 5.1. The user then selects the "SIN" operation which has only one operand. The user is prompted to enter the angle, and the program prints 0.49999999999999994 which is the sine of 30 degrees. The user then selects "QUI" and the program terminates.

Listing 5-1. Calculator.java

```java
import java.util.function.*;
import java.util.Scanner;
class Calculator
{
    public static double getOp()
    {
        Scanner scan = new Scanner(System.in);
        System.out.print("Enter an operand:");
        return Double.parseDouble(scan.nextLine());
    }
    public static void main(String[] args)
    {
        Scanner scan = new Scanner(System.in);
        final String[] ops = {"+","-","*","/","POW","ABS","LOG",
                              "EXP","SIN","COS","TAN","QUI"};

        DoubleBinaryOperator sum = (x,y) -> x + y;
        DoubleBinaryOperator dif = (x,y) -> x - y;
        DoubleBinaryOperator mul = (x,y) -> x * y;
        DoubleBinaryOperator div = (x,y) -> x / y;
        DoubleBinaryOperator pow = (x,y) -> Math.pow(x,y);

        DoubleUnaryOperator  abs = x -> Math.abs(x);
        DoubleUnaryOperator  log = x -> Math.log(x);
        DoubleUnaryOperator  exp = x -> Math.exp(x);
        DoubleUnaryOperator  sin = x -> Math.sin(Math.toRadians(x));
        DoubleUnaryOperator  cos = x -> Math.cos(Math.toRadians(x));
        DoubleUnaryOperator  tan = x -> Math.tan(Math.toRadians(x));

        boolean done = false;
        while (!done)
        {
            System.out.println("Select an operation " +
                          "(select QUI to quit):");
            for (String s : ops)
```

```
        System.out.println(s);
    String op = scan.nextLine();

    switch (op)
    {
        case "+"  : System.out.println(
                    sum.applyAsDouble(getOp(),getOp()));
                    break;
        case "-"  : System.out.println(
                    dif.applyAsDouble(getOp(),getOp()));
                    break;
        case "*"  : System.out.println(
                    mul.applyAsDouble(getOp(),getOp()));
                    break;
        case "/"  : System.out.println(
                    div.applyAsDouble(getOp(),getOp()));
                    break;
        case "POW": System.out.println(
                    pow.applyAsDouble(getOp(),getOp()));
                    break;
        case "ABS": System.out.println(
                    abs.applyAsDouble(getOp()));
                    break;
        case "LOG": System.out.println(
                    log.applyAsDouble(getOp()));
                    break;
        case "EXP": System.out.println(
                    exp.applyAsDouble(getOp()));
                    break;
        case "SIN": System.out.println(
                    sin.applyAsDouble(getOp()));
                    break;
        case "COS": System.out.println(
                    cos.applyAsDouble(getOp()));
                    break;
        case "TAN": System.out.println(
```

```
                        tan.applyAsDouble(getOp()));
                        break;
               case "QUI": done = true;
                        break;
               default:   System.out.println("Invalid operation");
            }
         }
      }
}
```

PROGRAM OUTPUT (user input shown in **BOLD**):

```
Select an operation (select QUI to quit):
+
-
*
/ POW
ABS
LOG
EXP
SIN
COS
TAN
QUI
+
Enter an operand:4.0
Enter an operand:5.1
9.1
Select an operation (select QUI to quit):
+
-
*
/
POW
ABS
LOG
```

```
EXP
SIN
COS
TAN
QUI
SIN
Enter an operand:30.0
0.49999999999999994
Select an operation (select QUI to quit):
+
-
*
/
POW
ABS
LOG
EXP
SIN
COS
TAN
QUI
QUI
```

Short Problems

1) Write an operator that returns a string containing the odd characters of an input string (in other words, the characters located at positions 1, 3, 5, etc.).

2) Write a chain of operators that computes the following equation:

$$-4 * (x + 2)$$

3) Class A has int field x and double field y. Write a BinaryOperator that add the x field of two A objects while subtracting the y field of the two objects.

Long Problems

1) Using a single chain of operators, solve the following equation for
    x = 6 and y = 3:

    $$5 * (2x + 3y) / 2$$

2) Given the string "The fault lies not from our stars," use a single
    chain of operators to perform the following operations:

    – Concatenate the string with "but from ourselves."

    – Replace "from" with "in".

    – Convert the string to uppercase.

3) Recall that Discount Dave sells Hyundai Elantras, Toyota Priuses,
    and Honda Odysseys. Dave is running a sale that takes 10% off the
    Hyundai Elantras in stock, 7% off the Toyota Priuses in stock, and
    5% off the Honda Odysseys in stock. His cars in stock are modeled
    using a list of Car objects.

    Using a single chain of operators, apply these discounts to Dave's
    cars, and print out the resulting list.

CHAPTER 6

Consumers

Section 6.1: The Consumer Interface

Consumer is a functional interface that is used to process data. A Consumer object is specified with type parameter T. Its functional method, called accept, takes an argument of type T and has return type void.

```
@FunctionalInterface
public interface Consumer<T>
{
    void accept(T t);
    ...
}
```

A Consumer of Integer type whose accept method adds its argument to a static field called sum is defined as follows:

```
Consumer<Integer> con = x -> sum += x;
```

The program in Listing 6-1 uses the consumer to add the numbers 4 and 5 and then prints the sum:

Listing 6-1. TestConsumer.java

```
import java.util.function.Consumer;
public class TestConsumer
{
    private static int sum = 0;
    public static void main(String[] args)
    {
        Consumer<Integer> con = x -> sum += x;
        con.accept(4);
```

© Ralph Lecessi 2019
R. Lecessi, *Functional Interfaces in Java*, https://doi.org/10.1007/978-1-4842-4278-0_6

```
        con.accept(5);
        System.out.println(sum);
    }
}
```

PROGRAM OUTPUT:

9

Section 6.2: Using Chains of Consumers to Compute Equations

The Consumer interface's default andThen method further processes the input argument after the accept method completes.

```
default Consumer<T> andThen(Consumer<? super T> after);
```

The following program computes the sum and the product of 4 and 5. The consumer chain creates a composed consumer consisting of the code in both consum and conprod. The code in the calling Consumer object, consum, is executed first, and the argument 4 is added to sum. Then the code in conprod, the consumer passed to the andThen method, is executed, and the argument 4 is multiplied by prod. The process is repeated for the argument 5.

Listing 6-2. TestConsumerAndThen.java

```
import java.util.function.Consumer;
public class TestConsumerAndThen
{
    private static int sum  = 0;
    private static int prod = 1;
    public static void main(String[] args)
    {
        Consumer<Integer> consum  = x -> sum  += x;
        Consumer<Integer> conprod = x -> prod *= x;

        consum.andThen(conprod)
              .accept(4);
        consum.andThen(conprod)
```

```
        .accept(5);

    System.out.println("sum = " + sum + " prod =" + prod);
    }
}
```

PROGRAM OUTPUT:

```
sum = 9 prod =20
```

Long chains of consumers can be composed to perform an operation that does not require a result to be returned. As with other functional interfaces, the composed consumer of the first two operations becomes the first operand of the second composed consumer, and so on.

This technique can be used to solve equations one term at a time. Consider the following polynomial:

$$fx = 5x^4 + 7x^3 + 4x^2 + 3x + 8$$

The value of the polynomial for a given x can be solved by computing the fourth-degree term using the calling consumer and then computing the third degree through the constant term using consumers passed to the andThen method in a consumer chain and so on.

Listing 6-3. ComputePolynomial.java

```
import java.util.function.Consumer;
public class ComputePolynomial
{
    private static int fx = 0;
    public static void main(String[] args)
    {
        Consumer<Integer> poly = x -> fx += 5 * (int)Math.pow(x, 4);

        poly.andThen(x -> fx += 7 * (int)Math.pow(x, 3))
            .andThen(x -> fx += 4 * (int)Math.pow(x, 2))
            .andThen(x -> fx += 3 * x)
            .andThen(x -> fx += 8)
            .andThen(x -> System.out.println(fx))
            .accept(2);

    }
}
```

111

PROGRAM OUTPUT:

166

Section 6.3: Using Consumers with println as the Terminal Operation

The last link in the consumer chain for the program in Listing 6-3 contained a System.out. println statement that printed the result of the equation. Method chains frequently end in a consumer that displays the result of the processing that occurred along the chain.

Section 6.4: Non-generic Specializations of Consumers

The Java API provides IntConsumer, LongConsumer, and DoubleConsumer, which are non-generic specializations of the Consumer interface. They process int, long, and double primitive types, respectively.

```
@FunctionalInterface
public interface IntConsumer
{
    void accept(int value);
    ...
}

@FunctionalInterface
public interface LongConsumer
{
    void accept(long value);
    ...
}

@FunctionalInterface
public interface DoubleConsumer
{
    void accept(double value);
    ...
}
```

The program in Listing 6-4 demonstrates. `IntConsumer` ic assigns the sum of `int` argument 2 and the value 3 to static field a. `LongConsumer` lc assigns the quotient of `long` argument 6 and the value 2 to static field b. `DoubleConsumer` dc assigns the product of `double` argument 4.0 and static field c to static field c.

Listing 6-4. ConsumerSpecials.java

```java
import java.util.function.*;
public class ConsumerSpecials
{
    private static int    a = 0;
    private static long   b = 0;
    private static double c = 1.0;
    public static void main(String[] args)
    {
        IntConsumer    ic = x -> a = x + 3;
        LongConsumer   lc = x -> b = x / 2L;
        DoubleConsumer dc = x -> c = x * c;

        ic.andThen(x -> System.out.println(a))
          .accept(2);
        lc.andThen(x -> System.out.println(b))
          .accept(6L);
        dc.andThen(x -> System.out.println(c))
          .accept(4.0);
    }
}
```

PROGRAM OUTPUT:

```
5
3
4.0
```

Section 6.5: The BiConsumer Interface

It is often useful to process inputs of two different generic types. The BiConsumer functional interface specifies type parameters T and U. Its accept method takes arguments of types T and U and has return type void.

```
@FunctionalInterface
public interface BiConsumer<T,U>
{
    void accept(T t, U u);
    ...
}
```

In the following example, a sum is accumulated using an Integer parameter, which is the first type of the BiConsumer. A descriptor for its components is accumulated using a String parameter, which is the second type of the BiConsumer. The first call to BiConsumer bi's accept method adds 6 to sum and concatenates "Term 1" to components. The second call to BiConsumer bi's accept method adds 7 to sum and concatenates "Term 2" to components.

Listing 6-5. TestBiConsumer.java

```
import java.util.function.BiConsumer;
public class TestBiConsumer
{
    private static int sum = 0;
    private static String components = "";
    public static void main(String[] args)
    {
        BiConsumer<Integer,String> bi = (x,y) -> {
            sum += x;
            components += y;
        };

        bi.andThen( (x,y) -> System.out.println(x + " " + y))
          .accept(6, "Term 1");
```

```
        bi.andThen( (x,y) -> System.out.println("add " + x + " ." + y
                         + " result = " + sum + " " + components))
            .accept(7, ",Term 2");
    }
}
```

PROGRAM OUTPUT:

```
6 Term 1
add 7 ,Term 2 result = 13 Term 1,Term 2
```

Section 6.6: Specializations of BiConsumer

The Java API provides the ObjIntConsumer, ObjLongConsumer, and ObjDoubleConsumer interfaces which specialize the second argument to the apply method.

```
@FunctionalInterface
public interface ObjIntConsumer<T> {
    void accept(T t, int value);
}
```

```
@FunctionalInterface
public interface ObjLongConsumer<T> {
    void accept(T t, long value);
}
```

```
@FunctionalInterface
public interface ObjDoubleConsumer<T> {
    void accept(T t, double value);
}
```

The following example demonstrates. ObjIntConsumer oic prints String argument "Value" followed by " = " followed by int argument 4. ObjLongConsumer olc parses String argument "7" as long and then adds it to long argument 2. ObjDoubleConsumer odc prints String argument "DBL" followed by double argument 4.1 formatted as a String.

```
ObjIntConsumer<String> oic    = (x,y) ->
    System.out.println(x + " = " + y);
ObjLongConsumer<String> olc   = (x,y) ->
    System.out.println(Long.parseLong(x) + y);
ObjDoubleConsumer<String> odc = (x,y) ->
    System.out.println(x + (new Double(y)).toString());

oic.accept("Value", 4);
olc.accept("7", 2L);
odc.accept("DBL", 4.1);
```

OUTPUT:

```
Value = 4
9
DBL4.1
```

PROJECT 6: Bank Transactions

Problem Statement

The High Interest Bank wants a program with a command line interface that performs transactions on a database consisting of bank accounts. The program should be able to open, close, deposit into, and withdraw from an account. Bank accounts consist of the customer's name, an id which is a random integer from 0 to 10000, and the customer's balance.

When an account is opened, the customer's name and initial deposit are requested. A bank account containing the customer's name, initial balance, and generated id is added to the database. The account creation is then verified, and a message indicating its success or failure is displayed.

When a deposit is performed, the customer's id and the deposit amount are requested. If a bank account matching the customer's id is found in the database, the deposit amount is added to the balance. The deposit is then verified, and a message indicating its success or failure is displayed.

When a withdrawal is performed, the customer's id and the withdrawal amount are requested. If a bank account matching the customer's id is found in the database and if sufficient funds are available, the withdrawal amount is subtracted from the balance. The withdrawal is then verified, and a message indicating its success or failure is displayed.

When an account is closed, the customer's id is requested. If a bank account matching the customer's id is found in the database, the account is removed from the database. The account closure is then verified, and a message indicating its success or failure is displayed.

Solution

First, a BankAccount class with fields name, id, and balance should be written.

```
class BankAccount
{
    String name;
    int    id;
    double balance;
    public BankAccount(String n, int i, double b)
    {
        name = n;
        id = i;
        balance = b;
    }
    @Override
    public boolean equals(Object ba)
    {
        return id == ((BankAccount)ba).id;
    }
    @Override
    public String toString()
    {
        return "name = " + name + " id = " + id
            + " balance = " + balance;
    }
}
```

Next, a few static fields shared by the consumers need to be created. These include the accounts database, the number of accounts, and the previous balance.

```
private static ArrayList<BankAccount> accounts
    = new ArrayList<>();
private static int numAccounts = 0;
private static double prevBalance = 0.0;
```

Accounts are opened using the customer's name and an initial deposit amount. Therefore, a BiConsumer<String, Double> object should be created. The BiConsumer will first save the current number of bank accounts in the database. Then, it will generate a random number between 0 and 10000, and use the customer's name, the random number, and the initial balance to create a new bank account and add it to the database.

```
BiConsumer<String,Double> open = (x,y) -> {
    numAccounts = accounts.size();
    Random generator = new Random();
    accounts.add(new BankAccount(x,
                generator.nextInt(10000), y));
};
```

The account creation is then verified by checking if an entry has been added to the accounts database and that the name field in the added entry matches the customer's name. If the entry matches, the corresponding bank account information is displayed.

```
BiConsumer<String,Double> openVerification = (x,y) -> {
    if ( accounts.size() == (numAccounts + 1)
     && accounts.get(numAccounts).name.equals(x) )
        System.out.println("ACCOUNT for " + x
                        + " OPENED SUCCESSFULLY.\n"
                        + accounts.get(numAccounts));
    else
        System.out.println("COULD NOT OPEN ACCOUNT for " + x);
};
```

Verification can be performed in the andThen method of the open BiConsumer. Methods that prompt the user for the customer's name and amount can be written.

```
open.andThen(openVerification)
    .accept(promptName(), promptAmount());
```

Deposits, withdrawals, and account closures need to look up a bank account based on id. Since the BankAccount class's equals method tests the id field, a BankAccount object containing the entered id can be passed to the indexOf method of ArrayList accounts.

```
public static BankAccount findBankAccount(int id)
{
    int index = accounts.indexOf(new BankAccount(null,id,0.0));
    return (index > -1) ? accounts.get(index) : null;
}
```

Deposits are performed using the customer's id and the deposit amount. Therefore, they can be implemented by a BiConsumer<Integer, Double> object. If an account matching the id is found, the previous balance in the account is stored. Then the deposit amount is added to the balance.

```
BiConsumer<Integer,Double> deposit = (x,y) -> {
    BankAccount account = findBankAccount(x);
    if (account != null)
    {
        prevBalance = account.balance;
        account.balance += y;
    }
};
```

The deposit is then verified by checking if an account matching the customer's id exists and its balance has been incremented by the deposit amount.

```
BiConsumer<Integer,Double> depositVerification = (x,y) -> {
    BankAccount account = findBankAccount(x);
    if (account != null
     && account.balance == (prevBalance + y) )
        System.out.println("DEPOSIT OF $" + y
                        + " INTO ACCOUNT " + x
                        + " SUCCESSFUL\n" + account);
    else
        System.out.println("ACCOUNT " + x + "NOT FOUND");
};
```

Verification can be performed in the andThen method of the deposit BiConsumer.

```
deposit.andThen(depositVerification)
      .accept(promptId(), promptAmount());
```

Withdrawals are performed using the customer's id and the withdrawal amount. Therefore, they can be implemented by a BiConsumer<Integer, Double> object. If an account matching the id is found, the previous balance in the account is stored. If sufficient funds exist in the account, the withdrawal amount is subtracted from the balance.

```
BiConsumer<Integer,Double> withdraw = (x,y) -> {
    BankAccount account = findBankAccount(x);
    if (account != null)
    {
        prevBalance = account.balance;
        if ((account.balance - y) >= 0.0)
            account.balance -= y;
    }
};
```

The withdrawal is then verified by checking if an account matching the customer's id exists and its balance has been decremented by the withdrawal amount. If the account exists and the funds were not withdrawn, the BiConsumer displays a message indicating insufficient funds.

```
BiConsumer<Integer,Double> withdrawVerification = (x,y) -> {
    BankAccount account = findBankAccount(x);
    if (account != null)
    {
        if (account.balance == (prevBalance - y))
            System.out.println("WITHDRAW OF $" + y
                            + " FROM ACCOUNT " + x
                            + " SUCCESSFUL\n" + account);
        else
```

```
            System.out.println("INSUFFICIENT FUNDS TO"
                    + " WITHDRAW $" + y
                    + " FROM ACCOUNT " + x + "\n"
                    + account);
    }
    else
        System.out.println("ACCOUNT " + x + "NOT FOUND");
};
```

Verification can be performed in the andThen method of the withdraw BiConsumer.

```
withdraw.andThen(withdrawVerification)
        .accept(promptId(), promptAmount());
```

Accounts are closed using the customer's id. A Consumer<Integer> can be used. If an account matching the id is found, it is removed from the database.

```
Consumer<Integer> close = x -> {
    numAccounts = accounts.size();
    BankAccount account = findBankAccount(x);
    if (account != null)
        accounts.remove(account);
};
```

The account closure is then verified by checking if an entry has been removed from the accounts database.

```
Consumer<Integer> closeVerification = x -> {
    if (accounts.size() == (numAccounts - 1) )
        System.out.println("ACCOUNT " + x +
                            " SUCCESSFULLY CLOSED");
    else
        System.out.println("COULD NOT CLOSE ACCOUNT " + x);
};
```

Verification can be performed in the andThen method of the close Consumer.

```
close.andThen(closeVerification)
    .accept(promptId());
```

121

The complete program is listed and demonstrated as follows. An account is opened for Harvey Smith with an initial balance of $500 dollars. The program responds that the account was opened successfully and assigns id 8485 to Mr. Smith. This id will be used for all deposits and withdrawals on the bank account and to close the account if the customer desires. Mr. Smith then deposits $100 dollars into his account bringing his balance to $600. Next, Mr. Smith attempts to withdraw $700 from his account and is told that there are insufficient funds to do so. He then withdraws $50 from his account bringing his balance to $550. Then, Mr. Smith closes his account. Lastly the program is terminated.

Listing 6-6. BankTransactions.java

```java
import java.util.function.*;
import java.util.*;
class BankAccount
{
    String name;
    int    id;
    double balance;
    public BankAccount(String n, int i, double b)
    {
        name = n;
        id = i;
        balance = b;
    }
    @Override
    public boolean equals(Object ba)
    {
        return id == ((BankAccount)ba).id;
    }
    @Override
    public String toString()
    {
        return "name = " + name + " id = " + id
            + " balance = " + balance;
    }
}
```

```
class BankTransactions
{
    private static ArrayList<BankAccount> accounts
        = new ArrayList<>();
    private static int numAccounts = 0;
    private static double prevBalance = 0.0;
    private static Scanner scan = new Scanner(System.in);
    public static String promptTransaction()
    {
        System.out.println("Enter Transaction Type:");
        System.out.println("OPENACCOUNT");
        System.out.println("DEPOSIT");
        System.out.println("WITHDRAWAL");
        System.out.println("CLOSEACCOUNT");
        System.out.print("QUIT:");
        return scan.nextLine();
    }
    public static double promptAmount()
    {
        System.out.print("Enter amount:");
        return Double.parseDouble(scan.nextLine());
    }
    public static String promptName()
    {
        System.out.print("Enter name:");
        return scan.nextLine();
    }
    public static int promptId()
    {
        System.out.print("Enter id:");
        return Integer.parseInt(scan.nextLine());
    }
    public static BankAccount findBankAccount(int id)
    {
        int index = accounts.indexOf(new BankAccount(null,id,0.0));
```

```
        return (index > -1) ? accounts.get(index) : null;
    }
    public static void main(String[] args)
    {
        BiConsumer<String,Double> open = (x,y) -> {
            numAccounts = accounts.size();
            Random generator = new Random();
            accounts.add(new BankAccount(x,
                        generator.nextInt(10000), y));
        };

        BiConsumer<String,Double> openVerification = (x,y) -> {
            if ( accounts.size() == (numAccounts + 1)
             &&  accounts.get(numAccounts).name.equals(x) )
                System.out.println("ACCOUNT for " + x
                                 + " OPENED SUCCESSFULLY.\n"
                                    + accounts.get(numAccounts));
            else
                System.out.println("COULD NOT OPEN ACCOUNT for "
                                 + x);
        };

        BiConsumer<Integer,Double> deposit = (x,y) -> {
            BankAccount account = findBankAccount(x);
            if (account != null)
            {
                prevBalance = account.balance;
                account.balance += y;
            }
        };

        BiConsumer<Integer,Double> depositVerification = (x,y) -> {
            BankAccount account = findBankAccount(x);
            if (account != null
             && account.balance == (prevBalance + y) )
                System.out.println("DEPOSIT OF $" + y
                                 + " INTO ACCOUNT " + x
```

```java
                                + " SUCCESSFUL\n" + account);
        else
            System.out.println("ACCOUNT " + x + "NOT FOUND");
};

BiConsumer<Integer,Double> withdraw = (x,y) -> {
    BankAccount account = findBankAccount(x);
    if (account != null)
    {
        prevBalance = account.balance;
        if ((account.balance - y) >= 0.0)
            account.balance -= y;
    }
};

BiConsumer<Integer,Double> withdrawVerification = (x,y) -> {
    BankAccount account = findBankAccount(x);
    if (account != null)
    {
        if (account.balance == (prevBalance - y))
            System.out.println("WITHDRAW OF $" + y
                                + " FROM ACCOUNT " + x
                                + " SUCCESSFUL\n" + account);
        else
            System.out.println("INSUFFICIENT FUNDS TO"
                                + " WITHDRAW $" + y
                                + " FROM ACCOUNT " + x + "\n"
                                + account);
    }
    else
        System.out.println("ACCOUNT " + x + "NOT FOUND");
};

Consumer<Integer> close = x -> {
    numAccounts = accounts.size();
    BankAccount account = findBankAccount(x);
    if (account != null)
```

```
            accounts.remove(account);
    };

    Consumer<Integer> closeVerification = x -> {
        if (accounts.size() == (numAccounts - 1) )
            System.out.println("ACCOUNT " + x +
                                " SUCCESSFULLY CLOSED");
        else
            System.out.println("COULD NOT CLOSE ACCOUNT " + x);
    };

    boolean done = false;
    while (!done)
    {
        String transactionSelected = promptTransaction();
        switch (transactionSelected)
        {
            case "OPENACCOUNT":
                open.andThen(openVerification)
                    .accept(promptName(), promptAmount());
                break;
            case "DEPOSIT":
                deposit.andThen(depositVerification)
                        .accept(promptId(), promptAmount());
                break;
            case "WITHDRAWAL":
                withdraw.andThen(withdrawVerification)
                        .accept(promptId(), promptAmount());
                break;
            case "CLOSEACCOUNT":
                close.andThen(closeVerification)
                    .accept(promptId());
                break;
            case "QUIT":
                done = true;
                break;
```

```
        default:
            System.out.println("Invalid selection");
        }
    }
  }
}
```

PROGRAM OUTPUT (user input shown in **BOLD**):

Enter Transaction Type:
OPENACCOUNT
DEPOSIT
WITHDRAWAL
CLOSEACCOUNT
QUIT:**OPENACCOUNT**
Enter name:**Harvey Smith**
Enter amount:**500.0**
ACCOUNT for Harvey Smith OPENED SUCCESSFULLY.
name = Harvey Smith id = 8485 balance = 500.0
Enter Transaction Type:
OPENACCOUNT
DEPOSIT
WITHDRAWAL
CLOSEACCOUNT
QUIT:**DEPOSIT**
Enter id:**8485**
Enter amount:**100.0**
DEPOSIT OF $100.0 INTO ACCOUNT 8485 SUCCESSFUL
name = Harvey Smith id = 8485 balance = 600.0
Enter Transaction Type:
OPENACCOUNT
DEPOSIT
WITHDRAWAL
CLOSEACCOUNT
QUIT:**WITHDRAWAL**
Enter id:**8485**
Enter amount:**700.0**

INSUFFICIENT FUNDS TO WITHDRAW $700.0 FROM ACCOUNT 8485

name = Harvey Smith id = 8485 balance = 600.0

Enter Transaction Type:

OPENACCOUNT

DEPOSIT

WITHDRAWAL

CLOSEACCOUNT

QUIT:**WITHDRAWAL**

Enter id:**8485**

Enter amount:**50.0**

WITHDRAW OF $50.0 FROM ACCOUNT 8485 SUCCESSFUL

name = Harvey Smith id = 8485 balance = 550.0

Enter Transaction Type:

OPENACCOUNT

DEPOSIT

WITHDRAWAL

CLOSEACCOUNT

QUIT:**CLOSEACCOUNT**

Enter id:**8485**

ACCOUNT 8485 SUCCESSFULLY CLOSED

Enter Transaction Type:

OPENACCOUNT

DEPOSIT

WITHDRAWAL

CLOSEACCOUNT

QUIT:**QUIT**

Short Problems

1) Use a chain of consumers to do the following:

   – Initialize a number to the value 5

   – Add 4 to the number

   – Multiply the number by 7

   – Print the number

2) Create an `ArrayList` of `Consumer` objects that process numeric wrapper class objects. Create a Java array of numeric wrapper class objects and use the consumers to process them in a loop.

3) Write a `BiConsumer` to populate an array of strings. One argument to the `BiConsumer` specifies the value to store, and the other argument specifies the index in the array at which to store the value. Demonstrate in a main program.

Long Problems

1) A dictionary is implemented as a map of keys and values. Using a single chain of consumers, create a string that contains a comma-separated list of the first word of each value whose key is five characters in length.

2) Your entertainment collection consists of the following:

   – DVDs organized by title, production company, and memory size in megabytes

   – Audio files organized by title, format, and memory size in megabytes

   – E-books organized by title, number of pages, and memory size in megabytes

   Use a chain of consumers to generate a list of all the titles in your collection and another list of all the memory sizes in your collection.

3) An apartment building contains two-bedroom and three-bedroom apartments of various sizes. Using the `Consumer` interface, compute the total square footage of all the rooms in the building.

CHAPTER 7

Suppliers

Section 7.1: The Supplier Interface

Supplier is a functional interface that is used to generate data. A Supplier object is specified with type parameter T. Its functional method, called get, takes no arguments and returns an object of type T.

```
@FunctionalInterface
public interface Supplier<T>
{
    T get();
}
```

A supplier that generates a random integer is defined as follows:

```
Supplier<Integer> generateInteger = () ->
{
    Random rand = new Random();
    return rand.nextInt(100);
};
```

A supplier that generates a string using a Scanner object is defined as follows:

```
Supplier<String> generateString = () ->
{
    Scanner scan = new Scanner(System.in);
    System.out.print("Enter a string:");
    return scan.nextLine();
};
```

© Ralph Lecessi 2019
R. Lecessi, *Functional Interfaces in Java*, https://doi.org/10.1007/978-1-4842-4278-0_7

The program in Listing 7-1 demonstrates the use of these two suppliers. The get method of generateInteger is called and integer value 30 is generated randomly. It is called again and integer value 24 is randomly generated. The get method of generateString is called which first prompts the user to enter a string and then uses a Scanner to enter the string "Hello" from the user. GenerateString's get method is called again, and the string "World" is obtained from the user.

Listing 7-1. TestSupplier.java

```java
import java.util.function.Supplier;
import java.util.Random;
import java.util.Scanner;
class TestSupplier
{
    public static void main(String[] args)
    {
        Supplier<Integer> generateInteger = () ->
        {
            Random rand = new Random();
            return rand.nextInt(100);
        };
        Supplier<String> generateString = () ->
        {
            Scanner scan = new Scanner(System.in);
            System.out.print("Enter a string:");
            return scan.nextLine();
        };

        System.out.println(generateInteger.get());
        System.out.println(generateInteger.get());
        System.out.println(generateString.get());
        System.out.println(generateString.get());
    }
}
```

PROGRAM OUTPUT (user input shown in **BOLD**):

```
30
24
Enter a string:Hello

Hello
Enter a string:World
World
```

Section 7.2: Wrapping User Prompts in a Supplier

Using suppliers to wrap each user prompt can help to simplify the logic of a program.

Suppose a program needs to prompt a user to select between three different operations. The following supplier wraps a Scanner object and code which prompts the user for the selection. The user is first presented with four choices: 1 for Operation 1, 2 for Operation 2, 3 for Operation 3, and 4 to quit the program. If the user selects a number out of this range, he or she is informed that the selection is invalid and is prompted to select again. If the selection is valid, the selected operation is returned.

```
Supplier<Integer> selectOperation = () -> {
    int operation = 0;
    Scanner userInput = new Scanner(System.in);

    while (operation < 1 || operation > 4)
    {
        System.out.println("Select an operation:");
        System.out.println("    1: Operation 1");
        System.out.println("    2: Operation 2");
        System.out.println("    3: Operation 3");
        System.out.println("    4: Quit");
        operation = Integer.parseInt(userInput.nextLine());
        if (operation < 1 || operation > 4)
            System.out.println("Invalid operation");
    }
    return operation;
};
```

Since the while loop and prompt have been moved to the Supplier implementation, the main loop is simplified considerably.

```
boolean done = false;
while (!done)
{
    switch (selectOperation.get())
    {
        case 1: System.out.println("Performing Operation 1");
                break;
        case 2: System.out.println("Performing Operation 2");
                break;
        case 3: System.out.println("Performing Operation 3");
                break;
        default: done = true;
    }
}
```

An execution of the main loop is shown as follows. The user selects 0 and is told that the operation is invalid. Then, the user selects 2 and the program performs Operation 2. Then, the user selects 4 and the program terminates.

OUTPUT (user input shown in **BOLD**):

```
Select an operation:
  1: Operation 1
  2: Operation 2
  3: Operation 3
  4: Quit
0
Invalid operation
Select an operation:
  1: Operation 1
  2: Operation 2
  3: Operation 3
  4: Quit
2
Performing Operation 2
```

```
Select an operation:
  1: Operation 1
  2: Operation 2
  3: Operation 3
  4: Quit
4
```

Section 7.3: Non-generic Specializations of Suppliers

The Java API provides BooleanSupplier, IntSupplier, LongSupplier, and DoubleSupplier, which are non-generic specializations of the Supplier interface. They generate boolean, int, long, and double primitive types, respectively.

```java
@FunctionalInterface
public interface BooleanSupplier {
    boolean getAsBoolean();
}
```

```java
@FunctionalInterface
public interface IntSupplier {
    int getAsInt();
}
```

```java
@FunctionalInterface
public interface LongSupplier {
    long getAsLong();
}
```

```java
@FunctionalInterface
public interface DoubleSupplier {
    double getAsDouble();
}
```

The program in Listing 7-2 demonstrates. The BooleanSupplier returns true if a random integer between 0 and 1 is 1, and returns false otherwise. The IntSupplier, LongSupplier, and DoubleSupplier return random int, long, and double primitive values, respectively.

Listing 7-2. TestSpecials.java

```java
import java.util.function.*;
import java.util.Random;
class TestSpecials
{
    public static Random rand = new Random();
    public static void main(String[] args)
    {
        BooleanSupplier genBol = () ->
            (rand.nextInt(2) == 1)? true:false;
        IntSupplier     genInt = () -> rand.nextInt();
        LongSupplier    genLng = () -> rand.nextLong();
        DoubleSupplier  genDbl = () -> rand.nextDouble();

        System.out.println(genBol.getAsBoolean());
        System.out.println(genInt.getAsInt());
        System.out.println(genLng.getAsLong());
        System.out.println(genDbl.getAsDouble());
    }
}
```

PROGRAM OUTPUT:

```
true
-1883978156
95506489147983601
0.050671447138405656
```

PROJECT 7: Ticketing System

Problem Statement

The Awesome Cheap Cell Phones company sells several types of phones, provides software apps which run on the phones, and has a web site where customers can purchase phones, purchase apps, manage their accounts, and post problems in the form of hardware or software trouble tickets.

All tickets contain the customer's name, the customer's id, a description of the problem, and an estimated completion date. Hardware tickets document problems with the cell phone itself. They also contain the device name, its model, and serial number. Software tickets document either bugs in a software app or problems using the web site. They also contain the application name, its version, and where the application is hosted (on phone or on the Internet).

Each day, a tech support specialist attempts to work on all the problems documented in the trouble ticket database; the order of tickets worked is based on estimated completion dates. When the tech works on a problem, it is marked as having been serviced today. If the tech can solve the problem, it is removed from the database. The tech proceeds until all the tickets in the database have been serviced or his or her shift is over. If the tech can service all the tickets in the database in a single day, he or she earns a $50 bonus.

Solution

A Ticket class that is comparable by due date can be written. The class should store the last date the ticket was serviced. When a ticket is created, the estimated repair time is added to the current date forming the due date. The service date is set to yesterday, so that the ticket will be serviced today by the tech specialist.

```
abstract class Ticket implements Comparable<Ticket>
{
    String customerName;
    int id;
    String description;
    LocalDate dueDate;
    LocalDate servicedDate;
    public Ticket(String cn, int i, String d, int due)
    {
        customerName = cn;
        id = i;
        description = d;
        dueDate = LocalDate.now().plusDays(due);
        servicedDate = LocalDate.now().minusDays(1);
    }
    @Override
```

```
    public String toString()
    {
        return "NAME:             " + customerName
            + "\nID:             " + id
            + "\nDESCRIPTION:    " + description
            + "\nDUE DATE:       " + dueDate
            + "\nSERVICED DATE:  " + servicedDate;
    }
    @Override
    public int compareTo(Ticket t)
    {
        return dueDate.compareTo(t.dueDate);
    }
}
```

HardwareTicket and SoftwareTicket subclasses can be created.

```
class HardwareTicket extends Ticket
{
    String device;
    String model;
    String serialNumber;
    public HardwareTicket(String cn, int i, String d, int due,
                        String dev, String mod, String sn)
    {
        super(cn, i, d, due);
        device = dev;
        model = mod;
        serialNumber = sn;
    }
    @Override
    public String toString()
    {
        return super.toString()
            + "\nDEVICE:         " + device
            + "\nMODEL:          " + model
```

```
                  + "\nSERIAL NUMBER:   " + serialNumber;
    }
}

enum Domain {WEB_HOSTED, PHONE_HOSTED}
class SoftwareTicket extends Ticket
{
    String application;
    String version;
    Domain domain;
    public SoftwareTicket(String cn, int i, String d, int due,
                          String app, String ver, Domain dom)
    {
        super(cn, i, d, due);
        application = app;
        version = ver;
        domain = dom;
    }
    @Override
    public String toString()
    {
        return super.toString()
            + "\nAPPLICATION:   " + application
            + "\nVERSION:       " + version
            + "\nDOMAIN:        " + domain;
    }
}
```

Tickets can be polymorphically stored in the database using an ArrayList<Ticket> object.

```
private static ArrayList<Ticket> tickets = new ArrayList<>();
tickets.add(new HardwareTicket("Kalpana Patel",54641,
                               "Cell phone won't power on",
                               5, "Smartie", "SM250",
                               "SN546497-S23"));
tickets.add(new SoftwareTicket("Chester Rodriguez",89034,
```

```
                        "MapApp can't find grandma's house",
                            2, "MapApp", "1.01",
                              Domain.PHONE_HOSTED));
tickets.add(new SoftwareTicket("Britney Delmonica",91472,
                            "Can't change banking info on website",
                              1, "awesomecheapcellphones.com",
                              "2.65", Domain.WEB_HOSTED));
tickets.add(new HardwareTicket("Kalpana Patel",54641,
                              "Cell phone's screen goes black",
                              7, "Rover", "RV100",
                              "SN456742-R31"));
```

Type wildcarding can be used to create a supplier that generates either a HardwareTicket or a SoftwareTicket. The supplier selects the entry in the database with the earliest due date that has not already been serviced today. The selected entry is then marked as serviced by changing its service date to today. If no entry has been selected, a reference to null is returned.

```
Supplier<? extends Ticket> nextTicket = () ->
{
    Ticket next = null;
    for (int i=0; i < tickets.size(); ++i)
    {
        Ticket t = tickets.get(i);
        if (t.servicedDate.compareTo(today) < 0)
        {
            if (next == null || t.compareTo(next) < 0)
                next = t;
        }
    }
    if (next != null)
        next.servicedDate = today;
    return next;
};
```

BooleanSuppliers can be written to prompt the specialist if he or she can close the ticket or if his or her shift is over.

```
BooleanSupplier canClose = () -> {
    boolean result = false;
    Scanner scan = new Scanner(System.in);
    System.out.print("\nCan you close the ticket (Y or N)?");
    if (scan.nextLine().charAt(0) == 'Y')
        result = true;
    return result;
};

BooleanSupplier isQuittingTime = () -> {
    boolean result = false;
    Scanner scan = new Scanner(System.in);
    System.out.print("Is it quitting time (Y or N)?");
    if (scan.nextLine().charAt(0) == 'Y')
        result = true;
    return result;
};
```

Supplier nextTicket's get method is called in a loop that terminates when either all the tickets have been serviced or the tech specialist's shift is over. If the tech can solve the problem, it is removed from the database. The BooleanSuppliers provide the necessary user input.

```
Ticket next;
boolean done = false;
do
{
    next = nextTicket.get();
    if (next != null)
    {
        System.out.println("\n" + next);
        if (canClose.getAsBoolean())
            tickets.remove(next);
        if (isQuittingTime.getAsBoolean())
            done = true;
    }
} while(next != null && !done);
```

141

```
if (next == null)
    System.out.println(
        "\nCongrats, you get a $50 bonus today!");
else
    System.out.println("\nSee you tomorrow");
```

The complete program is shown and demonstrated as follows. The tech support specialist starts her day, and the nextTicket Supplier returns the first ticket due that has not been worked on yet today. A SoftwareTicket which is due tomorrow for Britney Delmonica concerning the web site is displayed by the program. The specialist works on the ticket and then closes it, which causes the ticket to be removed from the database. NextTicket then displays a SoftwareTicket which is due 2 days from now for Chester Rodriguez concerning a cell phone app. The specialist works on the ticket and then closes it. NextTicket then displays a HardwareTicket which is due 5 days from now for Kalpana Patel concerning cell phone power. The specialist is unable to close this ticket. NextTicket then displays a HardwareTicket for Kalpana Patel which is due 7 days from now concerning the cell phone's screen. The specialist is unable to close this ticket. NextTicket then returns null since the specialist has serviced all open tickets today, and the loop terminates. Since the specialist got through all the tickets in the database, she gets a $50 bonus for the day.

Listing 7-3. TicketingSystem.java

```
import java.util.ArrayList;
import java.util.Scanner;
import java.time.LocalDate;
import java.util.function.Supplier;
import java.util.function.BooleanSupplier;

abstract class Ticket implements Comparable<Ticket>
{
    String customerName;
    int id;
    String description;
    LocalDate dueDate;
    LocalDate servicedDate;

    public Ticket(String cn, int i, String d, int due)
```

```java
    {
        customerName = cn;
        id = i;
        description = d;
        dueDate = LocalDate.now().plusDays(due);
        servicedDate = LocalDate.now().minusDays(1);
    }
    @Override
    public String toString()
    {
        return "NAME:            " + customerName
            + "\nID:             " + id
            + "\nDESCRIPTION:    " + description
            + "\nDUE DATE:       " + dueDate
            + "\nSERVICED DATE:  " + servicedDate;

    }
    @Override
    public int compareTo(Ticket t)
    {
        return dueDate.compareTo(t.dueDate);
    }
}

class HardwareTicket extends Ticket
{
    String device;
    String model;
    String serialNumber;
    public HardwareTicket(String cn, int i, String d, int due,
                        String dev, String mod, String sn)
    {
        super(cn, i, d, due);
        device = dev;
        model = mod;
        serialNumber = sn;
    }
```

```java
    @Override
    public String toString()
    {
        return super.toString()
            + "\nDEVICE:          " + device
            + "\nMODEL:           " + model
            + "\nSERIAL NUMBER:  " + serialNumber;
    }
}

enum Domain {WEB_HOSTED, PHONE_HOSTED}
class SoftwareTicket extends Ticket
{
    String application;
    String version;
    Domain domain;
    public SoftwareTicket(String cn, int i, String d, int due,
                          String app, String ver, Domain dom)
    {
        super(cn, i, d, due);
        application = app;
        version = ver;
        domain = dom;
    }
    @Override
    public String toString()
    {
        return super.toString()
            + "\nAPPLICATION:    " + application
            + "\nVERSION:        " + version
            + "\nDOMAIN:         " + domain;
    }
}

class TicketingSystem
{
```

```
private static ArrayList<Ticket> tickets = new ArrayList<>();
private static LocalDate today = LocalDate.now();
private static void populateDatabase()
{
    tickets.add(new HardwareTicket("Kalpana Patel",54641,
                            "Cell phone won't power on",
                            5, "Smartie", "SM250",
                            "SN546497-S23"));
    tickets.add(new SoftwareTicket("Chester Rodriguez",89034,
                            "MapApp can't find grandma's house",
                            2, "MapApp", "1.01",
                            Domain.PHONE_HOSTED));
    tickets.add(new SoftwareTicket("Britney Delmonica",91472,
                            "Can't change banking info on website",
                            1, "awesomecheapcellphones.com",
                            "2.65", Domain.WEB_HOSTED));
    tickets.add(new HardwareTicket("Kalpana Patel",54641,
                            "Cell phone's screen goes black",
                            7, "Rover", "RV100",
                            "SN456742-R31"));
}
public static void main(String[] args)
{
    Supplier<? extends Ticket> nextTicket = () ->
    {
        Ticket next = null;

        for (int i=0; i < tickets.size(); ++i)
        {
            Ticket t = tickets.get(i);
            if (t.servicedDate.compareTo(today) < 0)
            {
                if (next == null || t.compareTo(next) < 0)
                    next = t;
            }
        }
```

```
            if (next != null)
                next.servicedDate = today;
        return next;
    };

    BooleanSupplier canClose = () -> {
        boolean result = false;
        Scanner scan = new Scanner(System.in);
        System.out.print("\nCan you close the ticket (Y or N)?");
        if (scan.nextLine().charAt(0) == 'Y')
            result = true;
        return result;
    };

    BooleanSupplier isQuittingTime = () -> {
        boolean result = false;
        Scanner scan = new Scanner(System.in);
        System.out.print("Is it quitting time (Y or N)?");
        if (scan.nextLine().charAt(0) == 'Y')
            result = true;
        return result;
    };

    populateDatabase();
    Ticket next;
    boolean done = false;
    do
    {
        next = nextTicket.get();
        if (next != null)
        {
            System.out.println("\n" + next);
            if (canClose.getAsBoolean())
                tickets.remove(next);

            if (isQuittingTime.getAsBoolean())
                done = true;
```

```
          }
      } while(next != null && !done);

      if (next == null)
          System.out.println(
                "\nCongrats, you get a $50 bonus today!");
      else
          System.out.println("\nSee you tomorrow");
    }
}
```

PROGRAM OUTPUT (user input shown in **BOLD**):

```
NAME:           Britney Delmonica
ID:             91472
DESCRIPTION:    Can't change banking info on website
DUE DATE:       2018-05-26
SERVICED DATE:  2018-05-25
APPLICATION:    awesomecheapcellphones.com
VERSION:        2.65
DOMAIN:         WEB_HOSTED

Can you close the ticket (Y or N)?Y
Is it quitting time (Y or N)?N

NAME:           Chester Rodriguez
ID:             89034
DESCRIPTION:    MapApp can't find grandma's house
DUE DATE:       2018-05-27
SERVICED DATE:  2018-05-25
APPLICATION:    MapApp
VERSION:        1.01
DOMAIN:         PHONE_HOSTED

Can you close the ticket (Y or N)?Y
Is it quitting time (Y or N)?N

NAME:           Kalpana Patel
ID:             54641
```

```
DESCRIPTION:     Cell phone won't power on
DUE DATE:        2018-05-30
SERVICED DATE: 2018-05-25
DEVICE:          Smartie
MODEL:           SM250
SERIAL NUMBER:  SN546497-S23

Can you close the ticket (Y or N)?N
Is it quitting time (Y or N)?N

NAME:            Kalpana Patel
ID:              54641
DESCRIPTION:     Cell phone's screen goes black
DUE DATE:        2018-06-01
SERVICED DATE: 2018-05-25
DEVICE:          Rover
MODEL:           RV100
SERIAL NUMBER:  SN456742-R31

Can you close the ticket (Y or N)?N
Is it quitting time (Y or N)?N

Congrats, you get a $50 bonus today!
```

Short Problems

1) The Fibonacci sequence is the following series of numbers:

   0, 1, 1, 2, 3, 5, 8, 13, 21 ...

   where Fn = Fn-2 + Fn-1 is true for n >= 2. Write a supplier that generates the Fibonacci numbers in order. Demonstrate in a main program.

2) Write a supplier that generates the words of the sentence "To be or not to be" in order. The supplier should generate null when all the words have been processed. Demonstrate in a main program that stores the words in an ArrayList and then prints the contents of the ArrayList.

3) Use suppliers to create a dictionary that is stored in a map.
    Write a supplier that prompts the user for a word. If the word is
    already present in the dictionary, print an error message. Write
    another supplier that prompts the user for the word's definition.
    Write a third supplier that asks the user if he or she is finished
    entering words. After the user is finished, print the contents of the
    dictionary.

Long Problems

1) File `entertainmentCollection.txt` contains records that
    describe the entertainment collection discussed in homework
    problem #2 from Chapter 6. The first field in each comma-
    separated record is a tag documenting if the record pertains to a
    DVD, an audio file, or an E-book. For example:

    ```
    DVD,Great Java Programmers,Big Hit Cinema,8123
    AUD,Tunes to Program By,mp4,57
    DVD,Tax tips for Programmers,Accountant Cinema Co,5439
    EBK,The Zen of Java Programming,257,912
    ```

    Use the `Supplier` interface to read file `entertainmentCollection.`
    `txt` and generate an object corresponding to each record. Call the
    supplier in a loop which prints the contents of the object.

2) Use the `Supplier` interface to implement a customer satisfaction
    survey that prompts the user for the answers to several customer
    service questions. The program also uses a supplier to allow the
    user to quit the test at any time.

3) Use the `Supplier` interface to implement a part of speech detector
    that parses a sentence by word and then determines the word's
    part of speech according to the following rules:

    ```
    Articles:     the, a, an
    Prepositions: of, in, on, beside, under, above
    Verbs:        is, was, compiled
    Noun:         (all other words)
    ```

For example, the sentence "The programmer compiled a program." should produce the following output:

```
The: ARTICLE
programmer: NOUN
compiled: VERB
a: ARTICLE
program: NOUN
```

CHAPTER 8

Use in Traversing Objects

The traversal of data structures has been simplified through the use of consumers which can be used to replace the while loops associated with iterators.

Section 8.1: Traversing Objects Using Iterators

Given the following Car class,

Listing 8-1. Car.java

```java
class Car
{
    private String make;
    private String model;
    public Car(String ma, String mo)
    {
        make = ma;
        model = mo;
    }
    @Override
    public String toString() {return make + " " + model; }
}
```

a program can create a list of cars.

```java
List<Car> cars = Arrays.asList(
    new Car("Nissan"   , "Sentra" ),
    new Car("Chevrolet", "Vega" ),
    new Car("Hyundai " , "Elantra")
);
```

© Ralph Lecessi 2019
R. Lecessi, *Functional Interfaces in Java*, https://doi.org/10.1007/978-1-4842-4278-0_8

The traditional way to traverse an object is to call its `Iterator`'s `hasNext` and `next` methods in a loop.

```
Iterator<Car> it = cars.iterator();
while (it.hasNext())
    System.out.println(it.next());
```

OUTPUT:

```
Nissan Sentra
Chevrolet Vega
Hyundai Elantra
```

In Java 8, the default `forEachRemaining` method which accepts a consumer was added to the `Iterator` interface.

```
public interface Iterator<E>
{
    default void forEachRemaining(Consumer<? super E> action);
    ...
}
```

The `forEachRemaining` method traverses each element while providing it to the specified `Consumer`'s `accept` method. This method can therefore be used to replace the while loop.

```
cars.iterator().forEachRemaining(x -> System.out.println(x));
```

OUTPUT:

```
Nissan Sentra
Chevrolet Vega
Hyundai Elantra
```

Section 8.2: Traversing Java Arrays of Primitive Types

An `Iterator<E>` can be used to traverse a `Collection<E>` or any object that implements the `Iterable<E>` interface. Is it possible to traverse a Java array in the same manner?

The `PrimitiveIterator` interface can be used to traverse a Java array of certain primitive types. It is generic for two types, T and T_CONS. Type T must be `Integer`, `Long`, or `Double`, and type T_CONS must be the corresponding specialization of `Consumer`.

```
public interface PrimitiveIterator<T,T_CONS> extends Iterator<T>
{
    void forEachRemaining(T_CONS action);
}
```

Suppose a program needs a class that can traverse a Java array of `int`s. This can be accomplished by implementing the `PrimitiveIterator` interface where the first type is `Integer` and the second type is `IntConsumer`.

```
class IntIteratorGen implements
PrimitiveIterator<Integer,IntConsumer>
{
    ...
```

The class should have a copy of the array and a cursor as fields.

```
private int[] array;
private int cursor;
public IntIteratorGen(int... a)
{
    cursor = 0;
    array = Arrays.copyOf(a,a.length);
}
```

The `forEachRemaining` method needs to be defined. It can simply call the `IntConsumer`'s `accept` method in a loop while incrementing the cursor.

```
@Override
public void forEachRemaining(IntConsumer c)
{
    while (hasNext())
    {
        c.accept(array[cursor]);
        cursor++;
    }
}
```

153

The hasNext and next methods inherited from Iterator also need to be defined.

```
@Override
public boolean hasNext() { return cursor < array.length; }
@Override
public Integer next()
{
    int i = 0;
    if (hasNext())
    {
        i = array[cursor];
        cursor++;
    }
    return i;
}
```

The class can now be used to traverse any Java array of ints. The Consumer needs to be cast to IntConsumer to avoid an ambiguous reference, since the Iterator interface's forEachRemaining method accepts a Consumer<X>.

```
IntIteratorGen it = new IntIteratorGen(1, 2, 3, 4, 5);
it.forEachRemaining((IntConsumer)x -> System.out.println(x));
```

The program in Listing 8-2 demonstrates. An IntIteratorGen object is used to traverse and print a Java array of ints that contains the numbers 1 through 5.

Listing 8-2. TestPrimitiveIteratorGen.java

```
import java.util.*;
import java.util.function.*;
class IntIteratorGen implements
PrimitiveIterator<Integer,IntConsumer>
{
    private int[] array;
    private int cursor;
    public IntIteratorGen(int... a)
    {
        cursor = 0;
```

```
        array = Arrays.copyOf(a,a.length);
    }
    @Override
    public void forEachRemaining(IntConsumer c)
    {
        while (hasNext())
        {
            c.accept(array[cursor]);
            cursor++;
        }
    }
    @Override
    public boolean hasNext() { return cursor < array.length; }
    @Override
    public Integer next()
    {
        int i = 0;

        if (hasNext())
        {
            i = array[cursor];
            cursor++;
        }
        return i;
    }
}
class TestPrimitiveIteratorGen
{
    public static void main(String[] args)
    {
        IntIteratorGen it = new IntIteratorGen(1, 2, 3, 4, 5);
        it.forEachRemaining((IntConsumer)x -> System.out.println(x));
    }
}
```

PROGRAM OUTPUT:

```
1
2
3
4
5
```

Section 8.2.1: Using Specializations of PrimitiveIterator

Non-generic specializations for Integer, Long, and Double are available as nested interfaces of PrimitiveIterator.

```
public static interface PrimitiveIterator.OfInt
extends PrimitiveIterator<Integer, IntConsumer>
{
    int nextInt();
    ...
}

public static interface PrimitiveIterator.OfLong
extends PrimitiveIterator<Long, LongConsumer>
{
    long nextLong();
    ...
}

public static interface PrimitiveIterator.OfDouble
extends PrimitiveIterator<Double, DoubleConsumer>
{
    double nextDouble();
    ...
}
```

The forEachRemaining, remove, and next methods have been defaulted, so only hasNext, nextInt, nextLong, and nextDouble need to be defined.

The IntIterator, LongIterator, and DoubleIterator classes defined as follows can be used to traverse Java arrays of int, long, and double primitive types, respectively.

Listing 8-3. IntIterator.java

```java
import java.util.*;
import java.util.function.*;
class IntIterator implements PrimitiveIterator.OfInt
{
    private int[] array;
    private int cursor;
    public IntIterator(int... a)
    {
        cursor = 0;
        array = Arrays.copyOf(a,a.length);
    }

    @Override
    public boolean hasNext() { return cursor < array.length; }

    @Override
    public int nextInt()
    {
        int i = 0;
        if (hasNext())
        {
            i = array[cursor];
            cursor++;
        }
        return i;
    }
}
```

Listing 8-4. LongIterator.java

```java
import java.util.*;
import java.util.function.*;
class LongIterator implements PrimitiveIterator.OfLong
{
    private long[] array;
    private int cursor;
```

```java
    public LongIterator(long... a)
    {
        cursor = 0;
        array = Arrays.copyOf(a,a.length);
    }
    @Override
    public boolean hasNext() { return cursor < array.length; }
    @Override
    public long nextLong()
    {
        long l = 0;
        if (hasNext())
        {
            l = array[cursor];
            cursor++;
        }
        return l;
    }
}
```

Listing 8-5. DoubleIterator.java

```java
import java.util.*;
import java.util.function.*;
class DoubleIterator implements PrimitiveIterator.OfDouble
{
    private double[] array;
    private int cursor;
    public DoubleIterator(double... a)
    {
        cursor = 0;
        array = Arrays.copyOf(a,a.length);
    }
    @Override
    public boolean hasNext() { return cursor < array.length; }
    @Override
```

```
public double nextDouble()
{
    double d = 0;
    if (hasNext())
    {
        d = array[cursor];
        cursor++;
    }
    return d;
}
}
```

The program in Listing 8-6 demonstrates these classes. IntIterator iit is used to traverse and print a Java array of ints containing the numbers 1 through 5. LongIterator lit is used to traverse and print a Java array of longs containing the numbers 6 through 10. DoubleIterator dit is used to traverse and print a Java array of doubles containing 20.1, 21.2, 22.3, 23.4, and 24.5.

Listing 8-6. TestPrimitiveIteratorSpecializations.java

```
import java.util.function.*;
class TestPrimitiveIteratorSpecializations
{
    public static void main(String[] args)
    {
        IntIterator iit = new IntIterator(1, 2, 3, 4, 5);

        iit.forEachRemaining((IntConsumer)x ->
                        System.out.println(x));

        System.out.println();
        LongIterator lit = new LongIterator(6, 7, 8, 9, 10);
        lit.forEachRemaining((LongConsumer)x ->
                        System.out.println(x));

        System.out.println();
        DoubleIterator dit = new DoubleIterator(
                        20.1, 21.2, 22.3, 23.4, 24.5);
```

```
        dit.forEachRemaining((DoubleConsumer)x ->
                            System.out.println(x));
    }
}
```

PROGRAM OUTPUT:

```
1
2
3
4
5

6
7
8
9
10

20.1
21.2
22.3
23.4
24.5 java
```

Section 8.3: Traversing Objects Using **Spliterators**

Like the Iterator interface, the Spliterator interface defines a default
forEachRemaining method which accepts a consumer. Spliterator is useful for
partitioning a collection into components through the use of its trySplit method.

```
public interface Spliterator<T>
{
    default void forEachRemaining(Consumer<? super T> action);
    Spliterator<T> trySplit();
    ...
}
```

Suppose a program creates a list of cars.

```
List<Car> cars = Arrays.asList(
    new Car("Nissan", "Sentra"),
    new Car("Chevrolet", "Vega"),
    new Car("Hyundai"  , "Elantra"),
    new Car("Buick"    , "Regal")
);
```

A Spliterator object can be made to traverse the list through the use of the spliterator's forEachRemaining method. Note that this spliterator contains all elements in the list.

```
Spliterator<Car> spliterator = cars.spliterator();
spliterator.forEachRemaining(x ->
                System.out.println("In spliterator: " + x));
```

OUTPUT:

```
In spliterator: Nissan Sentra
In spliterator: Chevrolet Vega
In spliterator: Hyundai Elantra
In spliterator: Buick Regal
```

The Spliterator interface's trySplit method can be used to partition the list. The result of the trySplit method is placed in a new spliterator named firstHalf. The original spliterator contains the remainder of the list elements (the second half of the list).

```
spliterator = cars.spliterator();
Spliterator<Car> firstHalf = spliterator.trySplit();
```

The Spliterator objects can then be traversed to display the first half and then the second half of the list.

```
firstHalf.forEachRemaining (x ->
                System.out.println("In 1st half: " + x));
spliterator.forEachRemaining(x ->
                System.out.println("In 2nd half: " + x));
```

OUTPUT:

```
In 1st half: Nissan Sentra
In 1st half: Chevrolet Vega
In 2nd half: Hyundai Elantra
In 2nd half: Buick Regal
```

The following program traverses a Java array of Integers using a Spliterator. This is accomplished using the ArraySpliterator class which implements Spliterator<Integer> and contains an Integer array with a cursor that tracks the current position of the Spliterator. The characteristics and estimatedSize methods are overridden. The trySplit method calculates the midpoint in the Integer array, returns the first half, and updates the array to contain only the second half. The tryAdvance method is called internally by forEachRemaining. It passes the array element at the cursor to the Consumer object and then advances the cursor.

Listing 8-7. ArraySpliterator.java

```java
import java.util.*;
import java.util.function.Consumer;
class ArraySpliterator implements Spliterator<Integer> {
    Integer[] array;
    int cursor;
    public ArraySpliterator(Integer... a)
    {
        array = Arrays.copyOf(a,a.length);
        cursor = 0;
    }
    @Override
    public int characteristics() {
        return SIZED|SUBSIZED|ORDERED|NONNULL;
    }
    @Override
    public long estimateSize() {
        return array.length;
    }
    @Override
```

```java
public Spliterator<Integer> trySplit() {
    int midpoint = array.length / 2;
    Integer[] temp = new Integer[midpoint];
    Integer[] temp2;
    if ( array.length %2 > 0)
        temp2 = new Integer[midpoint+1];
    else
        temp2 = new Integer[midpoint];
    for (int i = 0; i < midpoint; i++)
        temp[i] = array[i];
    for (int i = midpoint; i < array.length; i++)
        temp2[i-midpoint] = array[i];
    array = temp2;
    return new ArraySpliterator(temp);
}
@Override
public boolean tryAdvance(Consumer<? super Integer> action) {
    boolean result = true;
    action.accept(array[cursor]);
    cursor++;
    if (cursor >= array.length)
        result = false;
    return result;
}
public static void main(String[] args)
{
    ArraySpliterator aspliterator =
        new ArraySpliterator(1,2,3,4,5);
    Spliterator<Integer> firstHalf = aspliterator.trySplit();
    firstHalf.forEachRemaining(x ->
            System.out.println("First half: " + x));
    aspliterator.forEachRemaining(x ->
            System.out.println("Second half: " + x));
}
}
```

PROGRAM OUTPUT:

```
First half: 1
First half: 2
Second half: 3
Second half: 4
Second half: 5
```

Section 8.4: Traversing **Iterable** Objects

In Java 8, the default forEach method, which accepts a consumer, was added to the Iterable interface.

```
public interface Iterable<T>
{
    default void forEach(Consumer<? super T> action);
    ...
}
```

As discussed in Section 1, an Iterator instance is an object that can be used to traverse another object through the use of its hasNext and nextMethods. An Iterable object provides an Iterator instance whenever its iterator method is called.

Any Iterable object can be traversed using its forEach method and a consumer instead of obtaining the object's Iterator and traversing with a while loop.

```
List<Car> cars = Arrays.asList(
    new Car("Nissan" , "Sentra" ),
    new Car("Chevrolet", "Vega" ),
    new Car("Hyundai" , "Elantra")
);
cars.forEach(x -> System.out.println(x));
```

OUTPUT:

```
Nissan Sentra
Chevrolet Vega
Hyundai Elantra
```

Section 8.5: Traversing **Iterable** Objects That Contain Java Arrays of Primitives

When an Iterable object consists of Java array of ints, longs, or doubles, the objects' Iterator method can return a PrimitiveIterator.

The MyInts class shown as follows implements Iterable<Integer> and contains a Java array of int.

```
class MyInts implements Iterable<Integer>
{
    private int[] array;

    public MyInts(int... a)
    {
        array = Arrays.copyOf(a,a.length);
    }
    ...
```

The iterator method of MyInts can return a PrimitiveIterator<Integer, IntConsumer>, which is a subclass of Iterator<Integer>.

```
    public PrimitiveIterator<Integer,IntConsumer> iterator()
    {
        return new IntIter();
    }
```

Class IntIter is a private inner class of MyInts that directly accesses the array field and uses a cursor to navigate.

```
private class IntIter implements
    PrimitiveIterator<Integer,IntConsumer>
{
    private int cursor;
    public IntIter()
    {
        cursor = 0;
    }
    ...
```

The forEachRemaining method calls the IntConsumer interface's accept method in a loop while incrementing the cursor.

```
@Override
public void forEachRemaining(IntConsumer c)
{
    while (hasNext())
    {
        c.accept(array[cursor]);
        cursor++;
    }
}
```

The non-default hasNext and next methods inherited from Iterator must also be defined.

```
@Override
public boolean hasNext() { return cursor < array.length; }
@Override
public Integer next()
{
    int i = 0;
    if (hasNext())
    {
        i = array[cursor];
        cursor++;
    }
    return i;
}
```

The MyInts class can be used to traverse any Java array of ints by calling its forEach method and providing a consumer.

```
MyInts my = new MyInts(1, 2, 3, 4, 5);
my.forEach(x -> System.out.println(x));
```

Note that the array can also be iterated by obtaining the MyInts object's Iterator and calling its forEachRemaining method.

```
my.iterator().forEachRemaining((IntConsumer)x ->
                              System.out.println(x));
```

The program in Listing 8-8 contains the complete definition of the MyInts class and demonstrates its usage. A MyInts object is used to traverse and print an array of ints containing the numbers 1 through 5. The first traversal is performed using the MyInts object's forEach method. The second traversal is performed by obtaining the MyInts object's Iterator and calling the Iterator's forEachRemaining method.

Listing 8-8. TestMyInts.java

```
import java.util.*;
import java.util.function.*;
class MyInts implements Iterable<Integer>
{
    private int[] array;
    public MyInts(int... a)
    {
        array = Arrays.copyOf(a,a.length);
    }
    public PrimitiveIterator<Integer,IntConsumer> iterator()
    {
        return new IntIter();
    }

    private class IntIter implements
            PrimitiveIterator<Integer,IntConsumer>
    {
        private int cursor;
        public IntIter()
        {
            cursor = 0;
        }
        @Override
        public void forEachRemaining(IntConsumer c)
        {
```

167

```
                    while (hasNext())
                    {
                        c.accept(array[cursor]);
                        cursor++;
                    }
                }
                @Override
                public boolean hasNext() { return cursor < array.length; }

                @Override
                public Integer next()
                {
                    int i = 0;
                    if (hasNext())
                    {
                        i = array[cursor];
                        cursor++;
                    }
                    return i;
                }
            }
        }

        class TestMyInts
        {
            public static void main(String[] args)
            {
                MyInts my = new MyInts(1, 2, 3, 4, 5);
                my.forEach(x -> System.out.println(x));
                System.out.println();
                my.iterator().forEachRemaining((IntConsumer)x ->
                    System.out.println(x));
            }
        }
```

PROGRAM OUTPUT:

1
2
3
4
5

1
2
3
4
5

Section 8.5.1: Using Specializations of `PrimitiveIterator`

The `iterator` method of the `MyInts` class could also have returned a
`PrimitiveIterator.OfInts`. The inner class would then implement
`PrimitiveIterator.OfInts` instead of `PrimitiveIterator<Integer, IntConsumer>`.

The program in Listing 8-9 traverses and prints an array of `ints` using `MyIntsP`,
whose inner class implements `PrimitiveIterator.OfInts`. `IntIterP` differs
from `IntIter` of Listing 8-8 in that it has no `forEachRemaining` method (a *default*
implementation is provided) and method `nextInt` replaces method `next`.

Listing 8-9. TestMyIntsP.Java

```java
import java.util.*;
import java.util.function.*;
class MyIntsP implements Iterable<Integer>
{
    private int[] array;

    public MyIntsP(int... a)
    {
        array = Arrays.copyOf(a,a.length);
    }
    public PrimitiveIterator.OfInt iterator()
    {
```

```java
        return new IntIterP();
    }

    private class IntIterP implements PrimitiveIterator.OfInt
    {
        int cursor;
        public IntIterP()
        {
            cursor = 0;
        }
        @Override
        public boolean hasNext() { return cursor < array.length; }

        @Override
        public int nextInt()
        {
            int i = 0;

            if (hasNext())
            {
                i = array[cursor];
                cursor++;
            }
            return i;
        }
    }
}

class TestMyIntsP
{
    public static void main(String[] args)
    {
        MyIntsP my = new MyIntsP(1, 2, 3, 4, 5);
        my.forEach(x -> System.out.println(x));
        System.out.println();
        my.iterator().forEachRemaining((IntConsumer)x ->
                System.out.println(x));

    }
}
```

PROGRAM OUTPUT:

1
2
3
4
5

1
2
3
4
5

Section 8.6: Traversing Maps

Java maps are not iterable. However, a forEach method has been provided for traversal.
Unlike Iterable objects, whose forEach method accepts a consumer, the forEach
method of the Map interface accepts a BiConsumer object which processes the map
entry's key and value.

Suppose a program defines a TreeMap containing employee's names and salaries.

```
TreeMap<String, Double> employeeSalaries = new TreeMap<>();
employeeSalaries.put("Joe Smith", 100000.0);
employeeSalaries.put("Maggie Jones", 110000.0);
employeeSalaries.put("Larry Rodriguez", 105000.0);
```

The following example uses the Map interface's forEach method to traverse the map
and print each employee's name and salary:

```
employeeSalaries.forEach( (x,y) ->
        System.out.println(x + " makes $" + y + " annually."));
```

OUTPUT:

```
Joe Smith makes $100000.0 annually.
Larry Rodriguez makes $105000.0 annually.
Maggie Jones makes $110000.0 annually.
```

Section 8.7: Traversing Sets

Since a Java set is iterable, the forEachRemaining method of its Iterator<E> can be passed a consumer which can print each element in the set. The example in Listing 8-10 traverses and prints a set in a manner similar to the list example in Section 1.

Listing 8-10. TestSet.java

```java
import java.util.*;
public class TestSet
{
  public static void main(String[] args)
  {
    Set<String> colors = new TreeSet<>();
    colors.add("red");
    colors.add("green");
    colors.add("blue");
    colors.iterator().forEachRemaining(x -> System.out.println(x));
  }
}
```

PROGRAM OUTPUT:

```
blue
green
red
```

PROJECT 8: Payroll

Problem Statement

The MomAndPop startup company is committed to sharing profits with all their employees. In addition to their base salary and sign-on bonus, employees share in annual profits as follows:

- The CEO receives 15%.

- The Vice President receives 15%.

- 30% is split between two district managers.

- 40% is split between four programmers.

MomAndPop earned $120,000 last year. Write a program that will traverse each employee of the MomAndPop company adding the portion of the profit to the bonus as described in the preceding list and printing the employee's name, base salary, and bonus to the display.

Solution

An Employee class can be written to model each employee of MomAndPop. In addition to name, baseSalary, and bonus, the class can have a multiplier field which determines the portion of the profit to add to the sign-on bonus.

```
class Employee
{
    String name;
    double baseSalary;
    double bonus;
    double multiplier;
    public Employee(String n, double bs, double bn, double m)
    {
        name = n;
        baseSalary = bs;
        bonus = bn;
        multiplier = m;
    }
    @Override
    public String toString()
    {
        return name + ": base salary = " + baseSalary
            + " bonus = " + bonus;
    }
}
```

A MomAndPop class can be written to represent the company. The class contains Employee fields for the CEO and Vice President and lists of employees for the district managers and programmers.

```
class MomAndPop implements Iterable<Employee>
{
    static int NUM_EXECS = 2;
    static double profit;
    Employee CEO;    .
    Employee vicePresident;
    List<Employee> districtManagers;
    List<Employee> programmers;
    public MomAndPop()
    {
        CEO = new Employee("Mr. Bucks", 1000000.0, 75000.0, 0.15);
        vicePresident = new Employee("Highly Mobile", 750000.0,
                                     25000.0, 0.15);
        districtManagers = Arrays.asList(
            new Employee("Joe Johnston", 200000.0, 10000.0, 0.15),
            new Employee("Sarah Smith" , 210000.0, 9000.0, 0.15 ));
        programmers = Arrays.asList(
            new Employee("Javier Rodriguez", 150000.0, 2000.0, 0.10),
            new Employee("Kalpana Patel",    155000.0, 1500.0, 0.10),
            new Employee("Cyndy Altavera",   140000.0, 1200.0, 0.10),
            new Employee("Sam Jones",        130000.0, 1300.0, 0.10)
        );
    }
    ...
```

MomAndPop implements Iterable<Employee> since it needs to traverse all the employees in the company. Inner class EmployeeIterator utilizes a cursor to select each Employee object in the following order:

0	CEO
1	Vice President
2–3	District managers
4–7	Programmers

```java
public Iterator<Employee> iterator() {
    return new EmployeeIterator();
}

private class EmployeeIterator implements Iterator<Employee>
{
    private int cursor;
    private final int limit;
    public EmployeeIterator()
    {
        cursor = 0;
        limit = NUM_EXECS + districtManagers.size()
                + programmers.size();
    }
    @Override
    public boolean hasNext() { return cursor < limit; }
    @Override
    public Employee next()
    {
        Employee emp = null;
        if (hasNext())
        {
            if (cursor == 0)
                emp = CEO;
            else if (cursor == 1)
                emp = vicePresident;
            else if (cursor < (NUM_EXECS
                    + districtManagers.size()))
                emp = districtManagers.get(cursor - NUM_EXECS);

            else if (cursor < (NUM_EXECS + districtManagers.size()
                    + programmers.size()))
                emp = programmers.get(cursor - NUM_EXECS
                                    - districtManagers.size());

            cursor++;
        }
        return emp;
    }
}
```

A consumer which adds a portion of the profit to an Employee 's bonus using its multiplier can be written.

```
Consumer<Employee> applyProfit = x ->
            x.bonus += MomAndPop.profit * x.multiplier;

MomAndPop company = new MomAndPop();
MomAndPop.profit = 120000.0; // 40% PRG 30%MGR 15% VP 15% CEO
```

Company's forEach method can be called to iterate each Employee object. The argument to forEach is a chain of consumers composed of applyProfit and a consumer that prints the Employee object.

```
company.forEach(applyProfit
            .andThen(x -> System.out.println(x)));
```

The complete program is shown and demonstrated as follows. The first iteration of company selects Employee CEO and adds 15% of the $120,000 profit to his bonus resulting in $93,000. The second iteration selects Employee vicePresident and adds 15% of the profit to his or her bonus resulting in $43,000. The next two iterations select the two district managers and distribute 30% of the profit among the two managers resulting in $28,000 and $27,000, respectively. The next four iterations select the four programmers and distribute 40% of the profit among the four programmers resulting in $14,000, $13,500, $13,200, and $13,300, respectively.

Listing 8-11. Payroll.java

```java
import java.util.*;
import java.util.function.Consumer;
class Employee
{
    String name;
    double baseSalary;
    double bonus;
    double multiplier;
    public Employee(String n, double bs, double bn, double m)
    {
        name = n;
        baseSalary = bs;
```

```java
        bonus = bn;
        multiplier = m;
    }
    @Override
    public String toString() {
        return name + ": base salary = " + baseSalary
            + " bonus = " + bonus;
    }
}

class MomAndPop implements Iterable<Employee>
{
    static int NUM_EXECS = 2;
    static double profit;
    Employee CEO;
    Employee vicePresident;
    List<Employee> districtManagers;
    List<Employee> programmers;
    public MomAndPop()
    {
        CEO = new Employee("Mr. Bucks", 1000000.0, 75000.0, 0.15);

        vicePresident = new Employee("Highly Mobile", 750000.0,
                                    25000.0, 0.15);
        districtManagers = Arrays.asList(
            new Employee("Joe Johnston", 200000.0, 10000.0, 0.15),
            new Employee("Sarah Smith" , 210000.0, 9000.0, 0.15 ));
        programmers = Arrays.asList(
            new Employee("Javier Rodriguez", 150000.0, 2000.0, 0.10),
            new Employee("Kalpana Patel"    , 155000.0, 1500.0, 0.10),
            new Employee("Cyndy Altavera"   , 140000.0, 1200.0, 0.10),
            new Employee("Sam Jones"        , 130000.0, 1300.0, 0.10)
        );
    }
    public Iterator<Employee> iterator()
    {
```

```java
        return new EmployeeIterator();
    }

    private class EmployeeIterator implements Iterator<Employee>
    {
        private int cursor;
        private final int limit;
        public EmployeeIterator()
        {
            cursor = 0;
            limit = NUM_EXECS + districtManagers.size()
                    + programmers.size();
        }
        @Override
        public boolean hasNext() { return cursor < limit; } @Override
        public Employee next()
        {
            Employee emp = null;
            if (hasNext())
            {
                if (cursor == 0)
                    emp = CEO;
                else if (cursor == 1)
                    emp = vicePresident;
                else if (cursor < (NUM_EXECS
                                + districtManagers.size())))
                    emp = districtManagers.get(cursor - NUM_EXECS);
                else if (cursor < (NUM_EXECS
                                + districtManagers.size()
                                + programmers.size())))
                    emp = programmers.get(cursor - NUM_EXECS
                                    - districtManagers.size());
                cursor++;
            }
            return emp;
        }
    }
}
```

```
class Payroll {
    public static void main(String[] args)
    {
        Consumer<Employee> applyProfit = x ->
            x.bonus += MomAndPop.profit * x.multiplier;

        MomAndPop company = new MomAndPop();
        MomAndPop.profit = 120000.0; // 40% PRG 30%MGR 15% VP 15% CEO

        company.forEach(applyProfit
                    .andThen(x -> System.out.println(x)));
    }
}
```

PROGRAM OUTPUT:

```
Mr. Bucks: base salary = 1000000.0 bonus = 93000.0
Highly Mobile: base salary = 750000.0 bonus = 43000.0
Joe Johnston: base salary = 200000.0 bonus = 28000.0
Sarah Smith: base salary = 210000.0 bonus = 27000.0
Javier Rodriguez: base salary = 150000.0 bonus = 14000.0
Kalpana Patel: base salary = 155000.0 bonus = 13500.0
Cyndy Altavera: base salary = 140000.0 bonus = 13200.0
Sam Jones: base salary = 130000.0 bonus = 13300.0
```

Short Problems

1) Use the forEachRemaining method to create a string containing a comma-separated list of models from the list of cars shown in Section 1 of this chapter.

2) Write a program that uses the techniques discussed in this chapter to compute and print a running sum of the elements in an array of ints. Feel free to utilize one of the prewritten iterators.

3) Write a class called MyDouble that implements Iterable<Double>. Demonstrate the class in a main program.

Long Problems

1) Write a class that iterates a string. Use its forEach method to convert each character in the string to uppercase, and then print the character (**Hint**: the class implements Iterable<Character>).

2) Using the techniques described in this chapter, write a class that will iterate a Java array of ints in reverse order. Demonstrate in a main program.

3) Write a Deck class that iterates a deck of cards. Use its forEach method to print each card, and then produce a poker hand every five cards. Use the predicates defined in homework problem #3 of Chapter 3 to determine if the hand is a straight, a flush, or a full house.

CHAPTER 9

Use in Collections

Functional interfaces can be used to perform several important operations on collections.

Section 9.1: Removing Elements from a Collection

The removeIf method can be used to remove elements from a Collection object whose Iterator supports the remove operation.

```
default boolean removeIf(Predicate<? super E> filter);
```

If the predicate supplied to the removeIf method is true for an element of the collection, that element is removed from the collection. If the Collection object's Iterator does not support the remove operation, an UnsupportedOperationException will be thrown. In the following example, a Predicate<String> is used to remove all elements beginning with "S" from the collection.

```
ArrayList<String> list = new ArrayList<>();
list.add("Super");
list.add("Random");
list.add("Silly");
list.add("Strings");

list.removeIf(x -> x.charAt(0) == 'S');
list.forEach(x -> System.out.println(x));
```

OUTPUT:

```
Random
```

© Ralph Lecessi 2019
R. Lecessi, *Functional Interfaces in Java*, https://doi.org/10.1007/978-1-4842-4278-0_9

Section 9.2: Populating an Array

The Arrays class has several setAll methods that will populate each element of an array passed as the first argument using an operator or function passed as the second argument. The first parameter of the operator or function is the subscript corresponding to the array element.

```
static void setAll(int[] array, IntUnaryOperator generator)
static void setAll(long[] array, IntToLongFunction generator)
static void setAll(double[] array, IntToDoubleFunction generator)
static <X> void setAll(X[] array, IntFunction<? extends X> generator)
```

The following example sets each element of int array iarr equal to its subscript.

```
IntUnaryOperator iop = x -> x;
int[] iarr = new int[4];
Arrays.setAll(iarr, iop);
for (int i : iarr)
    System.out.println(i);
```

OUTPUT:

```
0
1
2
3
```

The following example sets each element of long array larr equal to 5.

```
IntToLongFunction gen5 = x -> 5;
long[] larr = new long[4];
Arrays.setAll(larr, gen5);
for (long l : larr)
    System.out.println(l);
```

OUTPUT:

```
5
5
5
5
```

The following example sets each element of double array darr equal to a random number between 0.0 and 1.0.

```
IntToDoubleFunction i2d = x -> (new Random()).nextFloat();
double[] darr = new double[4];
Arrays.setAll(darr, i2d);
for (double d : darr)
    System.out.println(d);
```

OUTPUT:

```
0.40630531311035156
0.9486522674560547
0.8432348370552063
0.7855687737464905
```

The following example populates an array of strings such that each element contains the letter "S" repeated the number of subscript times.

```
IntFunction<String> is = x -> {
    String s = "";
    for (int i=0; i<=x; ++i)
        s += "S";
    return s;
};
```

```
String[] sarr = new String[4];
Arrays.setAll(sarr, is);
for (String s : sarr)
    System.out.println(s);
```

OUTPUT:

```
S
SS
SSS
SSSS
```

Section 9.3: Replacing the Elements of a List or a Map

All the elements in a list can be modified using the default `replaceAll` method and a `UnaryOperator` that specified how to perform the modification.

```
default void replaceAll(UnaryOperation<E> operator);
```

The following example divides each element in a list of integers by 4.

```
List<Integer> list = Arrays.asList(16,12,8,4);
UnaryOperator<Integer> div4 = x -> x / 4;
list.replaceAll(div4);
list.forEach(x -> System.out.println(x));
```

OUTPUT:

```
4
3
2
1
```

All the element in a map can also be modified using the default `replaceAll` method and a `BiFunction`.

```
default void replaceAll(BiFunction<? super K, ? super V, ? extends V>
function);
```

The following example adds the prefix "Mr. " to each entry of a map.

```
Map<String,String> map = new TreeMap<>();
map.put("Smith", "Robert");
map.put("Jones", "Alex");
BiFunction<String,String,String> bi = (k,v) -> "Mr. " + v;

map.replaceAll(bi);
map.forEach( (x,y) -> System.out.println(y + " " + x));
```

OUTPUT:

```
Mr. Alex Jones
Mr. Robert Smith
```

Section 9.4: Parallel Computations on Arrays

Computations on arrays can be performed in parallel to make programs run faster as long as doing so does not change the results of the computations.

The Arrays class has several parallelPrefix methods that perform parallel computations on the elements of an array or on a subrange of the elements in the array. The methods accept the array and a binary operator that specifies the computation to be performed.

```
static void parallelPrefix(double[] array, int fromIndex, int toIndex,
DoubleBinaryOperator op);
static void parallelPrefix(double[] array, DoubleBinaryOperator op);
static void parallelPrefix(int[] array, int fromIndex, int toIndex,
IntBinaryOperator op);
static void parallelPrefix(int[] array, IntBinaryOperator op);
static void parallelPrefix(long[] array, int fromIndex, int toIndex,
LongBinaryOperator op);
static void parallelPrefix(long[] array, LongBinaryOperator op);
static void parallelPrefix(T[] array, int fromIndex, int toIndex,
BinaryOperator<X> op);
static void parallelPrefix(T[] array, BinaryOperator<x> op);
```

The following example defines an int array. An IntBinaryOperator specifies the multiplication of two elements of the array to be performed in parallel.

The first element of the array is not modified. The second element contains the product of the first and second elements (2 * 3 = 6). The third element contains that product multiplied by the third element (6 * 4 = 24). The fourth element contains that product multiplied by the fourth element (24 * 3 = 72).

```
int[] arr = {2,3,4,3};
IntBinaryOperator op = (x,y) -> x * y;

Arrays.parallelPrefix(arr, op);
for (int i: arr)
    System.out.println(i);
```

OUTPUT:

```
2
6
24
72
```

Section 9.5: Map Computations

The Map interface provides the following methods which perform inline computations on an entry in a map.

```
default V compute<K key, BiFunction<? super K, ? super V, ? extends V>
remappingFunction);
default V computeIfAbsent<K key, Function<? super K, ? extends V>
mappingFunction);
default V computeIfPresent<K key, BiFunction<? super K, ? super V, ?
extends V>
    remappingFunction);
```

The Map interface's default compute method performs its computation on an entry in a map using the specified BiFunction. If the function results in null, the entry is removed from the map.

In the following example, a mapping BiFunction is defined that returns null if the value is null (or if the key is not present), and returns the value divided by 4 otherwise.

The first call to the compute method divides the value 32 by 4 resulting in 8. The second call results in null since the value corresponding to the key "GREEN" is null, and the entry "GREEN" is removed from the map. The third call operates on the key "YELLOW" which is not present and results in null, so nothing is added to the Map.

```
BiFunction<String,Integer,Integer> bin = (k,v) -> v ==
    null? null : v / 4;

Map<String,Integer> map = new TreeMap<>();
map.put("RED", 32);
map.put("GREEN", null);
System.out.println(map.compute("RED", bin));
```

CHAPTER 9   USE IN COLLECTIONS

```
System.out.println(map.compute("GREEN", bin));
System.out.println(map.compute("YELLOW", bin));

System.out.println();
map.forEach( (x,y) -> System.out.println(x + " " + y));
```

OUTPUT:

```
8
null
null

RED 8
```

The default `computeIfPresent` method performs its computation if the entry is present and the value is not null. If the `BiFunction` results in null, the entry is removed from the map.

In the following example, the mapping `BiFunction` divides the value by 4 and never returns null.

The first call to the `computeIfPresent` method divides the value 8 by 4 resulting in 2. The second call does not perform the computation since the value corresponding to the key "GREEN" is null. Entry "GREEN" remains in the map. The third call operates on the key "YELLOW" which is not present, so no calculation is performed.

```
BiFunction<String,Integer,Integer> bi = (k,v) -> v / 4;

Map<String,Integer> map = new TreeMap<>();
map.put("RED", 8);
map.put("GREEN", null);
System.out.println(map.computeIfPresent("RED", bi));
System.out.println(map.computeIfPresent("GREEN", bi));
System.out.println(map.computeIfPresent("YELLOW", bi));

System.out.println();
map.forEach( (x,y) -> System.out.println(x + " " + y));
```

OUTPUT:

```
2
null
null

GREEN null
RED 2
```

The default `computeIfAbsent` method performs its computation if the entry is not present or its value is `null`. If the function results in null, no entry is added to the map. It accepts a `Function` object instead of a `BiFunction`, since no existing value needs to be processed.

In the following example, the value resulting from the mapping function `fi` is the length of the key and the value resulting from the mapping function `finull` is `null`.

The first call to the `computeIfAbsent` method performs no computation since entry "RED" is present and its value is not null. The second call computes a new value 5 which is the length of the key "GREEN", since the original value was `null`. The third call computes 6 which is the length of the key "YELLOW" which is absent from the map. Although entry "BLACK" is absent from the map, the fourth call does not add an entry for it because mapping function `finull` results in null.

```java
Function<String,Integer> fi     = k -> k.length();
Function<String,Integer> finull = k -> null;

Map<String,Integer> map = new TreeMap<>();
map.put("RED", 2);
map.put("GREEN", null);
System.out.println(map.computeIfAbsent("RED"   , fi));
System.out.println(map.computeIfAbsent("GREEN" , fi));
System.out.println(map.computeIfAbsent("YELLOW", fi));
System.out.println(map.computeIfAbsent("BLACK" , finull));

System.out.println();
map.forEach( (x,y) -> System.out.println(x + " " + y));
```

OUTPUT:

```
2
5
6
null

GREEN 5
RED 2
YELLOW 6
```

Section 9.6: Map Merging

The Map interface's default merge method is mainly used to modify an existing value by merging portions of a new value with it according to a mapping function. If the entry does not exist, a new entry is created with the specified key and value. If the mapping function results in a null value, the entry is removed from the map. The new value is not allowed to be null.

```
default V merge(K key, V value, BiFunction<? super V, ? super V, ? extends
V> remappingFunction);
```

Given the following class,

```
class MyClass
{
    int i1;
    int i2;
    String s;
    public MyClass(int x, int y, String z)
    {
        i1 = x;
        i2 = y;
        s = z;
    }
    @Override
    public String toString() { return i1 + " " + i2 + " " + s; }
}
```

a program can create a map whose values are of the type MyClass and whose keys are of type String.

```
Map<String,MyClass> m = new TreeMap<>();
m.put("k1",new MyClass(1, 2, "Dog"));
```

A BiFunction can be written that returns a new MyClass composed of the i1 and s fields of the existing MyClass value and the i2 field of a new MyClass value.

```
BiFunction<MyClass,MyClass,MyClass> changeI2 =
    (ov,nv) -> new MyClass(ov.i1, nv.i2, ov.s);
```

A different mapping BiFunction can be written that returns a new MyClass composed of the i1 and i2 fields of the existing MyClass value and the s field of a new MyClass value.

```
BiFunction<MyClass,MyClass,MyClass> changeS =
    (ov,nv) -> new MyClass(ov.i1, ov.i2, nv.s);
```

BiFunction changeI2 and the merge method can be used to change field i1 of entry "k1" to 5. BiFunction changeS and the merge method can be used to change field s of entry "k1" to "Cat". Entry "k2" does not exist, so a new entry is created with the specified value without using the mapping function.

```
System.out.println(m.merge("k1", new MyClass(0, 5, null ),
                        changeI2));
System.out.println(m.merge("k1", new MyClass(0, 0, "Cat" ),
                        changeS));
System.out.println(m.merge("k2", new MyClass(6, 7, "Bird"),
                        changeS));

System.out.println();
m.forEach( (x,y) -> System.out.println(x + " " + y));
```

OUTPUT:

```
1 5 Dog
1 5 Cat
6 7 Bird

k1 1 5 Cat
k2 6 7 Bird
```

Section 9.7: Functional Interfaces and Sets

Since the Set interface supports the remove operation, the removeIf method can be used to remove elements from a set. If the supplied predicate is true for an element, that element is removed from the set.

```
Set<String> names = new TreeSet<>();
names.add("Jeremy");
names.add("Javier");
names.add("Rose");

names.removeIf(x -> x.charAt(0) == 'J');
names.forEach(x -> System.out.println(x));
```

OUTPUT:

Rose

Unlike the List interface, the Set interface does not provide a replaceAll method.

PROJECT 9: Department of Motor Vehicles

Problem Statement

The Department of Motor Vehicles has asked you to write a program that maintains a database of all licensed drivers. Drivers' licenses are organized by license id. The expiration date, privilege status (active or suspended), insurance policy, and a list of registered vehicles are stored with each license. The program needs to support the following operations:

- Add a driver's license

- Remove a driver's license

- Change a driver's insurance policy

- Suspend a driver's license

- Renew a driver's license

- Add a vehicle to a driver's license

- Remove a vehicle from a driver's license

191

Solution

A Vehicle class can be written which contains fields for the make, model, and year of a vehicle.

```
class Vehicle
{
    String make;
    String model;
    int year;
    public Vehicle(String ma, String mo, int y)
    {
        make = ma;
        model = mo;
        year = y;
    }
    @Override
    public String toString()
    {
        return year + " " + make + " " + model;
    }
}
```

A License class can be written with fields for the expiration date, insurance policy, privilege status, and the list of vehicles associated with the license. The class needs constructors that will accept either a variable length list of vehicles or an ArrayList<Vehicle> object. The class should also have a copy constructor.

```
enum STATUS {ACTIVE, SUSPENDED}
class License
{
    LocalDate expDate;
    String insurance;
    STATUS status;
    ArrayList<Vehicle> vehicles;
    public License(LocalDate e, String i, Vehicle... v)
    {
```

```
        expDate = e;
        insurance = i;
        status = STATUS.ACTIVE;
        vehicles = new ArrayList<>();
        for (Vehicle r : v)
            vehicles.add(r);
    }
    public License(LocalDate e, String i, STATUS s,
                 ArrayList<Vehicle> vs)
    {
        expDate = e;
        insurance = i;
        status = s;
        vehicles = new ArrayList<>(vs);
    }
    public License(License l)
    {
        expDate = l.expDate;
        insurance = l.insurance;
        status = l.status;
        vehicles = new ArrayList<>(l.vehicles);
    }
    @Override
    public String toString()
    {
        return expDate + " " + insurance + " " + status
        + " " + vehicles;
    }
}
```

The program can use a map to store the driver's license database where the key is the license id and the value is a license record.

```
Map<String,License> d = new TreeMap<>();
```

Suppliers can be written to prompt the user for the driver's license id, the insurance policy, the expiration date, and the vehicle information.

```java
Supplier<String> licenseId = () -> {
    Scanner input = new Scanner(System.in);
    System.out.print("Enter licenseId:");
    return input.nextLine();
};

Supplier<String> insurance = () -> {
    Scanner input = new Scanner(System.in);
    System.out.print("Enter insurance:");
    return input.nextLine();
};

Supplier<LocalDate> expDate = () -> {
    Scanner input = new Scanner(System.in);
    System.out.print("Enter year:");
    int year = Integer.parseInt(input.nextLine());
    System.out.print("Enter month:");
    Month month = Month.valueOf(input.nextLine());
    System.out.print("Enter day:");
    int day = Integer.parseInt(input.nextLine());
    return LocalDate.of(year, month, day);
};

Supplier<Vehicle> vehicle = () -> {
    Scanner input = new Scanner(System.in);
    System.out.print("Enter make:");
    String make = input.nextLine();
    System.out.print("Enter model:");
    String model = input.nextLine();
    System.out.print("Enter year:");
    int year = Integer.parseInt(input.nextLine());
    return new Vehicle(make, model, year);
};
```

The Map interface's merge method can be used to add a driver to the database. If an entry whose key matches the license id is not present in the map, an entry will be added with the provided value that only specifies the expiration date. If the entry is present, the BiFunction returns the existing License value, so attempting to add the driver will have no effect.

194

```
BiFunction<License,License,License> addDriver = (ov,nv) -> ov;
System.out.println(d.merge(licenseId.get(),
                           new License(expDate.get(), null),
                           addDriver));
```

The Map class's computeIfPresent method can be used to remove a driver from the database. If an entry whose key matches the license id is present, the BiFunction returns a null value, and the ComputeIfPresent method removes the entry from the map.

```
BiFunction<String,License,License> remove = (k,v) -> null;
System.out.println(d.computeIfPresent(licenseId.get(),remove));
```

To change a driver's insurance policy, the Map class's merge method can be used to merge an existing License value with one containing a new insurance policy. The BiFunction creates a License object using the insurance field from the new value and the remaining fields from the existing value.

```
BiFunction<License,License,License> changeInsurance = (ov,nv) ->
    new License(ov.expDate, nv.insurance, ov.status, ov.vehicles);
System.out.println(d.merge(licenseId.get(),
                           new License(null, insurance.get()),
                           changeInsurance));
```

Since suspending an existing license does not require input of any License fields, the Map class's computeIfPresent method can be used. The BiFunction modifies the existing value, setting the status field to STATUS.SUSPENDED.

```
BiFunction<String,License,License> suspend = (k,v) ->
    new License(v.expDate, v.insurance, STATUS.SUSPENDED,
v.vehicles);
System.out.println(d.computeIfPresent(licenseId.get(),suspend));
```

To renew a driver's license, a new License value containing a new expiration date can be merged with an existing value. The BiFunction can also set the status field in the new License object to STATUS.ACTIVE.

```
BiFunction<License,License,License> renew = (ov,nv) ->
    new License(nv.expDate, ov.insurance, STATUS.ACTIVE,
ov.vehicles);
```

```
System.out.println(d.merge(licenseId.get(),
                           new License(expDate.get(), null),
                           renew));
```

To add a vehicle to a driver's license, an existing License value can be merged with one containing the new vehicle. The BiFunction creates a License object that adds the vehicle from the new value to any existing vehicles.

```
BiFunction<License,License,License> addVehicle = (ov,nv) -> {
    License temp = new License(ov);
    temp.vehicles.add(nv.vehicles.get(0));
    return temp;
};

System.out.println(d.merge(licenseId.get(),
                           new License(null, null,vehicle.get()),
                           addVehicle));
```

To add a vehicle to a driver's license, an existing License value can be merged with one containing the vehicle to be removed. The BiFunction can use the ArrayLists object's removeIf method to remove the vehicle from the list.

```
BiFunction<License,License,License> removeVehicle = (ov,nv) -> {
    License temp = new License(ov);
    Vehicle r = nv.vehicles.get(0);
    temp.vehicles.removeIf(x -> x.make.equals(r.make)
                           && x.model.equals(r.model)
                           && x.year == r.year);
    return temp;
};
System.out.println(d.merge(licenseId.get(),
                           new License(null, null,vehicle.get()),
                           removeVehicle));
```

The complete program is shown and demonstrated as follows. First, a driver with license id 123 is added to the database with an expiration date of May 7, 2022. Then, driver 123's insurance policy is changed to INS22. Next, the driver's privilege is suspended. Then, driver 123's license is renewed with an expiration date of

June 11, 2022. Then, a 2017 Honda Accord is added to the driver's license. Next, the Accord is removed from the license. Then, driver 123 is removed from the database. The user then quits, and the program terminates.

Listing 9-1. DMV.java

```java
import java.util.*;
import java.util.function.*;
import java.time.*;
enum STATUS {ACTIVE, SUSPENDED}
class Vehicle
{
    String make;
    String model;
    int year;

    public Vehicle(String ma, String mo, int y)
    {
        make = ma;
        model = mo;
        year = y;
    }
    @Override
    public String toString()
    {
        return year + " " + make + " " + model;
    }
}

class License
{
    LocalDate expDate;
    String insurance;
    STATUS status;
    ArrayList<Vehicle> vehicles;

    public License(LocalDate e, String i, Vehicle... v)
    {
```

```java
        expDate = e;
        insurance = i;
        status = STATUS.ACTIVE;
        vehicles = new ArrayList<>();
        for (Vehicle r : v)
            vehicles.add(r);
    }

    public License(LocalDate e, String i, STATUS s,
                    ArrayList<Vehicle> vs)
    {
        expDate = e;
        insurance = i;
        status = s;
        vehicles = new ArrayList<>(vs);
    }

    public License(License l)
    {
        expDate = l.expDate;
        insurance = l.insurance;
        status = l.status;
        vehicles = new ArrayList<>(l.vehicles);
    }
    @Override
    public String toString()
    {
        return expDate + " " + insurance + " " + status
            + " " + vehicles;
    }
}
class DMV
{
    public static void main(String[] args)
    {
        Map<String,License> d = new TreeMap<>();
```

```java
System.out.println(
    "Welcome to the Department of Motor Vehicles.");

Supplier<Integer> selectOperation = () -> {
    int selection = -1;
    Scanner input = new Scanner(System.in);
    while (selection < 0 || selection > 7)
    {
        System.out.println("Select and Operation:");
        System.out.println(
        " 0 - Add Driver 1 - Remove Driver 2 - Change Ins");
        System.out.println(
        " 3 - Suspend Lic 4 - Renew License 5 - Add Veh");
        System.out.print (
        " 6 - Remove Veh 7 - Quit:");
        selection = Integer.parseInt(input.nextLine());
        if (selection < 0 || selection > 7)
            System.out.println("Imvalid selection");
    }
    return selection;
};

Supplier<String> licenseId = () -> {
    Scanner input = new Scanner(System.in);
    System.out.print("Enter licenseId:");
    return input.nextLine();
};
Supplier<String> insurance = () -> {
    Scanner input = new Scanner(System.in);
    System.out.print("Enter insurance:");
    return input.nextLine();
};

Supplier<LocalDate> expDate = () -> {
    Scanner input = new Scanner(System.in);
    System.out.print("Enter year:");
    int year = Integer.parseInt(input.nextLine());
```

```
        System.out.print("Enter month:");
        Month month = Month.valueOf(input.nextLine());
        System.out.print("Enter day:");
        int day = Integer.parseInt(input.nextLine());
        return LocalDate.of(year, month, day);
};

Supplier<Vehicle> vehicle = () -> {
        Scanner input = new Scanner(System.in);
        System.out.print("Enter make:");
        String make = input.nextLine();
        System.out.print("Enter model:");
        String model = input.nextLine();
        System.out.print("Enter year:");
        int year = Integer.parseInt(input.nextLine());
        return new Vehicle(make, model, year);
};

int operation = 0;
while (operation != 7)
{
        operation = selectOperation.get();

switch (operation)
{
        case 0: // Add Driver
            BiFunction<License,License,License> addDriver
                = (ov,nv) -> ov;
            System.out.println(
                d.merge(licenseId.get(),
                        new License(expDate.get(), null),
                        addDriver));
            break;

        case 1: // Remove Driver
          BiFunction<String,License,License> remove
              = (k,v) -> null;
```

```
    System.out.println(
        d.computeIfPresent(licenseId.get(),remove));
    break;

case 2: // Change Insurance
    BiFunction<License,License,License> changeInsurance
        = (ov,nv) -> new License(ov.expDate,
                                 nv.insurance,
                                 ov.status,
                                 ov.vehicles);
    System.out.println(
        d.merge(licenseId.get(),
                new License(null, insurance.get()),
                changeInsurance));
    break;

case 3: // Suspend License
    BiFunction<String,License,License> suspend
        = (k,v) -> new License(v.expDate, v.insurance,
                               STATUS.SUSPENDED,
                               v.vehicles);

    System.out.println(
        d.computeIfPresent(licenseId.get(),suspend));
    break;

case 4: // Renew License
    BiFunction<License,License,License> renew
        = (ov,nv) -> new License(nv.expDate,
                                 ov.insurance,
                                 STATUS.ACTIVE,
                                 ov.vehicles);

    System.out.println(
        d.merge(licenseId.get(),
                new License(expDate.get(), null),
                renew));
    break;
```

```
    case 5: // Add Vehicle
      BiFunction<License,License,License>
          addVehicle = (ov,nv) -> {
              License temp = new License(ov);
              temp.vehicles.add(nv.vehicles.get(0));
              return temp;
          };

      System.out.println(
          d.merge(licenseId.get(),
                  new License(null, null,vehicle.get()),
                  addVehicle));
      break;

    case 6: // Remove Vehicle
      BiFunction<License,License,License>
          removeVehicle = (ov,nv) -> {
              License temp = new License(ov);
              Vehicle r = nv.vehicles.get(0);
              temp.vehicles.removeIf(
                  x -> x.make.equals(r.make)
                      && x.model.equals(r.model)
                      && x.year == r.year);
              return temp;
          };

    System.out.println(
            d.merge(licenseId.get(),
                    new License(null, null,vehicle.get()),
                    removeVehicle));
    }
  }
 }
}
```

PROGRAM OUTPUT (user input shown in **BOLD**):

```
Welcome to the Department of Motor Vehicles.
Select and Operation:
 0 - Add Driver 1 - Remove Driver 2 - Change Ins
 3 - Suspend Lic 4 - Renew License 5 - Add Veh
 6 - Remove Veh 7 - Quit:0
Enter licenseId:123
Enter year:2022
Enter month:MAY
Enter day:7
2022-05-07 null ACTIVE []
Select and Operation:
 0 - Add Driver 1 - Remove Driver 2 - Change Ins
 3 - Suspend Lic 4 - Renew License 5 - Add Veh
 6 - Remove Veh 7 - Quit:2
Enter licenseId:123
Enter insurance:INS22
2022-05-07 INS22 ACTIVE []
Select and Operation:
 0 - Add Driver 1 - Remove Driver 2 - Change Ins
 3 - Suspend Lic 4 - Renew License 5 - Add Veh 6 - Remove Veh
 7 - Quit:3
Enter licenseId:123
2022-05-07 INS22 SUSPENDED []
Select and Operation:
 0 - Add Driver 1 - Remove Driver 2 - Change Ins
 3 - Suspend Lic 4 - Renew License 5 - Add Veh
 6 - Remove Veh 7 - Quit:4
Enter licenseId:123
Enter year:2022
Enter month:JUNE
Enter day:11
2022-06-11 INS22 ACTIVE []
Select and Operation:
 0 - Add Driver 1 - Remove Driver 2 - Change Ins
```

```
 3 - Suspend Lic 4 - Renew License 5 - Add Veh
 6 - Remove Veh 7 - Quit:5
Enter licenseId:123
Enter make:Honda
Enter model:Accord
Enter year:2017
2022-06-11 INS22 ACTIVE [2017 Honda Accord]
Select and Operation:
 0 - Add Driver 1 - Remove Driver 2 - Change Ins
 3 - Suspend Lic 4 - Renew License 5 - Add Veh
 6 - Remove Veh 7 - Quit:6
Enter licenseId:123
Enter make:Honda
Enter model:Accord
Enter year:2017
2022-06-11 INS22 ACTIVE []
Select and Operation:
 0 - Add Driver 1 - Remove Driver 2 - Change Ins
 3 - Suspend Lic 4 - Renew License 5 - Add Veh
 6 - Remove Veh 7 - Quit:1
Enter licenseId:123
null
Select and Operation:
 0 - Add Driver 1 - Remove Driver 2 - Change Ins
 3 - Suspend Lic 4 - Renew License 5 - Add Veh
 6 - Remove Veh 7 - Quit:7
```

Short Problems

1) Use a setAll method of the Arrays class to populate each
    element in a Java array of ints with the length of the array minus its
    subscript. Then, use the removeIf method to remove the element
    whose value is 1. Print the resulting array.

2) Write a map with Integer keys and Integer values. Both the keys and the values are initially the numbers 1 through 5. Using the techniques described in this chapter, triple the values of all entries in the map whose keys contain odd values. Print the resulting map.

3) Given the following Car class,

```
class Car
{
    String make;
    String model;
    public Car(String ma, String mo)
    {
        make = ma;
        model = mo;
    }
    @Override
    public String toString() {return make + " " + model; }
}
```

create a map whose key is a serial number String and whose value is a Car. Use the merge method of the Map interface to do the following:

– Insert a Hyundai Excel with serial number "S123" into the map

– Insert a Buick Skylark with serial number "S456" into the map

– Insert a Toyota Prius with serial number "S789" into the map

– Change the make of entry "S123" to "Chevy"

– Change the model of entry "S123" to "Vega"

– Remove the Toyota Prius from the map

When the merge operations are finished, print the resulting map.

Long Problems

1) Simulate a round of poker where one player competes against the dealer. The player randomly draws five cards and adds them to his or her hand. If any of the cards drawn are already present in the hand, the card is removed and a new card is drawn. After the cards are drawn, it is desirable to remove cards from the hand whose face value is ten or less, and replace them with new cards drawn from the deck. The player may remove up to three cards and replace them with new ones. If any of the cards drawn are already present in the hand, the card is removed and a new card is drawn. When then player has five cards after the second series of draws, the round is finished. If the player has a straight, a flush, or a full house, he or she wins. Otherwise, the dealer wins.

2) A dictionary is implemented as a map containing the following entries:

key: automobile   **value:** ground-powered vehicle with wheels
key: boat   **value:** vehicle that travels on water
key: airplane   **value:** powered vehicle that flies

Using the techniques described in this chapter, translate the definitions into Spanish as follows:

automobile: vehiculo tierra-accionado con las ruedas
boat: vehiculo que viaja en el agua
airplane: vehiculo motorizado que vuela

3) A book reseller's database consists of a map with entries whose key is the book's title and whose values are an object consisting of the book's author, price, and the number of copies available. The database initially contains the following books:

Book Title	Author	Price	Copies Available
Moby-Dick	Herman Melville	$19.99	25
The Zen of Java Programming	Java J. Guru	$15.99	5
Frankenstein	Mary Shelley	$12.99	10

Using the techniques described in this chapter, make the following modifications to the book database:

– Delete the book *Frankenstein* from the database

– Add the book *Dracula* by Bram Stoker for $14.99 with 13 copies available

– Change the price of *The Zen of Java Programming* to $13.99

– Change the copies available for *Moby-Dick* to 24

CHAPTER 10

Use in Comparing Objects

Functional interfaces have changed the way data is compared in Java. This is due to the enhancements to the Comparator interface and the addition of several methods that utilize it in the Java API.

Section 10.1: The Comparator Interface

Comparator is a functional interface that is used to compare two objects. A Comparator is specified with type parameter T. Its functional method, called compare, takes two arguments of type T and returns an integer.

```
@FunctionalInterface
public interface Comparator<T>
{
    int compare(T o1, T o2);
    ...
}
```

The result of the compare method is as follows:

```
a positive integer: if o1 > o2
a negative integer: if o1 < o2
0:                  if o1 = o2
```

Suppose a program needs to compare two names using consonants only. It can define a method to remove all vowels from a name.

```
public static String removeVowels(String s)
{
    return s.replaceAll("[aeiou]","");
}
```

© Ralph Lecessi 2019
R. Lecessi, *Functional Interfaces in Java*, https://doi.org/10.1007/978-1-4842-4278-0_10

A Comparator<String> object can be written that compares two names after removing their vowels.

```
Comparator<String> byConsonants = (x,y) ->
          removeVowels(x).compareTo(removeVowels(y));
```

When the Comparator object's functional method is called, it lexicographically compares the two names using only consonants. The following statement displays 16 because "r" follows "b" in the alphabet by 16 letters.

```
System.out.println(byConsonants.compare("Larry", "Libby"));
```

OUTPUT:

```
16
```

The following example creates a Comparator<Integer> object that uses the Integer class's compareTo method. The compareTo method returns 1 if the calling object is greater than its argument, -1 if the calling object is less than its argument, and 0 if they are the same.

```
Comparator<Integer> byIntCompareTo = (x,y) -> x.compareTo(y);
```

If the integer values 1000 and 1002 are compared using this comparator, -1 will be displayed.

```
System.out.println(byIntCompareTo.compare(1000,1002));
```

OUTPUT:

```
-1
```

In order to see the difference of two integers as a result of the comparison, another comparator can be written that subtracts the numbers and displays -2 instead.

```
Comparator<Integer> byIntDifference = (x,y) -> x - y;
System.out.println(byIntDifference.compare(1000,1002));
```

OUTPUT:

```
-2
```

Section 10.2: Some Useful Comparator Methods

The following Comparator methods are useful.

```
static<T extends Comparable<? super T>> Comparator<T> naturalOrder();
static<T extends Comparable<? super T>> Comparator<T> reverseOrder();
static <T> Comparator<T> nullsFirst(Comparator<? super T> comparator);
static <T> Comparator<T> nullsLast(Comparator<? super T> comparator);
default Comparator<T> reversed();
```

A comparator can be created that compares two names using natural order which for String objects lexicographically compares each character. The following example displays -8 since "a" precedes "i" in the alphabet by eight letters.

```
Comparator<String> natural = Comparator.naturalOrder();
System.out.println(natural.compare("Larry", "Libby"));
```

OUTPUT:

-8

If a comparator is written that uses reversed natural ordering, 8 is displayed.

```
Comparator<String> reversed = Comparator.reverseOrder();
System.out.println(reversed.compare("Larry", "Libby"));
```

OUTPUT:

8

Passing a null string to the Comparator object's compare method will cause a NullPointerException. This can be prevented by passing the comparator to the nullsFirst method which creates a new comparator. A comparator built by the nullsFirst method treats nulls as being less than non-null objects, so the following statement displays 1.

```
System.out.println(Comparator.nullsFirst(byConsonants)
                    .compare("Larry", null));
```

OUTPUT:

1

The nullsLast method creates a comparator that treats nulls as being greater than non-null objects, so the following statement displays -1.

```
System.out.println(Comparator.nullsLast(byConsonants)
                         .compare("Larry", null));
```

OUTPUT:

-1

A new comparator can be created from byConsonants that compares consonants in reverse order. Therefore, the following statement displays -16.

```
System.out.println(byConsonants.reversed()
                         .compare("Larry", "Libby"));
```

OUTPUT:

-16

Note   The reverseOrder method creates a new comparator that compares in the reverse of the natural ordering. The reverse method takes an existing comparator and reverses the ordering of its comparisons.

Section 10.3: The Comparator comparing Methods

The static comparing methods of the Comparator interface create comparators that extract the field to be compared (the key) from an object before performing the comparison.

```
static <T, U extends Comparable<? super U>> Comparator<T>
        comparing(Function<? super T, ? extends U> keyExtractor);
static <T, U> Comparator<T>
        comparing(Function<? super T, ? extends U> keyExtractor,
                Comparator<? super U> comparator);
```

Consider the following class:

Listing 10-1. Student.java

```java
class Student
{
    String name;
    Integer id;
    Double gpa;
    public Student(String n, int i, double g)
    {
        name = n;
        id = i;
        gpa = g;
    }
    @Override
    public String toString() { return name + " " + id + " " + gpa; }

}
```

Since the Student class does not implement the Comparable<Student> interface, a comparator cannot be built by simply calling the object's compareTo method, as was done by the byConsonants comparator. Also, a program may need to compare two students based on name, id, or GPA.

Suppose a program needs to compare students based on grade point average. The program should write a function that extracts the gpa field from a Student object. This will be the key used for comparison of two students.

```java
Function<Student,Double> gpaKey = x -> x.gpa;
```

A Comparator<Student> object can be created that uses the function to extract the gpa field from two Student objects and then compare them based on the natural ordering of Doubles.

```java
Comparator<Student> byGpa = Comparator.comparing(gpaKey);
```

The byGpa Comparator displays 1 when comparing students s1 and s2, since 3.82 is greater than 3.76.

```
Student s1 = new Student("Larry", 1000, 3.82);
Student s2 = new Student("Libby", 1001, 3.76);
System.out.println(byGpa.compare(s1,s2));
```

OUTPUT:

1

Since the Java compiler is able to infer the types of the Function object based on the type of the Comparator object and the return type of the function's lambda, the lambda expression is typically written in the Comparator object's argument list.

```
Comparator<Student> byGpa2 = Comparator.comparing(x -> x.gpa);
```

Another comparator can be defined that compares students based on id instead of GPA. This comparator compares the two ids using the natural order of Integers, and displays -1 when comparing students s1 and s2, since 1000 is less than 1001.

```
Comparator<Student> byId = Comparator.comparing(x -> x.id);
System.out.println(byId.compare(s1,s2));
```

OUTPUT:

-1

A third comparator can be defined that compares students based on name. This comparator lexicographically compares each character in the two name strings and displays -8, since "a" precedes "i" in the alphabet by eight letters.

```
Comparator<Student> byName
    = Comparator.comparing(x -> x.name);
System.out.println(byName.compare(s1,s2));
```

OUTPUT:

-8

Since the Double, Integer, and String classes implement the Comparable interface, the previous examples were able to use the comparing method signature that accepts a single argument which is the key extraction function. If the key is not Comparable, or the program needs to override the natural ordering of the Comparable key, a comparator must be provided as the second parameter to the comparing method.

Suppose a program needs to override the comparison of String objects based on natural ordering, and compare the name strings using consonants only. A comparator that calls the removeVowel method must be provided as the second parameter of the comparing method. This comparator displays 16 because "r" follows "b" in the alphabet by 16 letters.

```
Comparator<Student> byNameConsonants =
    Comparator.comparing( x -> x.name,
                    (x,y) -> removeVowels(x).compareTo(
                                        removeVowels(y)));

System.out.println(byNameConsonants.compare(s1,s2));
```

OUTPUT:

16

Suppose a program needs to override the comparison of Doubles based on natural ordering, and compare grade point averages using the ceiling of the floating point number. This could be used to identify all students with grade point averages between 2.0 and 3.0, so they can be requested to take academic enrichment. A comparator that calls the Math class's ceil method must be provided as the second parameter of the comparing method. This comparator displays 0 because both 3.82 and 3.76 have a ceiling of 4.0 and are therefore considered equal.

```
Comparator<Student> byGpaCeil =
    Comparator.comparing( x -> x.gpa,
                    (x,y) -> (int)(Math.ceil(x)
                            - Math.ceil(y)));

System.out.println(byGpaCeil.compare(s1,s2));
```

OUTPUT:

0

Consider the following class:

```
class ListWrapper
{
    List<Integer> list;
```

```
    public ListWrapper(Integer... i)
    {
        list = Arrays.asList(i);
    }
}
```

If a comparator is written using only a function which extracts the list from a ListWrapper object, a compilation error occurs because lists are not comparable.

```
Comparator<ListWrapper> byList
    = Comparator.comparing(x -> x.list); // ERROR: list not
                                         // comparable
```

A comparator must be provided to specify how to compare the lists. The following comparator compares two List<Integer> objects by their first elements:

```
Comparator<List<Integer>> byElement0 =
        (x,y) -> x.get(0).compareTo(y.get(0));
```

This comparator can be used as the second argument to the comparing method in Comparator byList to specify that the lists extracted from the ListWrapper objects should be compared by their first elements. The following example outputs 1 since 2 (list1.list element 0) is 1 greater than 1 (list2.list element 0).

```
ListWrapper list1 = new ListWrapper(2, 4, 6);
ListWrapper list2 = new ListWrapper(1, 3, 5);

Comparator<ListWrapper> byList
    = Comparator.comparing(x -> x.list, byElement0);

System.out.println(byList.compare(list1,list2));
```

OUTPUT:

1

Section 10.4: Specializations of the Comparator comparing Method

The Java API provides specializations to the Comparator's comparing method that extract Doubles, Integers, and Long keys from objects before comparing them based on natural ordering.

```
static <T> Comparator<T>
        comparingDouble(ToDoubleFunction<? super T>keyExtractor);
static <T> Comparator<T>
        comparingInt(ToIntFunction<? super T>keyExtractor);
static <T> Comparator<T>
        comparingLong(ToLongFunction<? super T>keyExtractor);
```

The comparingDouble method compares two Doubles based on natural ordering using the key extracted by a ToDoubleFunction. In the following example, 1 is displayed because the GPA value 3.82 is greater than 3.76.

```
ToDoubleFunction<Student> gpaKey2 = x -> x.gpa;
System.out.println(Comparator.comparingDouble(gpaKey2)
                        .compare(s1, s2));
```

OUTPUT:

1

The comparingInt method compares two Integers based on natural ordering using the key extracted by a ToIntFunction.

The comparingInt method expects an argument of type ToIntFunction<? super T>. If a lambda expression were passed as the argument instead of a reference to ToIntFunction<Student>, the compiler would not be able to infer that the type of lambda parameter x is Student, and an error would be generated.

```
System.out.println(Comparator.comparingInt(x -> x.id) // ERROR
                        .compare(s1, s2));
```

217

The type of lambda parameter x can be provided in order to avoid the error. In the following example, -1 is displayed because the id value 1000 is less than 1001.

```
System.out.println(Comparator.comparingInt( (Student x) -> x.id)
                          .compare(s1, s2));
```

OUTPUT:

```
-1
```

The comparingLong method compares two Longs based on natural ordering using the key extracted by a ToLongFunction.

The following LongWrapper class wrap a Long value.

```
class LongWrapper
{
    Long l;
    public LongWrapper(long a) { l = a; }
}
```

In the following example, 0 is displayed because the value of l is 4 for both Longs.

```
LongWrapper l1 = new LongWrapper(4L);
LongWrapper l2 = new LongWrapper(4L);
ToLongFunction<LongWrapper> lKey = x -> x.l;
System.out.println(Comparator.comparingLong(lKey)
            .compare(l1, l2));
```

OUTPUT:

```
0
```

Section 10.5: Building Chains of Comparators

The default thenComparing methods return a comparator that is used for further comparison if the calling comparator determines that the objects being compared are equal.

```
default Comparator<T>
    thenComparing(Comparator<? super T> other);
default <U extends Comparable<? super U>> Comparator<T>
```

218

```
    thenComparing(Function<? super T, ? extends U> keyExtractor);
default <U> Comparator<T>
    thenComparing(Function<? super T, ? extends U> keyExtractor,
                  Comparator<? super U> keyComparator);
```

Three Comparator<Student> objects can be defined, each of which extracts a different field of the Student class and uses it for comparison based on the natural ordering of the field.

```
Comparator<Student> byName = Comparator.comparing(x -> x.name);
Comparator<Student> byId   = Comparator.comparing(x -> x.id);
Comparator<Student> byGpa  = Comparator.comparing(x -> x.gpa);
```

Suppose two students were named "Joseph" and had with the same grade point average.

```
Student s1 = new Student("Joseph", 1000, 3.82);
Student s2 = new Student("Joseph", 1002, 3.82);
```

If these students were compared by name, the result would be 0.

```
System.out.println(byName.compare(s1, s2));
```

OUTPUT:

0

The students could then be further compared by grade point average by specifying the byGpa Comparator in the thenComparing call of the comparator's method chain. The comparisons are performed in the reverse of the order they are listed, and only if the prior comparison returns 0. Since comparison by name returns 0, comparison by GPA is performed. This also returns 0.

```
System.out.println(byName.thenComparing(byGpa)//byName->byGpa
                          .compare(s1, s2));
```

OUTPUT:

0

The students could then be further compared by id by specifying the `byId` Comparator in an additional `thenComparing` call. This returns -1 since 1000 is less than 1002.

```
System.out.println(byName.thenComparing(byId)//byName->byGpa->byId
                          .thenComparing(byGpa)
                          .compare(s1, s2));
```

OUTPUT:

```
-1
```

If the order of the `thenComparing` calls in the comparator chain were switched, the byGpa comparison would not be performed because the byId comparison already resulted in a non-zero value. In the following example, byName is performed first resulting in 0, and then byId is performed resulting in -1 since 1000 is less than 1002. The byGpa comparison is not performed.

```
System.out.println(byName.thenComparing(byGpa)
                          .thenComparing(byId)
                          .compare(s1, s2));
```

OUTPUT:

```
-1
```

The previous examples have used the `thenComparing` signature that accepts a comparator. If natural order comparisons are desired, the `thenComparing` signature that accepts a function can be used.

```
System.out.println(byName.thenComparing(x -> x.id)
                          .thenComparing(x -> x.gpa)
                          .compare(s1, s2));
```

OUTPUT:

```
-1
```

A third signature of the `thenComparing` method accepts both a function and a comparator and can be used to perform comparisons that are not in natural order.

```
Comparator<Student> byNameConsonants
        = Comparator.comparing( x -> x.name,
                                (x,y) ->
                    removeVowels(x).compareTo(removeVowels(y)));

Comparator<Integer> byDifference = (x,y) -> x - y;

Comparator<Double> byCeil =
        (x,y) -> (int)(Math.ceil(x) - Math.ceil(y));
```

In the following example, the byNameConsonants Comparator removes the vowels from "Jean" and "Jen" creating strings that are equal. Therefore, the byCeil Comparator is invoked on the extracted grade point average to compare the ceiling of 3.86 with the ceiling of 3.69, again resulting in equality since both are 4. Finally, the byDifference Comparator is invoked on the extracted id and -2 is displayed.

```
Student s3 = new Student("Jean", 1003, 3.86);
Student s4 = new Student("Jen" , 1005, 3.69);

System.out.println(byNameConsonants.thenComparing(x -> x.id,
                                                  byDifference)
                            .thenComparing(x -> x.gpa,
                                           byCeil)
                            .compare(s3, s4));
```

OUTPUT:

-2

Section 10.6: Specializing Comparator Chain Components

The Java API provides specializations to the Comparator interface's thenComparing signature that accepts a specialized function object. These specializations extract Doubles, Integers, and Long keys from objects before comparing them based on natural ordering.

```
default Comparator<T> thenComparingInt(ToIntFunction<? super T>
keyExtractor);
default Comparator<T> thenComparingLong(ToLongFunction<? super T>
keyExtractor);
default Comparator<T> thenComparingDouble(ToDoubleFunction<? super T>
keyExtractor);
```

In the following example, the byGpa Comparator result determines that students s5 and s6 are equal. Next, thenComparingInt extracts the id field and compares 1006 to 1007 by natural ordering, which results in -1.

```
Student s5 = new Student("Kaitlyn", 1006, 3.69);
Student s6 = new Student("Jane" , 1007, 3.69);

System.out.println(byGpa.thenComparingInt( x-> x.id )
                    .compare(s5,s6));
```

OUTPUT:

```
-1
```

In the following example, the byName Comparator result determines that students s7 and s8 are equal. Next, thenComparingDouble extracts the gpa field and compares 3.86 to 3.69 by natural ordering, which results in 1.

```
Student s7 = new Student("Robert", 1008, 3.86);
Student s8 = new Student("Robert", 1009, 3.69);

System.out.println(byName.thenComparingDouble( x-> x.gpa )
                    .compare(s7,s8));
```

OUTPUT:

```
1
```

Section 10.7: Using Comparators to Sort Lists

Comparators will most frequently be used to sort lists and streams.

The List<X> interface has a method named sort which accepts a Comparator<X> argument that is used for the comparisons during the sort.

Suppose a program needs to sort the following list of students first by GPA ceiling, then by name, and then by id:

```
List<Student> students = Arrays.asList(
        new Student("Joseph"  , 1623, 3.54),
        new Student("Annie"   , 1923, 2.94),
        new Student("Sharmila", 1874, 1.86),
        new Student("Harvey"  , 1348, 1.78),
        new Student("Grace"   , 1004, 3.90),
        new Student("Annie"   , 1245, 2.87)
);
```

In its first version, the program sorts the list by GPA ceiling only. A comparator is written that performs the GPA ceiling comparison. The comparator is passed to the List object's sort method. The resulting list is grouped by GPA ceiling (contrasted by bold), but the entries within the groups are unsorted.

```
Comparator<Student> byGpaCeil =
    Comparator.comparing( x -> x.gpa,
                     (x,y) -> (int)(Math.ceil(x)
                                - Math.ceil(y)));

students.sort(byGpaCeil);
students.forEach(x-> System.out.println(x));
```

OUTPUT:

```
Sharmila 1874 1.86
Harvey 1348 1.78
Annie 1923 2.94
Annie 1245 2.87
Joseph 1623 3.54
Grace 1004 3.9
```

In its next version, the program further sorts the list by name. This is accomplished by adding a thenComparing call that extracts the student's name to the end of the comparator chain. The 4.0 and 2.0 GPA ceiling groups are now sorted, but the 3.0 GPA ceiling group is unsorted since both students are named "Annie".

```
students.sort(byGpaCeil
            .thenComparing(x -> x.name));
students.forEach(x-> System.out.println(x));
```

OUTPUT:

Harvey 1348 1.78
Sharmila 1874 1.86
Annie 1923 2.94
Annie 1245 2.87
Grace 1004 3.9
Joseph 1623 3.54

In its final version, the program further sorts the list by id. This is accomplished by adding a thenComparing call that extracts the student's id to the end of the comparator chain. The list is now fully sorted.

```
students.sort(byGpaCeil
            .thenComparing(x -> x.id)
            .thenComparing(x -> x.name));
students.forEach(x-> System.out.println(x));
```

OUTPUT:

Harvey 1348 1.78
Sharmila 1874 1.86
Annie 1245 2.87
Annie 1923 2.94
Grace 1004 3.9
Joseph 1623 3.54

Section 10.8: Using Comparators to Sort Java Arrays

Comparators can operate on Java arrays in a fashion similar to lists through the use of the Arrays class. Suppose the program stored the students in a Java array instead.

```
Student[] students = {
        new Student("Joseph"  , 1623, 3.54),
        new Student("Annie"   , 1923, 2.94),
```

```
                new Student("Sharmila", 1874, 1.86),
                new Student("Harvey"  , 1348, 1.78),
                new Student("Grace"   , 1004, 3.90),
                new Student("Annie"   , 1245, 2.87)
};
```

The students array is copied in order to perform two different sorts on its elements.

```
Student[] studentsCopy = Arrays.copyOf(students, students.length);
```

The Array class's static sort method sorts a Java array using a specified comparator. In the following example, the Java array is sorted in the same order as the list.

```
Comparator<Student> byGpaCeil =
Comparator.comparing( x -> x.gpa,
                      (x,y) -> (int)(Math.ceil(x)
                                   - Math.ceil(y)));

Arrays.sort(students,
            byGpaCeil
          .thenComparing(x -> x.id)
          .thenComparing(x -> x.name));

for (Student s : students)
    System.out.println(s);
```

OUTPUT:

```
Harvey 1348 1.78
Sharmila 1874 1.86
```
Annie 1245 2.87
Annie 1923 2.94
```
Grace 1004 3.9
Joseph 1623 3.54
```

The Array class's sort method can be used to sort a range of elements. In the following example, the second through fourth elements of the Java array are sorted by name.

```
Arrays.sort(studentsCopy, 2, 5,
            Comparator.comparing(x -> x.name));
```

```
for (Student s : studentsCopy)
    System.out.println(s);
```

OUTPUT:

```
Joseph 1623 3.54
Annie 1923 2.94
Grace 1004 3.9
Harvey 1348 1.78
Sharmila 1874 1.86
Annie 1245 2.87
```

A binary search can be performed on a sorted Java array using the `Arrays` class if a comparator is provided. Suppose a program models a student body that consists of 1000 students named "S000" through "S999".

```
final int NUM_STUDENTS = 1000;
NumberFormat fmt = NumberFormat.getNumberInstance();
fmt.setMinimumIntegerDigits(3);
Student[] studentBody = new Student[NUM_STUDENTS];
for (int i = 0; i < NUM_STUDENTS; ++i)
    studentBody[i] = new Student("S" + fmt.format(i), i, 0.0);
```

The `Array` class's `binarySearch` method can be used to quickly search for the student with name "S647" if a comparator which compares students by name is specified. In the following code, the student with name "S647" is found at index 647 of the student body array.

```
int index = Arrays.binarySearch(studentBody,
                        new Student("S647",0,0.0),
                        Comparator.comparing(x -> x.name));

System.out.println("index = " + index + " "
                + studentBody[index]);
```

OUTPUT:

```
index = 647 S647 647 0.0
```

Section 10.9: Using Comparators to Organize Maps

Several implementations of the Map interface can be instantiated with a comparator to organize its entries in a particular order. For example, the entries in a TreeMap are normally organized by the natural ordering of their keys. In the following example, the byConsonants Comparator is used to only consider consonants in the keys when organizing the entries. Therefore, guinea pig is placed before gerbil and cat is placed before chicken.

```
Comparator<String> byConsonants = (x,y) ->
        removeVowels(x).compareTo(removeVowels(y));

TreeMap<String,String> pets = new TreeMap<>(byConsonants);

pets.put("gerbil", "small cute rodents");
pets.put("guinea pig", "rodents, not pigs");
pets.put("cat", "have nine lives");
pets.put("chicken", "more populous than people");

pets.forEach((x,y) -> System.out.println(x + ", " + y));
```

OUTPUT:

```
chicken, more populous than people
cat, have nine lives
guinea pig, rodents, not pigs
gerbil, small cute rodents
```

Comparators can also be used to compare Map.Entry objects. In the following example, two Map.Entry objects are compared by key using the comparingByKey method. Therefore, -7 is displayed because the "h" in "chicken" is seven letters after the "a" in "cat".

```
Comparator<Map.Entry<String,String>> cmap =
    Map.Entry.comparingByKey();

Map.Entry<String,String> cat = pets.ceilingEntry("cat");
Map.Entry<String,String> chicken = pets.ceilingEntry("chicken");

System.out.println(cmap.compare(cat, chicken));
```

OUTPUT:

```
-7
```

The comparingByKey method can also accept a comparator. In the following example, the byConsonants Comparator is used, and 12 is displayed because the "h" in "chicken" is 12 letters before the "t" in "cat".

```
Comparator<Map.Entry<String,String>> cmapCons =
    Map.Entry.comparingByKey(byConsonants);

System.out.println(cmapCons.compare(cat, chicken));
```

OUTPUT:

```
12
```

Map.Entry objects can be compared by value using the comparingByValue method. In the following example, -5 is displayed because the "h" in "have" is five letters before the "m" in "more".

```
Comparator<Map.Entry<String,String>> cval =
    Map.Entry.comparingByValue();

System.out.println(cval.compare(cat, chicken));
```

OUTPUT:

```
-5
```

Section 10.10: Using Comparators in BinaryOperator Methods

The BinaryOperator<T> maxBy and minBy methods compare two objects of type X based on a Comparator<T>. In the following example, a Comparator which compares two Integers based on absolute value is defined. BinaryOperators are created using the static maxBy and minBy methods which accept a comparator. The BinaryOperator object's apply methods now compare two Integers based on their absolute values.

```
Comparator<Integer> abscompare =
    Comparator.comparing(x -> Math.abs(x));
BinaryOperator<Integer> bigint =
```

```
     BinaryOperator.maxBy(abscompare);
BinaryOperator<Integer> smallint =
     BinaryOperator.minBy(abscompare);

System.out.println(bigint.apply(2,-5));
System.out.println(smallint.apply(2,-5));
```

OUTPUT:

```
-5
2
```

PROJECT 10: Real Estate Broker
Problem Statement

Reba the realtor shows homes in the Forest Acres, Happy Gardens, and Comfy Condos communities to prospective buyers. Customers are usually interested in only one community, but sometimes, Reba gets a customer who will consider all three communities. Priorities vary among customers, but they usually include the following:

  – Price

  – Number of bedrooms

  – Property size

  – Distance to the nearest school

  – Distance to train station

Customers find it very frustrating when they are shown homes in which they are not interested, so Reba wants a program that will eliminate homes that are not in their desired community, if any, and list the remaining homes in order of the top three of the customer's priorities. The fractional components of both property size and distance are ignored while sorting the listing.

Solution

A class that contains values for the community and the customer priorities can be written.

```java
class Home
{
    String community;
    double price;
    int numBedrooms;
    double acres;
    double schoolDistance;
    double trainDistance;
    public Home(String co, double pr, int bed, double ac,
                double sd, double td)
    {
        community = co;
        price = pr;
        numBedrooms = bed;
        acres = ac;
        schoolDistance = sd;
        trainDistance = td;
    }
    @Override
    public String toString()
    {
        return numBedrooms + " bedroom house in " + community
            + " for $" + price + " on " + acres + " acres\n "
            + schoolDistance + " miles from school "
            + trainDistance + " miles from train";
    }
}
```

The Home class can be used to create a list of homes that Reba has available for sale.

```java
List<Home> homes = Arrays.asList(
    new Home( "Forest Acres" , 425000.0, 4, 1.7, 5.1, 4.5),
    new Home( "Happy Gardens", 510000.0, 4, 2.3, 5.1, 4.5),
```

```
    new Home( "Comfy Condos" , 190000.0, 2, 0.9, 2.1, 4.5),
    new Home( "Comfy Condos" , 190000.0, 2, 0.9, 0.7, 4.5),
    new Home( "Happy Gardens", 470000.0, 4, 2.1, 5.1, 4.5),
    new Home( "Forest Acres" , 345000.0, 3, 1.5, 3.2, 5.9),
    new Home( "Happy Gardens", 375000.0, 3, 1.5, 2.3, 2.4),
    new Home( "Comfy Condos" , 190000.0, 2, 0.3, 0.5, 2.4)
);
```

A separate Comparator can be created for each priority using the Comparator.
comparing method and a function that selects the appropriate field in the Home object.
The byPrice Comparator compares homes by price in ascending order. Since homes
with more bedrooms should be listed first, the byBedrooms Comparator calls the
reversed method to compare homes by number of bedrooms in descending order.

```
Comparator<Home> byPrice
    = Comparator.comparing(x -> x.price);
Comparator<Home> byBedroomsAsc
    = Comparator.comparing(x -> x.numBedrooms);
Comparator<Home> byBedrooms
    = byBedroomsAsc.reversed();
```

Since the fractional component of property size, school distance, and train distance
can be ignored, a comparator that extracts the ceiling of each floating point number
can be passed into each comparing method. Note that the order is reversed in the
byProperty Comparator so that larger properties are listed first.

```
Comparator<Home> byProperty =
    Comparator.comparing( x -> x.acres,
                        (x,y) -> (int)(Math.ceil(y) -
Math.ceil(x)));
Comparator<Home> bySchool =
    Comparator.comparing( x -> x.schoolDistance,
                        (x,y) -> (int)(Math.ceil(x) -
Math.ceil(y)));
Comparator<Home> byTrain =
    Comparator.comparing( x -> x.trainDistance,
                        (x,y) -> (int)(Math.ceil(x) -
Math.ceil(y)));
```

Reba only wants to show customers homes in the community in which they are interested, if any. Therefore, a copy of the home listing with homes from the other communities can be created. This can be accomplished using the `ArrayList` class's removeIf method with a predicate that checks the home's community. The comm object is a supplier that prompts the Reba to enter the customer's desired community.

```
String community = comm.get();
List<Home> homesTemp = new ArrayList<>(homes);
if (!community.equals("any"))
    homesTemp.removeIf(x -> !x.community.equals(community));
```

Reba then asks the customer their three top priorities and selects from one of the five available `Comparators`. `PriorityNumber` is a supplier that prompts Reba to enter one of the customer's priorities.

```
Supplier<Comparator<Home> > priority = () -> {
    Comparator<Home> pr;
    int prNumber = priorityNumber.get();
    switch (prNumber)
    {
        case 0 : pr = byPrice;         break;
        case 1 : pr = byBedroomsRev;   break;
        case 2 : pr = byProperty;      break;
        case 3 : pr = bySchool;        break;
        default: pr = byTrain;
    }
    return pr;
};

Comparator<Home> priority1, priority2, priority3;
priority1 = priority.get();
priority2 = priority.get();
priority3 = priority.get();
```

Reba can now create a listing sorted by the three priorities in order using the thenComparing method.

```
homesTemp.sort(priority1
            .thenComparing(priority2)
            .thenComparing(priority3)); homesTemp.forEach(x ->
```

```
System.out.println(x));
```

The complete program is shown as follows.

Listing 10-2. RealEstateBroker.java

```java
import java.util.*;
import java.util.function.*;
class Home
{
    String community;
    double price;
    int numBedrooms;
    double acres;

    double schoolDistance;
    double trainDistance;
    public Home(String co, double pr, int bed, double ac,
            double sd, double td)
    {
        community = co;
        price = pr;
        numBedrooms = bed;
        acres = ac;
        schoolDistance = sd;
        trainDistance = td;
    }
    @Override
    public String toString()
    {
        return numBedrooms + " bedroom house in " + community
            + " for $" + price + " on " + acres
            + " acres\n " + schoolDistance + " miles from school "
            + trainDistance + " miles from train";
    }
}
```

```
class RealEstateBroker
{
    public static void main(String[] args)
    {
        System.out.println("Home Listings for Forest Acres,"
                        + " Happy Gardens, and Comfy Condos\n");
        List<Home> homes = Arrays.asList(
            new Home( "Forest Acres" , 425000.0, 4, 1.7, 5.1, 4.5),
            new Home( "Happy Gardens", 510000.0, 4, 2.3, 5.1, 4.5),
            new Home( "Comfy Condos" , 190000.0, 2, 0.9, 2.1, 4.5),
            new Home( "Comfy Condos" , 190000.0, 2, 0.9, 0.7, 4.5),
            new Home( "Happy Gardens", 470000.0, 4, 2.1, 5.1, 4.5),
            new Home( "Forest Acres" , 345000.0, 3, 1.5, 3.2, 5.9),
            new Home( "Happy Gardens", 375000.0, 3, 1.5, 2.3, 2.4),
            new Home( "Comfy Condos" , 190000.0, 2, 0.3, 0.5, 2.4)
        );

        Comparator<Home> byPrice =
            Comparator.comparing(x -> x.price);

        Comparator<Home> byBedrooms =
            Comparator.comparing(x -> x.numBedrooms);

        Comparator<Home> byBedroomsRev =
            byBedrooms.reversed();

        Comparator<Home> byProperty =
            Comparator.comparing( x -> x.acres,
                    (x,y) -> (int)(Math.ceil(y) - Math.ceil(x)));

        Comparator<Home> bySchool =
            Comparator.comparing( x -> x.schoolDistance,
                    (x,y) -> (int)(Math.ceil(x) - Math.ceil(y)));
        Comparator<Home> byTrain =
            Comparator.comparing( x -> x.trainDistance,
                    (x,y) -> (int)(Math.ceil(x) - Math.ceil(y)));

        Supplier<Integer> priorityNumber = () -> {
```

```
    Scanner input = new Scanner(System.in);
    int prio = -1;
    while (prio < 0 || prio > 4)
    {
        System.out.println("Select a Priority:");
        System.out.println("0 - price");
        System.out.println("1 - number of bedrooms");
        System.out.println("2 - property size");
        System.out.println("3 - distance to nearest school");
        System.out.print("4 - distance to train station:");
        prio = Integer.parseInt(input.nextLine());
        if (prio < 0 || prio > 4)
            System.out.println("Invalid priority");
    }
    return prio;
};

Supplier<String> comm = () -> {
    Scanner input = new Scanner(System.in);
    String[] communities = {"Forest Acres", "Happy Gardens",
                            "Comfy Condos", "any"};
    int selection = -1;
    while (selection < 0 || selection > 3)
    {
        System.out.println("Select community:");
        System.out.println("0 - Forest Acres");
        System.out.println("1 - Happy Gardens");
        System.out.println("2 - Comfy Condos");
        System.out.print("3 - any:");
        selection = Integer.parseInt(input.nextLine());
        if ((selection < 0 || selection > 3))
            System.out.println("Invalid community");
    }
    return communities[selection];
};
```

```
        Supplier<Comparator<Home> > priority = () -> {
            Comparator<Home> pr;
            int prNumber = priorityNumber.get();
            switch (prNumber)
            {
                case 0 : pr = byPrice;          break;
                case 1 : pr = byBedroomsRev; break;
                case 2 : pr = byProperty;       break;
                case 3 : pr = bySchool;         break;
                default: pr = byTrain;
            }
            return pr;
        };

        Comparator<Home> priority1, priority2, priority3;
        String community = comm.get();

        List<Home> homesTemp = new ArrayList<>(homes);
        if (!community.equals("any"))
            homesTemp.removeIf(x -> !x.community.equals(community));

        priority1 = priority.get();
        priority2 = priority.get();

        priority3 = priority.get();
        homesTemp.sort(priority1
                    .thenComparing(priority2)
                    .thenComparing(priority3));
        homesTemp.forEach(x -> System.out.println(x));
    };
}
```

Reba's first customer wants a home in Happy Gardens and is most concerned with the number of bedrooms, then the property size, and then the price. Only the Happy Gardens homes are listed with the four-bedroom homes displayed before the three-bedroom homes. Within the four-bedroom home group, the ceilings of both property sizes are the same, so price is used to list the 470,000 home first.

PROGRAM OUTPUT (user input shown in **BOLD**):

Home Listings for Forest Acres, Happy Gardens, and Comfy Condos

Select community:
0 - Forest Acres
1 - Happy Gardens
2 - Comfy Condos
3 - any: **1**
Select a Priority:
0 - price
1 - number of bedrooms
2 - property size
3 - distance to nearest school
4 - distance to train station: **1**
Select a Priority:
0 - price
1 - number of bedrooms
2 - property size
3 - distance to nearest school
4 - distance to train station: **2**
Select a Priority:
0 - price
1 - number of bedrooms
2 - property size
3 - distance to nearest school
4 - distance to train station: **0**
4 bedroom house in Happy Gardens for $470000.0 on 2.1 acres
    5.1 miles from school 4.5 miles from train
4 bedroom house in Happy Gardens for $510000.0 on 2.3 acres
    5.1 miles from school 4.5 miles from train
3 bedroom house in Happy Gardens for $375000.0 on 1.5 acres
    2.3 miles from school 2.4 miles from train

Reba's next customer doesn't care which community the home is in and cares mostly about the number of bedrooms, then the home price, and then the distance to the nearest school. All homes are listed with the four-bedroom homes listed first followed by the three-bedroom homes and then the two-bedroom homes. Within the two-bedroom home group, all homes are the same price, so distance to school is used to list the 0.7 and 0.5 mile homes before the 2.1 mile home.

PROGRAM OUTPUT (user input shown in **BOLD**):

```
Home Listings for Forest Acres, Happy Gardens, and Comfy Condos

Select community:
0 - Forest Acres
1 - Happy Gardens
2 - Comfy Condos
3 - any :3
Select a Priority:
0 - price
1 - number of bedrooms
2 - property size
3 - distance to nearest school
4 - distance to train station: 1
Select a Priority:
0 - price
1 - number of bedrooms
2 - property size
3 - distance to nearest school
4 - distance to train station: 0
Select a Priority:
0 - price
1 - number of bedrooms
2 - property size
3 - distance to nearest school
4 - distance to train station: 3
4 bedroom house in Forest Acres for $425000.0 on 1.7 acres
    5.1 miles from school 4.5 miles from train
4 bedroom house in Happy Gardens for $470000.0 on 2.1 acres
```

5.1 miles from school 4.5 miles from train
4 bedroom house in Happy Gardens for $510000.0 on 2.3 acres
   5.1 miles from school 4.5 miles from train
3 bedroom house in Forest Acres for $345000.0 on 1.5 acres
   3.2 miles from school 5.9 miles from train
3 bedroom house in Happy Gardens for $375000.0 on 1.5 acres
   2.3 miles from school 2.4 miles from train
2 bedroom house in Comfy Condos for $190000.0 on 0.9 acres
   0.7 miles from school 4.5 miles from train
2 bedroom house in Comfy Condos for $190000.0 on 0.3 acres
   0.5 miles from school 2.4 miles from train
2 bedroom house in Comfy Condos for $190000.0 on 0.9 acres
   2.1 miles from school 4.5 miles from train

Short Problems

1) Write a comparator that compares two integers based on their natural ordering but treats all even integers as equal.

2) Given the following class,

```
class A implements Comparable<A>
{
    String s1;
    String s2;
    int i;
    public A(String a, String b, int c) { s1 = a; s2 = b;
    i = c; } @Override
    public String toString() { return s1 + " " + s2 + " " + i; }

    @Override
    public int compareTo(A a) { return s1.compareTo(a.s1); }
}
```

write the following comparators:

- A comparator that compares two As

- A comparator that compares two As by their reverse ordering

- A comparator that compares two As by the reverse ordering of field s2

- A comparator that compares two As by the natural ordering of field i

Demonstrate the comparators in a main program.

3) Sort the following list of A objects first by field s1, then by the reverse ordering of field s2, and then by field i:

    Sally   Jones   3
    Sally   Seashell   4
    Harry   Jones   1
    Harry   Homeowner   5
    Harry   Homeowner   2

Print the sorted list.

Long Problems

1) Design a rock-paper-scissors game that uses a comparator to compare a player's selection vs. the computer's selection according to the following rules:

    - Rock smashes scissors

    - Scissors cuts paper

    - Paper covers rock

    - All other combinations are a tie

    Write a supplier which prompts the user for his or her selection, another supplier which randomly generates the computer's selection, and a third supplier which prompts the user if he or she wants to play again. Keep score of the winner of each round. Print the final score and the overall winner at the end of the competition.

2) The following list contains baseball's career leaders in batting
    average, hits, home runs, and runs batted in:

	Avg	Hits	HR	RBI
Ty Cobb	.367	4191	117	1961
Rogers Hornsby	.358	2930	301	1584
Tris Speaker	.346	3514	117	1529
Ted Williams	.345	2654	521	1839
Babe Ruth	.344	2873	714	2213
Lou Gehrig	.340	2721	493	1995
George Sisler	.340	2812	102	1178
Tony Gwynn	.338	3141	135	1138
Stan Musial	.331	3630	475	1951
Wade Boggs	.328	3010	118	1024
Rod Carew	.328	3053	92	1015
Honus Wagner	.327	3415	101	1732
Joe DiMaggio	.325	2214	361	1539
Pete Rose	.303	4256	160	1314
Hank Aaron	.305	3771	755	2297
Derek Jeter	.310	3465	260	1311
Willie Mays	.302	3283	660	1903
Alex Rodriguez	.295	3115	696	2086
Barry Bonds	.298	2935	762	1996
Albert Pujols	.302	3081	644	1995

Hitters can be rated using combinations of the four statistics listed
previously. For example:

Finesse hitter: AVG, then Hits, then HRs, then RBIs
Endurance hitter: Hits, then AVG, then RBIs, then HRs
Power hitter: HRs, then RBIs, then Hits, then AVG
Clutch hitter: RBIs, then HRs, then AVG, then Hits

Write comparators for each of the four criteria listed previously,
and display lists that rate the hitters accordingly.

3)   A deck of playing cards when first opened is sorted by suite and then by face value. In other words, the first card is the Two of Hearts followed by the Three of Hearts through the Ace of Hearts, followed by the Two of Clubs, then the Three of Clubs, etc.

Write a comparator that sorts the deck by face value and then by suite. In other words, the first card should be the Two of Hearts followed by the Two of Clubs, then the Two of Spades, then the Two of Diamonds, then the Three of Hearts followed by the Three of Clubs, etc.

CHAPTER 11

Use in Optionals

It is useful to wrap an object inside an Optional to avoid checking for nullness. Optionals can also be used inside method chains to simplify the logic of a program.

Section 11.1: Creating an Optional

The Optional class wraps an object of type parameter T.

```
public final class Optional <T> {
    ...
}
```

The Optional class provides the following static methods which are used to create Optionals of type T:

```
static <T> Optional<T> of(T value);
static <T> Optional<T> ofNullable(T value);
static <T> Optional<T> empty();
```

The of method creates an Optional from a non-null argument. If called with a null argument, it throws a NullPointerException.

```
try {
    Optional<String> o1 = Optional.of(null);
} catch (NullPointerException e) {
    System.out.println("NullPointerException");
}
Optional<String> o2 = Optional.of("Hello");
System.out.println("OK");
```

© Ralph Lecessi 2019
R. Lecessi, *Functional Interfaces in Java*, https://doi.org/10.1007/978-1-4842-4278-0_11

OUTPUT:

```
NullPointerException
OK
```

If the object wrapped by an Optional can be null, the ofNullable method should be used.

```
Optional<String> o3 = Optional.ofNullable(null);
System.out.println("OK");
```

```
Optional<String> o4 = Optional.ofNullable("Hello");
System.out.println("OK");
```

OUTPUT:

```
OK
OK
```

The empty method can also be used to create an Optional that wraps a null object.

```
Optional<String> o5 = Optional.empty();
```

Section 11.2: Determining If an **Optional** Is Present

The isPresent method returns true if the Optional contains a non-null object and returns false otherwise.

```
boolean isPresent();
```

The following example produces no output.

```
if (o5.isPresent())
    System.out.println("o5 is non-null");
```

In Java 11, the isEmpty method was added. This method returns true if the Optional wraps a null object and false otherwise. This method gives the opposite result of isPresent.

```
bool isEmpty();      [JAVA 11]
```

244

The following example displays "Empty" since `Optional imNull` contains a null value.

```
Optional<String> imNull = Optional.ofNullable(null);
if (imNull.isEmpty())
    System.out.println("Empty");
```

OUTPUT:

```
Empty
```

Section 11.3: Retrieving the Contents of an `Optional`

The get method returns the object wrapped by an `Optional`.

```
T get();
```

The get method throws a `NoSuchElementException` if called on an `Optional` that contains `null`.

```
try {
    o5.get();
} catch (NoSuchElementException e) {
    System.out.println("NoSuchElementException");
}
```

OUTPUT:

```
NoSuchElementException
```

Always check `ifPresent` before calling get.

```
if (o4.isPresent())
    System.out.println(o4.get());
if (o5.isPresent())
    System.out.println(o5.get());
else
    System.out.println("o5 is null");

if (!o5.isEmpty())
```

```
    System.out.println(o5.get());
else
    System.out.println("o5 is null");
```

OUTPUT:

```
Hello
o5 is null
o5 is null
```

Section 11.4: Creating Chains of `Optionals`

The `Optional` class provides the following methods that can be used to create chains of `Optionals`:

```
T orElse(T other);
T orElseGet(Supplier<? extends T> supplier);
Optional<T> or(Supplier<? extends Optional<? extends T> > supplier);
<X extends Throwable> T orElseThrow(Supplier<? extends X>
exceptionSupplier);
T orElseThrow();        [JAVA10]
```

Suppose a program defines two strings t and u,

```
String t=null, u="Hello";
```

and the program needs to pick the first string that is non-null. That is, it needs to perform the following logic:

```
String s = t;
if (t == null)
    s = u;
```

The `Optional` class's `orElse` method provides a value to use if the `Optional` contains a null.

```
String s = Optional.ofNullable(t)      // Optional has null
                .orElse(u);            // Optional has "Hello"
```

The orElseGet method accepts a supplier which provides the value.

```
String s2 = Optional.ofNullable(t)          // null
                    .orElseGet( () -> u);   // "Hello"
```

The orElseThrow method accepts a supplier which provides an exception which is thrown if the value is not present. In the following example, the Optional contains null, so the orElseThrow method throws the Exception provided by its supplier. The exception is caught and "Null Optional" is displayed.

```
try {
    String s = null;
    String opt = Optional.ofNullable(s)
                         .orElseThrow(() ->
                             new Exception("Null Optional"));
}
catch (Exception e)
{
    System.out.println(e.getMessage());
}
```

OUTPUT:

```
Null Optional
```

In Java 10, an overloaded version of the orElseThrow method was provided. This version has no arguments and throws a NoSuchElementException. In the following example, the orElseThrow method throws a NoSuchElementException. The exception is caught and "No value present" is displayed.

```
try {
    String s = null;
    String opt = Optional.ofNullable(s)
                         .orElseThrow();
}
catch (Exception e)
{
    System.out.println(e.getMessage());
}
```

OUTPUT:

```
No value present
```

The orElse, orElseGet, and orElseThrow methods return a value of type X. The or method returns an Optional<X> that can be followed by additional links in an Optional chain.

The or method in the following example accepts a Supplier<Optional<String> >, which prompts the user to enter a string if the value contained in the Optional is null.

```
Supplier<Optional<String> > supplier = () -> {
    System.out.print("Enter a string:");
    return Optional.of((new Scanner(System.in)).nextLine());
};

String s = null;
Optional<String> os = Optional.ofNullable(s)
                            .or(supplier);

if (os.isPresent())
    System.out.println(os.get());
```

OUTPUT (Input shown in **BOLD**):

```
Enter a string:RED
RED
```

Section 11.5: Printing the Contents of an Optional

The Optional class's ifPresent method accepts a consumer and is frequently used to print the object that is wrapped by an Optional.

```
void ifPresent(Consumer<? super T> action);
```

Since ifPresent returns void, it must be the last method called if used in an Optional chain. The ifPresent method can be added as the final link in the Optional chain of the previous example.

```
String s = null;
Optional.ofNullable(s)
```

```
       .or(supplier)
       .ifPresent(x -> System.out.println(x));
```

OUTPUT (User input shown in **BOLD**):

```
Enter a string:Hello
Hello
```

Section 11.6: Filtering Optionals

The Optional class's filter method accepts a predicate and returns an Optional, so it can be used anywhere within an Optional chain.

```
Optional<T> filter(Predicate<? super T> predicate);
```

The filter method returns the Optional if the predicate is true and returns an empty Optional if the predicate is false.

The filter method is only called on non-null Optionals. This prevents NullPointerExceptions inside their predicates. If allowed to execute on null Optionals, the filter method in the following example would throw the exception when its predicate attempted to take the length of the string.

```
String t = null;
Optional.ofNullable(t)
        .filter(x -> x.length() > 2);
```

The filter method can be used to build chains of Optionals which result in the logical AND of their predicates. The chain stops executing after the first false predicate, since it returns a null Optional. In the following example, all predicates are true, so the ifPresent executes and "Hello" is displayed.

```
Optional.of("Hello")                        // Optional(Hello)
        .filter(x -> x.charAt(0) == 'H')    // Optional(Hello)
        .filter(x -> x.length() > 2)        // Optional(Hello)
        .filter(x -> x.charAt(1) == 'e')    // Optional(Hello)
        .ifPresent(x -> System.out.println(x)); // Prints "Hello"
```

OUTPUT:

```
Hello
```

In the following example, the first predicate is false, so the second and third predicates do not execute and no output is produced.

```
Optional.of("Hello")                              // Optional(Hello)
        .filter(x -> x.charAt(0) == 'i')          // Optional(null)
        .filter(x -> x.length() > 2)              // doesn't execute
        .filter(x -> x.charAt(1) == 'e')          // doesn't execute
        .ifPresent(x -> System.out.println(x));   // doesn't execute
```

Filter conditions can be logically OR'ed using the Predicate class's or method along a predicate chain. The following example filters the Optional using the logical OR of predicates which check if the first character is either "i" or "H." Since the first character is "H," "Hello" is printed.

```
Predicate<String> p = x -> x.charAt(0) == 'i';
Optional.of("Hello")                                  // Optional(Hello)
        .filter(p.or(x -> x.charAt(0) == 'H'))        // Optional(Hello)
        .ifPresent(x -> System.out.println(x));
```

OUTPUT:

```
Hello
```

Section 11.7: Optional Chains Involving map and flatmap

The Optional class's map method accepts a function that converts a non-null Optional<X> to an Optional<Y>.

```
<U> Optional<U> map(Function<? super T, ? extends U> mapper);
```

The following example converts an Optional<String> to an Optional<Integer> and then applies integer arithmetic operations in the predicates that follow. Since the predicates result in true, the value 4 is displayed.

```
Optional.of("4") // Optional("4")
        .map(x -> Integer.parseInt(x))            // Optional(4)
        .filter(x -> x > 2)                       // Optional(4)
        .filter(x -> (x%2) == 0)                  // Optional(4)
        .ifPresent(x -> System.out.println(x));   // Prints 4
```

Since the ifPresent method returns void, any modifications to the underlying object will not persist.

```
Optional<Integer> o1 = Optional.of(2);
o1.ifPresent(x -> ++x);
o1.ifPresent(x -> System.out.println(x)); // Prints 2
```

The map method can be used to modify the underlying object, since it returns a new Optional. Simply use the same input and output type in the function (by providing an implementation of UnaryOperator). The following example changes the underlying value in an Optional<Integer> from 2 to 3. Note the use of prefix notation in the map's function.

```
Optional.of(2)                           // Optional(2)
    .map(x -> ++x)                       // Optional(3)
    .ifPresent(x -> System.out.println(x)); // Prints 3
```

OUTPUT:

3

The flatMap method is similar to the map method, except that the result of its function is already wrapped in an Optional.

```
<U> Optional<U> flatMap(Function<? super T,
                        ? extends Optional<? extends U> > mapper);
```

In the following example, the flatMap method maps the String "4" to the Integer value 4 using a function that returns an Optional<Integer>.

```
Optional.of("4")                         // Optional("4")
    .flatMap(x ->
        Optional.of(Integer.parseInt(x)))   // Optional(4)
    .ifPresent(x -> System.out.println(x)); // Prints 4
```

OUTPUT:

4

An `Optional` chain can be used to track consumption of a resource. The `Resource` class defined as follows allows the user to consume a resource when its constructor is called and then decrements the number of resources remaining.

```
class Resource
{
    static int count = 3;
    public Resource()
    {
        count--;

        System.out.println("Resource consumed, " + count
                        + " remaining.");
    }
}
```

An `Optional` chain can be used to consume the resource by calling the `Resource` constructor in both the `of` and `map` methods. Then, the `filter` method is used to check if there are still resources remaining. Note that the last call to `map` does not execute, since `Resource`'s `count` field equals 0, and the previous predicate contains a null `Optional`. The result of this logic is that the resource will be completely consumed provided that the `Optional` chain is long enough to handle the number of items in the resource.

```
Optional.of(new Resource())          // Resource.count = 2
        .filter(x -> x.count > 0)
        .map(x -> new Resource())  // Resource.count = 1
        .filter(x -> x.count > 0)
        .map(x -> new Resource())  // Resource.count = 0
        .filter(x -> x.count > 0)  // Optional(null)
        .map(x -> new Resource()); // doesn't execute
```

OUTPUT:

```
Resource consumed, 2 remaining.
Resource consumed, 1 remaining.
Resource consumed, 0 remaining.
```

PROJECT 11: Guess a Number

Problem Statement

Using only an Optional chain, write a program that selects a number between 0 and 9 and then gives the user five attempts to guess the number. If the user is unable to guess the number after five attempts, print a message containing the number.

Solution

First, a Guess class should be written with fields for the number and the user's guess. The Guess(int) constructor is called by the Optional's of method to assign a random number between 0 and 9 to the number field. The Guess(int, int) constructor is called by Optional's map method to populate the user's guess and propagate the current number to the number field.

```
class Guess
{
    int number;
    int guess;
    public Guess(int n) { number = n; }
    public Guess(int g, int n) { guess = g; number = n; }
}
```

The function called by the Optional's map method will be a UnaryOperator that prompts the user to guess a number and passes the value input from a Scanner object along with the number to the Guess(int, int) constructor. The new Guess object is returned.

```
UnaryOperator<Guess> guessIt = x -> {
    System.out.print("Guess a number between 0 and 9:");
    return new Guess(new Scanner(System.in).nextInt(),
                     x.number);
};
```

Since the predicate called by Optional's filter method is used five times, it should be stored in a Predicate object.

253

```
Predicate<Guess> guessIsCorrect = x -> {
    if (x.guess != x.number)
        return true;
    System.out.println(x.number + " guessed correctly");
    return false;
};
```

The Optional's of method calls the Guess(int) constructor which initializes the number. Then, the map method executes with the UnaryOperator to make a guess. Next, the filter method's predicate checks if the guess is correct. If the user guesses correctly, the filter method returns a null Optional, and processing stops. If the user guesses incorrectly, processing continues and another guess is made. After the fifth attempt, if the user has not guessed correctly, the ifPresent method executes, and message showing the number is displayed.

```
Optional.of(new Guess(new Random().nextInt(10)))
        .map(guessIt)
        .filter(guessIsCorrect)
        .map(guessIt)
        .filter(guessIsCorrect)
        .map(guessIt)
        .filter(guessIsCorrect)
        .map(guessIt)
        .filter(guessIsCorrect)
        .map(guessIt)
        .filter(guessIsCorrect)
        .ifPresent(x -> System.out.println(
                    "Sorry, couldn't guess " + x.number));
```

The complete program is shown as follows.

Listing 11-1. GuessANumber.java

```
import java.util.*;
import java.util.function.*;
class Guess
{
```

```
    int number;
    int guess;
    public Guess(int n) { number = n; }
    public Guess(int g, int n) { guess = g; number = n; }
}
class GuessANumber
{
    public static void main(String[] args)
    {
        UnaryOperator<Guess> guessIt = x -> {
            System.out.print("Guess a number between 0 and 9:");
            return new Guess(new Scanner(System.in).nextInt(),
                             x.number);
        };

        Predicate<Guess> guessIsCorrect = x -> {
            if (x.guess != x.number)
                return true;
            System.out.println(x.number + " guessed correctly");
            return false;
        };

        Optional.of(new Guess(new Random().nextInt(10)))
                .map(guessIt)
                .filter(guessIsCorrect)
                .map(guessIt)
                .filter(guessIsCorrect)
                .map(guessIt)
                .filter(guessIsCorrect)
                .map(guessIt)
                .filter(guessIsCorrect)
                .map(guessIt)
                .filter(guessIsCorrect)
                .ifPresent(x -> System.out.println(
                        "Sorry, couldn't guess " + x.number));
    }
}
```

In the program's first execution, the `Optional`'s of method creates a `Guess` whose number is 3. The user makes five incorrect guesses for the number. Each call to the `map` method along the `Optional` chain prompts the user for a guess and stores it in a new `Guess` object. Each call to the `filter` method tests if the guess is not equal to 3. Since each predicate is `true`, the `ifPresent` method prints a message displaying the number 3.

PROGRAM OUTPUT 1 (user unable to guess number in five attempts) (input in **BOLD**):

```
Guess a number between 0 and 9: 9
Guess a number between 0 and 9: 5
Guess a number between 0 and 9: 2
Guess a number between 0 and 9: 7
Guess a number between 0 and 9: 4
Sorry, couldn't guess 3
```

In the program's second execution, the `Optional`'s of method creates a `Guess` whose number is 7. The user guesses the number correctly on the second guess. Since the second predicate is false, the second call to the `filter` method returns a null `Optional` and the chain stops executing.

PROGRAM OUTPUT 2 (user guesses correctly on second attempt) (input in **BOLD**):

```
Guess a number between 0 and 9: 3
Guess a number between 0 and 9: 7
7 guessed correctly
```

Short Problems

1) Write a supplier that returns an `Optional` object. The supplier prompts the user to select a number between 1 and 5 or enter "Q" to quit. The `Optional` should contain an integer value when a number is selected and contain `null` when "Q" was entered. Call the supplier in a loop that prints the contents of the `Optional` if populated. The loop terminates when the `Optional` is null. Demonstrate in a main program.

2) Write a program that uses the supplier you wrote in problem 1 in a chain of Optionals that throws an exception which prints the message "User has quit the program." if the user enters "Q".

3) Using a single chain of Optionals, do the following:

   – Create an Optional that contains the string "Optionals are optional"

   – Change the contents of the Optional to "Optionals are mandatory"

   – Check if the string contained by the Optional is greater than 20 characters in length

   – Print the contents of the Optional

Long Problems

1) The Internal Revenue Service allows you to specify your income as either a W-2 employee or a self-employed individual. Using the techniques described in this chapter, write a program that allows the user to input his or her income as either a W-2 employee or a self-employed person and then prints the resulting income.

2) Using the techniques described in this chapter, compute and print the result of the following polynomial equation where x equals 5:

$$x^3 + 4x^2 - 7x - 8$$

3) The words "of", "in", "on", "beside", "under", and "above" are prepositions. Using the techniques described in this chapter, find the first preposition in a sentence and replace it with the next preposition in the list of prepositions specified in the preceding text. Print the resulting sentence. If there are no prepositions in the sentence, throw an exception that states that the sentence contains no prepositions.

CHAPTER 12

Use in Streams

The Stream interface provides chainable operations that can be performed on a series of values. A Stream is generic for type parameter X which is the type of its values.

```
public interface Stream<T> extends BaseStream<T, Stream<T> >
{
    ...
}
```

An object that implements the Stream interface is like an Optional that can contain several values instead of just one. Stream has many of the same methods defined in the Optional class including of, filter, and map.

Since many of the methods in the Stream interface return streams, very powerful chains of streams can be created.

Section 12.1: Generating Stream Elements

The following static methods are used to create Stream objects of type T:

```
static <T> Stream<T> of(T... values);
static <T> Stream<T> generate(Supplier<? extends T> s);
```

A stream is easily created by providing a variable-length list of values to the static of method. The following example uses the of method to create a Stream of type Integer containing the values 1 through 4.

```
Stream<Integer> numbers = Stream.of(1, 2, 3, 4);
```

© Ralph Lecessi 2019
R. Lecessi, *Functional Interfaces in Java*, https://doi.org/10.1007/978-1-4842-4278-0_12

The static `generate` method can also be used to generate a stream. It accepts a Supplier that provides an infinite series of elements which are placed in the stream. The `limit` method can then be called in the stream chain to stop the series after a certain number of elements.

The following example creates a stream of 10 random numbers between 0 and 99.

```
Stream<Integer> tenRandomNumbers =
    Stream.generate( () -> (new Random()).nextInt(100))
        .limit(10);
```

Note   An example of an unbounded infinite stream is given in Section 1 of Chapter 13.

Section 12.2: Traversing Streams

Chapter 8 discussed how objects can be traversed by providing a consumer to the object's `forEach` method. Streams can be traversed in the same manner. Stream `tenRandomNumbers` from the previous example contains ten `Integer` values. The following statement prints each value in the stream.

```
tenRandomNumbers.forEach(x -> System.out.println(x));
```

OUTPUT:

```
17
50
97
8
22
76
31
24
78
92
```

Section 12.3: Filtering Stream Elements

The `filter` method removes elements from the stream that do not match its predicate.

```
Stream<T> filter(Predicate<? super T> predicate);
```

Filtering a stream may remove all its elements (recall that filtering an `Optional` will result in an `Optional` that either contains a null or a non-null object). In the following example, the `filter` method removes all elements from the stream, so nothing is displayed.

```
Stream.of("RED", "GREEN", "BLUE", "RED")
    .filter(x -> x.equals("YELLOW"))
    .forEach(x -> System.out.println(x));
```

In the following example, the two "RED" elements are matched, so "GREEN" and "BLUE" are removed.

```
Stream.of("RED", "GREEN", "BLUE", "RED")
    .filter(x -> x.equals("RED"))
    .forEach(x -> System.out.println(x));
```

OUTPUT:

```
RED
RED
```

Chained `filter` methods perform the logical AND operation on the results of their predicates. If the logical OR operation is desired, a composed predicate can be provided to the `filter` method. In the following example, elements that are either equal to "RED" or contain an "R" pass through the filtering.

```
Predicate<String> isRed = x -> x.equals("RED");

Stream.of("RED", "GREEN", "BLUE", "RED")
    .filter(isRed.or(x -> x.indexOf("R") > -1))
    .forEach(x -> System.out.println(x));
```

OUTPUT:

```
RED
GREEN
RED
```

Section 12.4: Converting an Object to a Stream

Any collection can be converted to a stream using the `stream` method specified in the `Collection` interface. The following example converts a list containing the elements "RED" and "GREEN" to a stream and then processes the elements using a chain of `Stream` methods.

```
List<String> list = Arrays.asList("RED","GREEN");


list.stream()
    .filter(x -> x.equals("GREEN"))
    .forEach(x -> System.out.println(x));
```

OUTPUT:

```
GREEN
```

An `Optional` can also be converted to a stream using its `stream` method.

```
Optional.of("RED")
        .stream()
        .forEach(x -> System.out.println(x));
```

OUTPUT:

```
RED
```

Section 12.5: Sorting Stream Elements

The following methods can be used to sort the elements in a stream:

```
Stream<T> sorted();
Stream<T> sorted(Comparator<? super T> comparator);
```

The no-arg version of the `sorted` method will arrange the elements in a stream by their natural order.

```
Stream.of("Kyle", "Jaquiline", "Jimmy")
      .sorted()
      .forEach(x -> System.out.println(x));
```

OUTPUT:

```
Jaquiline
Jimmy
Kyle
```

An overloaded version of the `sorted` method that accepts a comparator can be used if the elements are not comparable or their natural order is to be overridden. The following example builds a comparator using the `removeVowels` method from Chapter 10. The comparator is passed to the `sorted` method to produce a different order.

```
Stream.of("Kyle", "Jaquiline", "Jimmy")
    .sorted( (x,y) ->
        removeVowels(x).compareTo(removeVowels(y)))
    .forEach(x -> System.out.println(x));
```

OUTPUT:

```
Jimmy
Jaquiline
Kyle
```

Section 12.6: Selecting the Smallest or Largest Element in a Stream

The `min` method selects the smallest element in the stream according to the comparator provided in its argument. The `max` method selects the largest element in the stream according to the comparator provided in its argument. Both methods return an Optional of the same type as the stream elements.

```
Optional<T> min(Comparator<? super T> comparator);
Optional<T> max(Comparator<? super T> comparator);

Stream.of("Kyle", "Jaquiline", "Jimmy")    // Stream<String>
    .min( (x,y) ->                          // Optional<String>
      removeVowels(x).compareTo(removeVowels(y)))
    .ifPresent(x -> System.out.println(x));
```

OUTPUT:

```
Jimmy
```

```
Stream.of("Kyle", "Jaquiline", "Jimmy")          // Stream<String>
    .max( (x,y) ->                               // Optional<String>
      removeVowels(x).compareTo(removeVowels(y)))
    .ifPresent(x -> System.out.println(x));
```

OUTPUT:

```
Kyle
```

Section 12.7: flatMap vs. map

The flatMap method flattens a stream during the transformation of elements to a target type. For a transformation of a Stream of type T to a Stream of type R, the flatMap method accepts a function whose second type parameter is Stream<? extends R>.

```
<R> Stream<R> flatMap(Function<? super T, ? extends Stream<? extends R> >
mapper);
```

Suppose a Class was defined as a subject and a collection of students (see Chapter 10 for the Student class definition).

```
class Class
{
    String subject;
    Collection<Student> students;
    public Class(String su, Student... st)
    {
       subject = su;
       students = Arrays.asList(st);
    }
}
```

In the following example, a Stream of Class objects is created with elements for biology and physics. Each Class contains two students. The Function converts the Class's student collection to a stream which is flattened by flatMap to create a stream whose elements are the students in both classes.

```
Stream.of(new Class("Biology",
            new Student("Joe" ,1001,3.81),
            new Student("Mary",1002,3.91)),
        new Class("Physics",
            new Student("Kalpana",1003,3.61),
            new Student("Javier" ,1004,3.71))) // Stream<Class>
    .flatMap(x -> x.students.stream())          // Stream<Student>
    .forEach(x -> System.out.println(x));
```

OUTPUT:

```
Joe 1001 3.81
Mary 1002 3.91
Kalpana 1003 3.61
Javier 1004 3.71
```

The map method does not perform flattening. For a transformation of a Stream of type T to a Stream of type R, the map method accepts a function whose second type parameter is R.

```
<R> Stream<R> map(Function<? super T, ? extends R> mapper);
```

In the following example, the List<Student> resulting from the function is not flattened by the map method, which instead creates a Stream of List<Student> whose first element contains biology students and whose second element contains physics students.

```
Stream.of(
    new Class("Biology",
        new Student("Joe" ,1001,3.81),
        new Student("Mary",1002,3.91)),
    new Class("Physics",
        new Student("Kalpana",1003,3.61),
        new Student("Javier" ,1004,3.71))) // Stream<Class>
    .map(x -> x.students)                  // Stream<List<Student>>
    .forEach(x -> System.out.println(x));
```

OUTPUT:

```
[Joe 1001 3.81, Mary 1002 3.91]
[Kalpana 1003 3.61, Javier 1004 3.71]
```

Section 12.8: Reducing Stream Elements

The reduce method applies a binary operation to each element of the stream to produce a reduction in the form of an Optional object.

```
Optional<T> reduce(BinaryOperator<T> accumulator);
```

The following example uses the reduce method to compute the factorial of the elements of a stream of consecutive integers:

```
Stream.of(1, 2, 3, 4, 5)                    // Stream(Integer)
    .reduce( (x,y) -> x * y)                // Optional(Integer)
    .ifPresent(x -> System.out.println(x)); // Prints 120
```

OUTPUT:

120

The reduce method has an overloaded version which requires an *identity*, which is the initial value for the running computation. It returns a T, which is the type of the stream elements.

The following example computes the same factorial providing an identity of 1. Since the result is a T, it is wrapped in a println statement for display purposes.

```
System.out.println(
    Stream.of(1, 2, 3, 4, 5)            // Stream(Integer)
        .reduce(1, (x,y) -> x * y)); // Integer
```

OUTPUT:

120

The reduce method has another overloaded version which can transform complex objects into simpler reductions.

```
<U> U reduce(U identity, BiFunction<U,? super T,U> accumulator,
          BinaryOperator<U> combiner);
```

Suppose a program defines the TwoInts class that contains two integers

```
class TwoInts
{
```

```
    Integer i1;
    Integer i2;
    public TwoInts(int z1, int z2) { i1=z1; i2=z2;}
}
```

and the program needs to sum all second integers in a Stream of TwoInts.

```
Stream<TwoInts> two = Stream.of(new TwoInts(1,2),new TwoInts(8,9));
```

This calculation also requires an identity, which is zero for a summation.

An *accumulator* can be defined which extracts the i2 field from each TwoInts object and adds it to the running total of type Integer. This is implemented with a BiFunction which converts an Integer value and a TwoInts object to an Integer sum.

```
BiFunction<Integer,TwoInts,Integer> accumulator = (x,y) -> x + y.i2;
```

The following code combines the results of the accumulation using a BinaryOperator<Integer>.

```
BinaryOperator<Integer> combiner = (x,y) -> x += y;
Integer j = two.reduce(0,accumulator,combiner);
System.out.println(j);
```

OUTPUT:

11

Section 12.9: Collecting Stream Elements into a Mutable Reduction

Suppose a program needs to arrange the elements of a character stream such that alphabetic characters appear before numeric characters. A mutable reduction of the character stream can be created that is arranged in this order. This reduction is generated using an instance of the Collector interface.

```
public interface Collector<T,A,R>
{
    static <T,R> Collector<T,R,R> of(
        Supplier<R> supplier,
```

```
        BiConsumer<R,T> accumulator,
        BinaryOperator<R> combiner,
        Collector.Characteristics... characteristics);

    static <T,A,R> Collector<T,A,R> of(
        Supplier<A> supplier,
        BiConsumer<A,T> accumulator,
        BinaryOperator<A> combiner,
        Function<A,R> finisher,
        Collector.Characteristics... characteristics);
    ...
}
```

The Collector interface's static of methods create a mutable reduction of type R, which for this example will be List<Character>. The supplier generates containers of type R that are used for accumulation and then combined into the final reduction.

```
Supplier<List<Character>> supp = () -> new ArrayList<Character>();
```

The accumulator adds elements of type T into a container. In this example, alphabetic characters are added to the beginning of an ArrayList, while non-alphabetic characters are added to the end. Diagnostic print statements have been added for clarity.

The accumulator being used is of type BiConsumer<R, T>. An overloaded version of the Collector interface's of method uses a BiConsumer<A, T>, but the reduction needs to be transformed to type R using a *finisher* function (see the last example in this section).

```
BiConsumer<List<Character>, Character> acc = (x,y) -> {
    System.out.print("acc: x=" + x + " y=" + y+ " result=");
    if (Character.isAlphabetic(y))
        x.add(0,y);
    else
        x.add(y);
    x.forEach(z -> System.out.print(z));
    System.out.println();
};
```

The combiner combines containers into the final reduction. The combiner being used is of type BinaryOperator<R>. An overloaded version of the Collector interface's of method uses a BinaryOperator<A>, but the reduction needs to be transformed to type R using a finisher function (see the last example in this section).

```
BinaryOperator<List<Character>> comb1 = (x,y) -> {
    x.addAll(y);
    return x;
};
```

The collect method of the Stream interface uses a Collector to produce a mutable reduction of the elements in the stream.

```
<R,A> R collect(Collector<? super T,A,R> collector)
Stream.of('1','a','b','2')                        // Stream<Character>
    .collect(Collector.of(supp, acc, comb1)) // List<Character>
    .forEach(x -> System.out.println(x));
```

OUTPUT:

```
.accc: x=[] y=1 result=1
accc: x=[1] y=a result=a1
accc: x=[a, 1] y=b result=ba1
accc: x=[b, a, 1] y=2 result=ba12
b
a
1
2
```

Accumulator x is initially empty. Then, stream element '1' is placed at the end forming list [1]. Next, stream element 'a' is placed at the beginning forming list [a1]. Then, stream element 'b' is placed at the beginning forming list [ba1]. Finally, stream element '2' is placed at the end forming list [ba12].

An overloaded version of the collect method could also have been used which specifies the supplier, accumulator, and combiner without creating a Collector object. In this case, the combiner is of type BiConsumer<R, R> instead of BinaryOperator<R>.

```
<R> R collect(Supplier<R> supplier, BiConsumer<R,? super T> accumulator,
            BiConsumer<R,R> combiner);
```

```
BiConsumer<List<Character>,List<Character>> comb2 = (x,y) ->
            x.addAll(y);
```

```
Stream.of('1','a','b','2')
      .collect(supp, acc, comb2)
      .forEach(x -> System.out.println(x));
```

OUTPUT:

```
acc: x=[] y=1 result=1
acc: x=[1] y=a result=a1
acc: x=[a, 1] y=b result=ba1
acc: x=[b, a, 1] y=2 result=ba12
b
a
1
```

A mutual reduction can also be generated using the StringBuilder class. In the following example, the accumulator removes the vowels from a string before using the StringBuilder class's append(String) method to place at the end of the reduction.

```
Supplier<StringBuilder> supps = () -> new StringBuilder();
BiConsumer<StringBuilder,String> accs = (x,y) ->
        x.append(y.replaceAll("[aeiou]",""));
```

The StringBuilder class's append(StringBuilder) method is used in the combiner.

```
BinaryOperator<StringBuilder> combs = (x,y) -> {
    x.append(y);
    return x;
};
```

A finisher function is used to transform the final reduction to a String object.

```
Function<StringBuilder,String> fins = x -> x.toString();
```

```
String s = Stream.of("Joe","Kalpana","Christopher")
                .collect(Collector.of(supps, accs, combs, fins));
System.out.println(s);
```

OUTPUT:

```
JKlpnChrstphr
```

Section 12.9.1: Using Prewritten Collectors

The Collectors class contains static methods which create Collector objects that solve various problems. The following example uses the toList method to accumulate the stream elements into a list in the original order.

```
Stream.of('1', 'a' , 'b', '2')
    .collect(Collectors.toList())
    .forEach(x -> System.out.println(x));
```

OUTPUT:

```
1
a
b
2
```

The collectingAndThen method collects the elements of a stream using a Collector object and then transforms the result to another type using a function.

```
static <T,A,R,RR> Collector<T,A,RR> collectingAndThen(
    Collector<T,A,R> downstream,
    Function<R,RR> finisher);
```

The following example transforms a list of characters into a string using the collectingAndThen method and Function fins2:

```
BiConsumer<List<Character>,Character> accc2 = (x,y) -> {
    if (Character.isAlphabetic(y))
        x.add(0,y);
    else
        x.add(y);
};

Function<List<Character>,String> fins2 = x -> {
    String t="";
```

```
    for (Character c : x)
        t += c;
    return t;
};

String t =
  Stream.of('1','a','b','2')                    // Stream<Character>
        .collect(Collectors.collectingAndThen(
             Collector.of(supp, accc2, comb1), // List<Character>
             fins2));                           // String
System.out.println(t);                          // Prints ba12
```

OUTPUT:

ba12

The reducing method collects the elements of a stream into an Optional object. It accepts a BinaryOperator.

```
static <T> Collector<T,?,Optional<T>> reducing(BinaryOperator<T> op)
```

The following example uses the reduce method to create an Optional<Integer> that contains the factorial of 5.

```
Stream.of(1,2,3,4,5)                         // Stream<Integer>
      .collect(Collectors.reducing(((x,y) ->
             x *= y))                         // Optional<Integer>
      .ifPresent(x -> System.out.println(x)); // Prints 120
```

OUTPUT:

120

The joining method joins a stream of strings into a single String object.

```
static Collector<CharSequence,?,String> joining()
```

```
String s = Stream.of("RED", "GREEN", "BLUE")    // Stream<String>
        .collect(Collectors.joining());         // String

System.out.println(s);
```

OUTPUT:

REDGREENBLUE

A delimiter can also be specified.

```
String s = Stream.of("RED", "GREEN", "BLUE")    // Stream<String>
        .collect(Collectors.joining(","));      // String

System.out.println(s);                          // Prints RED,GREEN,BLUE
```

OUTPUT:

RED,GREEN,BLUE

The groupingBy method organizes the result by a key value. The resulting container is a map whose values are a list of stream elements. A function which transforms a stream element to a key value must be provided.

```
static <T,K> Collector<T,?,Map<K,List<T>>> groupingBy(
    Function<? super T,? extends K> classifier)
```

Given the following Car class,

```
class Car
{
    String manu;
    String model;
    int mpg;
    public Car(String ma, String mo, int mp)
    {
        manu = ma;
        model = mo;
        mpg = mp;
    }
    public String toString()
    {
        return manu + " " + model + " gets " + mpg + " mpg";
    }
}
```

a result can be created that organizes cars by manufacturer. The resulting container is a map whose key value is the manu field of type String. The value in each map element is the list of cars built by the manufacturer. A function which transforms a Car object to the map key (by obtaining the manufacturer) is provided to the groupingBy method.

```
Stream.of(new Car("Buick" ,"Regal" ,25),
         new Car("Hyundai","Elantra",27),
         new Car("Buick" ,"Skylark",26),
         new Car("Hyundai","Accent" ,30)) // Stream<Car>
    .collect(
         Collectors.groupingBy(x -> x.manu))// Map<String,List<Car>>
    .forEach( (x,y) ->
         System.out.println(x + ": " +y ));
```

OUTPUT:

```
Buick: [Buick Regal gets 25 mpg, Buick Skylark gets 26 mpg]
Hyundai: [Hyundai Elantra gets 27 mpg, Hyundai Accent gets 30 mpg]
```

An overloaded version of the groupingBy method accepts a Collector object as its second argument. The mapping method is frequently used as the second argument to transform the stream element and then generate a new list as the mapped value.

```
static <T,U,A,R> Collector<T,?,R> mapping(
    Function<? super T, ? extends U> mapper,
    Collector(<? super U,A,R> downstream);
```

The following example groups cars by manufacturer while applying the mapping method to each Car object's mpg field, and then uses the Collectors class's toList method to collect them into a list of integers:

```
Stream.of(new Car("Buick" ,"Regal" ,25),
         new Car("Hyundai","Elantra",27),
         new Car("Buick" ,"Skylark",26),
         new Car("Hyundai","Accent" ,30))// Stream<Car>
    .collect(Collectors.groupingBy(x ->// Map<String,List<Integer>>
         x.manu,
         Collectors.mapping(x -> x.mpg,
                 Collectors.toList())))) // List<Integer>>
```

```
.forEach( (x,y) ->
        System.out.println(x + ": " +y ));
```

OUTPUT:

```
Buick: [25, 26]
Hyundai: [27, 30]
```

The partitioningBy method splits the reduction into two components based on a pass/fail criterion. The map's key is of type Boolean, and a predicate is provided to specify the pass/fail criterion.

```
static <T> Collector<T,?,Map<Boolean,List<T>>> partitioningBy(
    Predicate<? super T> predicate)
```

The following example partitions the elements in a stream of cars using a predicate that specifies the pass/fail criterion of 30 or more miles per gallon.

```
Stream.of(new Car("Buick" ,"Regal" ,25),
        new Car("Hyundai","Elantra",27),
        new Car("Buick" ,"Skylark",26),
        new Car("Hyundai","Accent" ,30))  // Stream<Car>
    .collect(
        Collectors.partitioningBy(x ->
            x.mpg >= 30))                  // Map<Boolean,List<Car>>
    .forEach( (x,y) ->
            System.out.println(x + ": " +y ));
```

OUTPUT:

```
false: [Buick Regal gets 25 mpg, Hyundai Elantra gets 27 mpg, Buick Skylark
gets 26 mpg]
true: [Hyundai Accent gets 30 mpg]
```

The Collectors class has methods which produce a sum as the mutable reduction. These methods accept a function which transforms the stream element into the int, long, or double to be summed.

```
static <T> Collector<T, ? , Integer> summingInt(ToIntFunction<? super T>
mapper)
```

```
Integer sum =
    Stream.of(new Car("Buick" ,"Regal" ,25),
              new Car("Hyundai","Elantra",27),
              new Car("Buick" ,"Skylark",26),
              new Car("Hyundai","Accent" ,30))
          .collect(Collectors.summingInt(x -> x.mpg));

System.out.println("sum of mpg = " + sum);
```

OUTPUT:

```
sum of mpg = 108
```

Section 12.10: Building Streams Interactively

The Stream.Builder interface is a subinterface of Consumer. It can be used to interactively build a stream. The Stream interface's static builder method is used to create a Stream.Builder.

```
Stream.Builder<String> bld = Stream.builder();
```

The accept method can then be called to add elements.

```
bld.accept("RED");
bld.accept("GREEN");
bld.accept("BLUE");
```

The build method is used to create a stream from the builder. Once the stream has been generated, additional elements cannot be added to the builder. Note how attempting to add the element "YELLOW" to the builder after the stream has been generated causes an IllegalStateException and that yellow is not added to the stream.

```
Stream<String> st = bld.build();
try {
    bld.accept("YELLOW");
}
catch (IllegalStateException e) {
    System.out.println("IllegalStateException");
}
st.forEach(x -> System.out.println(x));
```

276

OUTPUT:

```
IllegalStateException
RED
GREEN
BLUE
```

Since the add method returns a `Stream.Builder` object, it can be used in a stream chain (the accept method returns void so it must be used as a separate statement).

```
Stream.builder()
     .add("RED")
     .add("GREEN")
     .add("BLUE")
     .build()
     .forEach(x -> System.out.println(x));
```

OUTPUT:

```
RED
GREEN
BLUE
```

Section 12.11: Displaying Intermediate Results

The peek method is useful for reporting and debugging purposes. It accepts a `Consumer` object of the same type as the stream elements.

```
Stream<T> peek(Consumer<? super T> action)
Stream.of(1,2,3,4)
     .peek(x -> System.out.println(x) )
     .reduce( (x,y) -> x += y)
     .ifPresent(x -> System.out.println(x));
```

OUTPUT:

```
1
2
3
4
10
```

Section 12.12: Stream Specializations

The Java API provides the non-generic IntStream, LongStream, and DoubleStream interfaces which support stream of Integers, Longs, and Doubles, respectively.

The Stream interface's mapToInt method uses its ToIntFunction argument to convert a generic Stream object to an IntStream.

```
IntStream ints =
    Stream.of(new Car("Buick" ,"Regal" ,25),
            new Car("Hyundai","Elantra",27),
            new Car("Buick" ,"Skylark",26),
            new Car("Hyundai","Accent" ,30))  // Stream<Car>
        .mapToInt(x -> x.mpg);                 // IntStream
```

The specializations have several methods that do not exist in the generic Stream interface. The max and min methods compute the largest and smallest elements in the stream, respectively. The methods return OptionalInt, OptionalLong, and OptionalDouble objects, respectively.

```
ints.max()
    .ifPresent(x -> System.out.println(x));

LongStream.of(1,2,3,4)
        .min()
        .ifPresent(x -> System.out.println(x));
```

OUTPUT:

```
30
1
```

The average method computes the average of the stream elements and returns an OptionalDouble.

```
DoubleStream.of(1.1,2.2,3.3,4.4)
        .average()
        .ifPresent(x -> System.out.println(x));
```

OUTPUT:

```
2.75
```

The sum method computes the sum of the stream elements and returns an int.

```
int sum = IntStream.of(1,2,3,4)
                    .sum();
System.out.println(sum);
```

OUTPUT:

10

PROJECT 12: Dave's Part Inventory
Problem Statement

Discount Dave's service department needs a program to keep an inventory of their car parts. Parts are organized by name, manufacturer, and installation time. Each part has a list of models containing the model, price, and quantity available.

The program should list the entire inventory organized by part. Customers often need several items of a particular part, and they specify the amount they are willing to pay for them.

Therefore, the program must find all models for a part in which there are enough available and that cost less than the specified price. The program should also print a list for the part sorted by price. The program needs to count the total quantity available in the inventory for a particular part.

Customers are frequently in a hurry and specify how long they can wait for repairs. Therefore the program should find all models for a part that can be installed in the specified time.

Solution

An Item class can be defined that contains the item's model, quantity, and price.

```
class Item
{
    String model;
    int quantity;
    double price;
```

```
    public Item(String m, int q, double p)
    {
        model = m;
        quantity = q;
        price = p;
    }
    @Override
    public String toString()
    {
        return model + ":" + quantity + " $" + price;
    }
}
```

A Part class can be defined that contains the part's name, manufacturer, installation time, and a list of items available in the inventory for the part made by the manufacturer.

```
class Part
{
    String name;
    String manu;
    int hoursToInstall;
    List<Item> models;
    public Part(String n, String m, int h, Item... it)
    {
        name = n;
        manu = m;
        hoursToInstall = h;
        models = new ArrayList<>();
        for (Item i : it)
            models.add(i);
    }
    @Override
    public String toString()
    {
        return manu + " " + hoursToInstall + "hrs " + models;
    }
}
```

The inventory database can be stored as a list of parts.

```
List<Part> parts = Arrays.asList(
    new Part("tires","Goodyear",2,
            new Item("RX2041",4,75.25),
            new Item("SX3355",2,90.50)),
    new Part("brakes","EBC",1,
            new Item("EX8426",2,125.35)),
    new Part("tires","Firestone",1,
            new Item("FS2112",3,60.47),
            new Item("FS2479",5,85.20)),
    new Part("brakes","Acme",3,
            new Item("AC25",1,90.74),
            new Item("AC26",4,130.22))
);
```

The program can be organized as a set of operations performed on the stream returned from the List implementation's stream method. Suppliers can be written to prompt the user to select an operation and to specify the part name, quantity, and price to check in the inventory. The part name, quantity, price, and installation time limit will be stored as fields in the program.

Listing the inventory by part is easily accomplished using Collectors.groupingBy. The result is a Map<String, List<Part>> which can be iterated using the forEach method of the Map implementation.

```
parts.stream()
    .collect(Collectors.groupingBy(x -> x.name))
    .forEach( (x,y) -> System.out.println(x + ": " + y));
```

A particular part can be searched by filtering the stream of parts by name. For reporting purposes, it is useful to call the peek method at this link in the chain to display the part's name and manufacturer. The list of items then needs to be flattened in order to test each item. Once flattened, we can filter each item based on quantity and price.

```
parts.stream()                                      // Stream<Part>
    .filter(x -> x.name.equals(partName))
    .peek(x -> System.out.println(
        x.name + " by " + x.manu + ":"))
```

```
    .flatMap(x -> x.models.stream())          // Stream<Item>
    .filter(x -> x.price <= price)
    .filter(x -> x.quantity >= quantity)
    .forEach(x -> System.out.println(x));
```

To create a list of items for the part sorted by price, the sorted method can be called after flattening. The Comparator.comparing method can be used to perform the sort if a Function<Item, Double> is provided to extract the price from each item.

```
parts.stream()                                // Stream<Part>
    .filter(x -> x.name.equals(partName))
    .flatMap(x -> x.models.stream())          // Stream<Item>
    .sorted( Comparator.comparing(x -> x.price))
    .forEach(x -> System.out.println(x));
```

To count the total quantity available for a part, the stream of items needs to be reduced to an Integer using the reduce method. The identity for the sum is zero. A BiFunction<Double, Item, Double> is used to accumulate each quantity. A BinaryOperator<Double> is used to combine the quantities.

```
Integer i =
  parts.stream()
      .filter(x -> x.name.equals(partName))
      .flatMap(x -> x.models.stream())
      .reduce(0,
              (x,z) -> x + z.quantity,
              (x,y) -> x += y);
System.out.println(i);
```

To find all models for a part that can be installed within a time limit, the stream of parts needs to be filtered by part name and installation time.

```
parts.stream()
    .filter(x -> x.name.equals(partName))
    .filter(x -> x.hoursToInstall < timeLimit)
    .forEach(x -> System.out.println(x));
```

The complete program is shown and demonstrated as follows. The service technician first selects "List Inventory," and the program lists all brake parts followed by all tire parts. The technician then searches for at least four tires that cost $80 or less each and finds the Goodyear RX2041 for $75.25 each. The technician then lists brakes by price, which lists the AC25 for $90.74 first, followed by the EX8426 for $125.35, and lastly the AC26 for $130.22. Next, the technician counts all tires, and the program displays 14. Finally, the technician searches for tires that can be installed in two hours and finds the Firestone FS2112:3 for $60.47 and the FS2479:5 for $85.20.

Listing 12-1. Inventory.java

```java
import java.util.stream.*;
import java.util.*;
import java.util.function.*;
class Item
{
    String model;
    int quantity;
    double price;
    public Item(String m, int q, double p)
    {
        model = m;
        quantity = q;
        price = p;
    }

    @Override
    public String toString()
    {
        return model + ":" + quantity + " $" + price;
    }
}

class Part
{
    String name;
    String manu;
```

```
    int hoursToInstall;
    List<Item> models;
    public Part(String n, String m, int h, Item... it)
    {
        name = n;
        manu = m;
        hoursToInstall = h;
        models = new ArrayList<>();
        for (Item i : it)
            models.add(i);
    }
    @Override
    public String toString()
    {
        return manu + " " + hoursToInstall + "hrs " + models;
    }
}
class Inventory
{
    static String partName = null;
    static int quantity=0;
    static double price = 0.0;
    static int timeLimit = 0;

    public static void main(String[] args)
    {
        List<Part> parts = Arrays.asList(
        new Part("tires","Goodyear",2,
              new Item("RX2041",4,75.25),
              new Item("SX3355",2,90.50)),
        new Part("brakes","EBC",1,
              new Item("EX8426",2,125.35)),
        new Part("tires","Firestone",1,
              new Item("FS2112",3,60.47),
              new Item("FS2479",5,85.20)),
        new Part("brakes","Acme",3,
```

```
                new Item("AC25",1,90.74),
                new Item("AC26",4,130.22))
);
Supplier<Integer> selectOperation = () -> {
    Scanner userInput = new Scanner(System.in);
    int operation = -1;
    while (operation < 0 || operation > 5)
    {
        System.out.println("Please select an operation:");
        System.out.println(
                "    0 - List inventory");
        System.out.println(
                "    1 - Find item by quantity and price");
        System.out.println(
                "    2 - List items by price");
        System.out.println(
                "    3 - Count items by part name");
        System.out.println(
                "    4 - Find items by installation time");
        System.out.print (
                "    5 - End program:");
        operation = Integer.parseInt(userInput.nextLine());
        if (operation < 0 || operation > 5)
            System.out.println("Invalid operation");
    }
    return operation;
};
Supplier<String> selectPartName = () ->
    (new Scanner(System.in)).nextLine();
Supplier<Integer> selectQuantity = () ->
    Integer.parseInt((new Scanner(System.in)).nextLine());
Supplier<Double> selectPrice = () ->
    Double.parseDouble((new Scanner(System.in)).nextLine());
Supplier<Integer> selectTimeLimit = () ->
    Integer.parseInt((new Scanner(System.in)).nextLine());
```

```
System.out.println(
    "Welcome to Discount Dave's Inventory Program.");
boolean done = false;
while (!done)
{
    switch (selectOperation.get())
    {
        case 0:
            parts.stream()
                    .collect(Collectors.groupingBy(x -> x.name))
                    .forEach(
                    (x,y) -> System.out.println(x + ": " + y));
            break;

        case 1:
            System.out.print("Select a part name:");
            partName = selectPartName.get();
            System.out.print("Select a minimum quantity:");
            quantity = selectQuantity.get();
            System.out.print("Select a price limit:");
            price = selectPrice.get();

            parts.stream()
                    .filter(x -> x.name.equals(partName))
                    .peek(x -> System.out.println(
                            x.name + " by " + x.manu + ":"))
                    .flatMap(x -> x.models.stream())
                    .filter(x -> x.price <= price)
                    .filter(x -> x.quantity >= quantity)
                    .forEach(x -> System.out.println(x));
            break;

        case 2:
            System.out.print("Select a part name:");
            partName = selectPartName.get();

            parts.stream()
```

```java
                .filter(x -> x.name.equals(partName))
                .flatMap(x -> x.models.stream())
                .sorted( Comparator.comparing(x -> x.price))
                .forEach(x -> System.out.println(x));
        break;

    case 3:
        System.out.print("Select a part name:");
        partName = selectPartName.get();

        Integer i =
            parts.stream()
                .filter(x -> x.name.equals(partName))
                .flatMap(x -> x.models.stream())
                .reduce(0,
                        (x,z) -> x + z.quantity,
                        (x,y) -> x += y);
        System.out.println(i);
        break;

    case 4:
        System.out.print("Select a part name:");
        partName = selectPartName.get();
        System.out.print(
            "Select installation time limit:");
        timeLimit = selectTimeLimit.get();

        parts.stream()
                .filter(x -> x.name.equals(partName))
                .filter(x -> x.hoursToInstall < timeLimit)
                .forEach(x -> System.out.println(x));
        break;

    default: // 5
        System.out.println("Bye Bye.");
        done = true;
    }
   }
  }
}
```

PROGRAM OUTPUT (user input in **BOLD**):

Welcome to Discount Dave's Inventory Program.
Please select an operation:
   0 - List inventory
   1 - Find item by quantity and price
   2 - List items by price
   3 - Count items by part name
   4 - Find items by installation time
   5 - End program: **0**
brakes: [EBC 1hrs [EX8426:2 $125.35], Acme 3hrs [AC25:1 $90.74, AC26:4 $130.22]]
tires: [Goodyear 2hrs [RX2041:4 $75.25, SX3355:2 $90.5], Firestone 1hrs [FS2112:3 $60.47, FS2479:5 $85.2]]
Please select an operation:
   0 - List inventory
   1 - Find item by quantity and price
   2 - List items by price
   3 - Count items by part name
   4 - Find items by installation time
   5 - End program: **1**
Select a part name: **tires**
Select a minimum quantity: **4**
Select a price limit: **80.00**
tires by Goodyear:
RX2041:4 $75.25
tires by Firestone:
Please select an operation:
   0 - List inventory
   1 - Find item by quantity and price
   2 - List items by price
   3 - Count items by part name
   4 - Find items by installation time
   5 - End program: **2**
Select a part name: **brakes**

```
AC25:1 $90.74
EX8426:2 $125.35
AC26:4 $130.22
Please select an operation:
   0 - List inventory
   1 - Find item by quantity and price
   2 - List items by price
   3 - Count items by part name
   4 - Find items by installation time
   5 - End program: 3
Select a part name: tires
14
Please select an operation:
   0 - List inventory
   1 - Find item by quantity and price
   2 - List items by price
   3 - Count items by part name
   4 - Find items by installation time
   5 - End program: 4
Select a part name: tires
Select installation time limit: 2
Firestone 1hrs [FS2112:3 $60.47, FS2479:5 $85.2]
Please select an operation:
   0 - List inventory
   1 - Find item by quantity and price
   2 - List items by price
   3 - Count items by part name
   4 - Find items by installation time
   5 - End program: 5
Bye Bye.
```

Short Problems

1) Create a stream containing the names "Robert", "Cheryl", "Rachel", "Jose", and "Rita". Remove all names that do not begin with the letter R. Sort the remaining elements by reverse ordering, and then print the results.

2) Create a stream containing the numbers 1 through 5. Add 4 to each element in the stream. Then, create a reduction that adds the elements in the stream that contain odd values, and double the value of the elements in the stream that contain even values. Print the result of the reduction.

3) Take the stream of characters from Section 9, and collect them into a map whose keys are the characters and whose values are each character's integer value (e.g., "1" is 49 and "a" is 97). Print the resulting map.

Long Problems

1) Using the techniques described in this chapter, produce an alphabetically sorted, comma-separated list of car models based on the Car class defined in Section 9a of this chapter. The cars are defined as follows:

Make	Model	MPG
Buick	Regal	25
Hyundai	Elantra	27
Buick	Skylark	26
Hyundai	Accent	30

2) Rewrite the part of speech detector you wrote in problem 3 of Chapter 7 using the techniques described in this chapter.

3) Using the Class example given in Section 7 of this chapter, compute and display the following:

- – The average grade point average of all the students

- – The average grade point average of the biology students

- – The average grade point average of the physics students

CHAPTER 13

Use in Multithreaded Programs

Section 13.1: Performing Computations Using Runnable and Callable

Runnable is an interface whose implementations contain computations meant to be performed in a thread separate from the calling thread. It is a functional interface containing functional method run which takes no arguments and returns no value.

```
@FunctionalInterface
public interface Runnable {
    void run();
}
```

The following example defines an implementation of Runnable. When its run method is called, "RED" is displayed.

```
Runnable r = () -> System.out.println("RED");
r.run();
```

OUTPUT:

RED

A Runnable is usually wrapped in a Thread object, which provides greater control over the execution of the computation. The Thread class includes a constructor that accepts a Runnable. The Thread class's start method begins the execution of the Runnable.

```
(new Thread(r)).start();
```

293

© Ralph Lecessi 2019
R. Lecessi, *Functional Interfaces in Java*, https://doi.org/10.1007/978-1-4842-4278-0_13

OUTPUT:

RED

Callable differs from Runnable in that it returns the result of its computation and can throw a checked exception. It is a functional interface that is generic for result type V, and with functional method call that returns an object of type V.

```
@FunctionalInterface
public interface Callable<V> {
    V call() throws Exception;
}
```

The following implementation of Callable returns the result "GREEN".

```
Callable<String> c1 = () -> "GREEN";
```

Since the Callable computation may throw a checked exception, its call method must be enclosed in a try block. The following example executes the call method of Callable c1 inside a try block. Since no exception occurs during the computation, "GREEN" is displayed.

```
try {
    String s1 = c1.call();
    System.out.println(s1);
} catch (Exception e) {}
```

OUTPUT:

GREEN

The following Callable implementation opens and reads a line from file my.txt.

```
Callable<String> c2 = () -> {
    BufferedReader br = new BufferedReader(
                        new FileReader("my.txt"));
    return br.readLine();
};
```

Assuming that file my.txt doesn't exist, the following example throws a FileNotFoundException when the call method executes. The exception is caught and displayed in the catch block.

```
try {
    String s1 = c2.call();
    System.out.println(s1);
} catch (Exception e) { System.out.println(e.getClass());}
```

OUTPUT:

```
class java.io.FileNotFoundException
```

The following Runnable creates an infinite stream of random integers between 0 and 99. It is run as a daemon thread which is terminated by the JVM when the main thread finishes. The main thread synchronizes with the Runnable using a semaphore which is acquired inside the peek method. The number is stored in static field number which is populated after the semaphore is acquired.

```
Runnable r = () -> {
    Stream.generate( () -> (new Random()).nextInt(100))
          .peek(acquire)
          .forEach(x -> number = x);
};

Consumer<Integer> acquire = x -> {
    try {
        sem.acquire();
    } catch (InterruptedException e) {}
};
```

The main thread releases the semaphore in a loop and then goes to sleep for 1 second to allow the Runnable to process. The main thread throttles execution by prompting the user to request another number or end the program. The complete program is shown as follows.

Listing 13-1. InfiniteStream.java

```
import java.util.stream.*;
import java.util.*;
import java.util.concurrent.Semaphore;
import java.util.function.*;
class InfiniteStream
```

```java
{
    private static Semaphore sem = new Semaphore(0);
    private static int number;
    public static void main(String[] args) throws Exception
    {
        Consumer<Integer> acquire = x -> {
            try {
                sem.acquire();
            } catch (InterruptedException e) {}
        };

        Runnable r = () -> {
            Stream.generate( () -> (new Random()).nextInt(100))
                    .peek(acquire)
                    .forEach(x -> number = x);
        };

        Thread generator = new Thread(r);
        generator.setDaemon(true);
        generator.start();

        Supplier<Boolean> finished = () -> {
            Scanner input = new Scanner(System.in);
            System.out.print("Do you want another number" +
                            "(Y for yes):");
            return input.nextLine().charAt(0) != 'Y';
        };

        do
        {
            sem.release();
            Thread.sleep(1000);
            System.out.println("The number is " + number);
        } while (!finished.get());
    }
}
```

PROGRAM OUTPUT (user input shown in **BOLD**):

```
The number is 5
Do you want another number(Y for yes): Y
The number is 61
Do you want another number(Y for yes): N
```

Section 13.1.1: Using **Runnable** in **Optionals**

The Optional class's ifPresentOrElse method accepts a Runnable as its second argument. If the Optional doesn't contain a value, the Runnable executes.

```
void ifPresentOrElse(Consumer<? super T> action, Runnable emptyAction);
```

The following example calls the ifPresentOrElse method on an Optional that contains null. Therefore the specified Runnable executes and "empty" is displayed.

```
String s = null;
Optional.ofNullable(s)
        .ifPresentOrElse(x -> System.out.println(x),
                        () -> System.out.println("empty"));
```

OUTPUT:

```
empty
```

Section 13.2: **Futures** and **FutureTasks**

Future is an interface that describes a generic computation to be performed in the future. It specifies methods to cancel and obtain the result of the computation.

FutureTask is a class that implements Future and Runnable. It is generic for the result of its computation. One of its constructors accepts a Callable argument. Another constructor accepts a Runnable and a specified result.

```
FutureTask(Callable<V> callable);
FutureTask(Runnable runnable, V result);
```

The following example creates two FutureTasks. The first executes a Callable that return a random number between 0 and 99. The second FutureTask results in -1 and executes a Runnable that displays "Runnable".

```
Callable<Integer> c = () -> (new Random()).nextInt(100);
Runnable r = () -> System.out.println("Runnable");

FutureTask<Integer> fc = new FutureTask(c);
FutureTask<Integer> fr = new FutureTask(r,-1);
```

The constructor does not perform the computation. It needs to be explicitly executed.

```
fc.run();
fr.run();
```

The Future interface specifies a get method which waits for the computation to complete, if necessary, and then returns the result. The get method may throw an InterruptedException or an ExecutionException.

```
try {
    int i = fc.get();
    int j = fr.get();
    System.out.println(i + " " + j);
} catch(InterruptedException|ExecutionException e) {}
```

OUTPUT:

```
Runnable
9 -1
```

Section 13.3: CompletionStages and CompletableFutures

Computations may be performed as a series of operations or stages which may depend on previous stages and kick off additional stages. The CompletionStage interface models computations that can be performed as part of a future chain.

CompletableFuture is a class that implements CompletionStage and also implements the Future interface. CompletableFuture provides static methods for creating instances and several terminal operations that are not defined in CompletionStage. CompletionStage and CompletableFuture are generic for the result of the computation. Both CompletionStage and CompletableFuture utilize functional interfaces.

```
public class CompletableFuture<T> implements Future<T>, CompletionStage<T>
{
    ....
}
```

Section 13.4: Creating CompletableFutures and Retrieving Their Results

CompletableFuture's static completedFuture method returns a CompletableFuture that immediately completes the computation with the value provided.

```
static <U> CompletableFuture<U> completedFuture(U value);
```

The CompletableFuture resulting from this method can be used as part of a chain. The following example creates a CompletableFuture<String> object that immediately completes with the result "RED". The get method is then called along the future chain to obtain the result of the computation which is passed to the System.out.println method.

```
try {
 System.out.println(
 CompletableFuture
     .completedFuture("RED")  // CompletableFuture<String>
     .get());                 // String
} catch (InterruptedException
       |ExecutionException e) {}
```

OUTPUT:

RED

The join method is similar to get except that it may only throw an unchecked exception. Use the get method if a checked exception can be thrown.

```
System.out.println(
CompletableFuture
    .completedFuture("BLUE") // CompletableFuture<String>
    .join());                     // String
```

OUTPUT:

BLUE

Neither the get method nor the join method blocks when the future is already completed. The static supplyAsync method accepts a supplier that returns an object of the result type.

```
static <U> CompletableFuture<U> supplyAsync(Supplier<U> supplier);
```

The future does not complete immediately and does not run in the calling thread. It executes asynchronously on a task in the ForkJoinPool common pool. In the following example, "NOT EXECUTED YET" is the first line in the displayed output, since the future has not executed before the println statement. The future executes when the join method is called, and therefore "EXECUTING THE FUTURE" and 4 are then displayed.

```
CompletableFuture<Integer> cf = CompletableFuture.supplyAsync( () ->
{
    System.out.println("EXECUTING THE FUTURE");
    return 4;
});
System.out.println("NOT EXECUTED YET");
System.out.println(cf.join());
```

OUTPUT:

```
NOT EXECUTED YET
EXECUTING THE FUTURE
4
```

Section 13.5: Using the **thenApply** and **thenAccept** Methods

CompletionStage's thenApply method accepts a function that operates on the result of the current stage. The method executes after the current stage completes and returns a new CompletionStage that can be used in a future chain.

```
<U> CompletionStage<U> thenApply(Function<? super T, ? extends U> fn);
```

In the following example, a function is used to transform the result of the first future from the String value "3" to the Integer value 3, resulting in a CompletableFuture<Integer>. A second function is used to transform the result from 3 to 4, also resulting in a CompletableFuture<Integer>. The join method is needed to begin the execution of the future generated by supplyAsync.

```
CompletableFuture<Integer> cf1 = CompletableFuture
    .supplyAsync( () -> "3")             // CompletableFuture<String>
    .thenApply(x -> Integer.parseInt(x)) // CompletableFuture<Integer>
    .thenApply(x -> ++x);                // CompletableFuture<Integer>

System.out.println(cf1.join());
```

OUTPUT:

4

CompletionStage's thenAccept method accepts a consumer that processes the result of the current CompletionStage. The result is of type CompletableFuture<Void>, so it can only occur at the end of a future chain.

```
CompletionStage<Void> thenAccept(Consumer<? super X> cons);
```

In the following example, a Consumer object prints "GREEN" which is the result of the current computation. Note that the join method is not required, since the consumer argument to thenAccept has already displayed the contents of the future.

```
CompletableFuture
    .supplyAsync( () -> "RED")                   // CompletableFuture<String>
    .thenApply(x ->
        x.equals("RED")? "GREEN":"BLUE")    // CompletableFuture<String>
    .thenAccept(x -> System.out.println(x));// CompletableFuture<Void>
```

OUTPUT:

GREEN

Section 13.6: Processing the First Asynchronous Future to Complete

It is possible to use the result of the first of two futures to complete. The acceptEitherAsync method accepts a CompletionStage to be compared with the current stage. The result of the first stage to complete is passed to the consumer.

```
CompletionStage<Void> acceptEitherAsync(
    CompletionStage<? extends T> other,
    Consumer<? super T> action,
    Executor executor);
```

Suppose a program creates a CompletableFuture that waits for 5 seconds before computing 4, and a second CompletableFuture that waits for 2 seconds before computing 5. The newCachedThreadPool can be used to execute the futures.

```
Supplier<Integer> s1 = () -> {
    try { Thread.sleep(5000);
    } catch (InterruptedException e) {}
    return 4;
};

Supplier<Integer> s2 = () -> {
    try { Thread.sleep(2000);
    } catch (InterruptedException e) {}
    return 5;
};

ExecutorService exec = Executors.newCachedThreadPool();
CompletableFuture<Integer> cf1
    = CompletableFuture.supplyAsync(s1,exec);
CompletableFuture<Integer> cf2
    = CompletableFuture.supplyAsync(s2,exec);
```

The first future to complete can be selected by passing the second future as an argument to the acceptEitherAsync method of the first. Since the second future completes first, its result is passed to a consumer that prints it.

```
CompletableFuture<Void> cf3
    = cf1.acceptEitherAsync(cf2,
                            x ->System.out.println(x),exec);
```

OUTPUT:

5

Section 13.7: Making a Future Dependent on Another Future

The execution of a future can be postponed until the completion of another future. The thenCompose method accepts a function that transforms the result of the calling stage into a new CompletionStage.

```
<U> CompletionState<U> thenCompose(Function<? super T,
                                ? extends CompletionStage<U>> fn)
```

Suppose a program creates a CompletableFuture<Integer> object that waits for 3 seconds before computing 4.

```
Supplier<Integer> s1 = () ->
{
    try { Thread.sleep(3000);
    } catch (InterruptedException e) {}
    return 4;
};

CompletableFuture<Integer> cf1
    = CompletableFuture.supplyAsync(s1);
```

A future that waits for the completion of another future can be created by calling the first future's thenCompose method. The function argument to the thenCompose method transforms the Integer result to a CompletableFuture<String> by creating a local CompletableFuture<String> object that uses the result and completing it immediately.

```
CompletableFuture<String> cf2 = cf1.thenCompose( x -> {
    CompletableFuture<String> c = new CompletableFuture();
    c.complete("HI" + Integer.toString(x));
    return c;
});
```

```
System.out.println(cf2.join());
```

OUTPUT:

```
HI4
```

Section 13.8: Cancelling a Future

If not already completed, the cancel method cancels a future's computation, resulting in a CancellationException. The method returns true if it was able to cancel the computation and returns false otherwise.

Suppose a program creates a future that waits 10 seconds and then computes the integer 5.

```
Supplier<Integer> s = () -> {
    try { Thread.sleep(10000);
    } catch (InterruptedException e) {}
    return 5;
};
```

```
CompletableFuture<Integer> cf1
    = CompletableFuture.supplyAsync(s);
```

Since the computation has not run yet, the future can be cancelled. The cancel method is called with argument true to allow interruption of the task in which the future runs.

```
if (cf1.cancel(true))
    System.out.println("Future cf1 cancelled.");
```

OUTPUT:

```
Future cf1 cancelled.
```

A cancelled computation results in a `CancellationException`. An exception is thrown if a program attempts to `join` or get the result of a cancelled future. The following example catches the exception throw when attempting to join the cancelled exception and displays "Cannot join cancelled future.".

```
try {
    System.out.println(cf1.join());
} catch (CancellationException e) {
    System.out.println("Cannot join cancelled future.");
}
```

OUTPUT:

```
Cannot join cancelled future.
```

A future that completes immediately cannot be cancelled. The `cancel` method returns `false`, and the result of the computation can be retrieved with `join` or `get`. The call to the `cancel` method in the following example returns `false`, since the future was completed immediately. The join method successfully retrieves the value of the computation and 6 is displayed.

```
CompletableFuture<Integer> cf2
    = CompletableFuture.completedFuture(6);

if (cf2.cancel(true))
    System.out.println("Future cf2 cancelled.");

try {
    System.out.println(cf2.join());
} catch (CancellationException e) {
    System.out.println("Cannot join cancelled future.");
}
```

OUTPUT:

```
6
```

`FutureTask` provides the `isDone` and `isCancelled` methods that can be used to check if a future has completed or has been cancelled.

```
if (cf2.isDone())
    System.out.println("Future cf2 has completed");
if (!cf2.isCancelled())
    System.out.println("Future cf2 has not been cancelled");
```

OUTPUT:

```
Future cf2 has completed
Future cf2 has not been cancelled
```

Section 13.9: When Futures Throw Unchecked Exceptions

Suppose the computation performed by a future throws an unchecked exception. The `return` statement in the following supplier causes an `ArrayIndexOutOfBoundsException`:

```
Supplier y = () -> { int[] a = {1,2,3}; return a[3]; };
```

The `exceptionally` method accepts a function which replaces the exception with an object of the computation result type. If an unchecked exception does not occur, the normal computation result is passed through. This method returns a `CompleteableFuture`, so it can be used along the future chain.

```
CompletableFuture<X> exceptionally(Function<Throwable, ? extends X> f);
```

The future in the following example throws an unchecked exception. Therefore, the function passed to the `exceptionally` method replaces it with zero. The value zero is wrapped in a new `CompleteableFuture` and printed by the `thenAccept` method.

```
CompletableFuture
    .supplyAsync(y)            // CompletableFuture<Integer>
    .exceptionally(x -> 0)     // CompletableFuture<Integer>
    .thenAccept(x ->
        System.out.println(x)); // CompletableFuture<Void>
```

OUTPUT:

```
0
```

If the previous example was repeated with a computation that does not throw an unchecked exception, the exceptionally method would do nothing and the supplyAsync result would be passed to the thenAccept method.

```
Supplier z = () -> { int[] a = {1,2,3,4}; return a[3]; };


CompletableFuture
    .supplyAsync(z)          // CompletableFuture<Integer>
    .exceptionally(x -> 0)   // CompletableFuture<Integer>
    .thenAccept(x ->
        System.out.println(x)); // CompletableFuture<Void>
```

OUTPUT:

4

Section 13.10: Running Futures in Parallel

The static allof method accepts a variable-length list of CompletableFutures and blocks until they all have completed.

```
static CompleteableFuture<Void> allOf(CompleteableFuture<?>... cfs)
```

This method is used to run several futures in parallel. It can be used when the order of computation is not important provided the futures do not share data (or are synchronized in some way). Since it creates a CompletableFuture<Void>, the results of each future are not available on the method chain. The following program runs three futures in parallel. It stores the result of each computation in a separate field.

Listing 13-2. AllOf.java

```
import java.util.concurrent.CompletableFuture;
class AllOf
{
    static String color1=null;
    static String color2=null;
    static String color3=null;
    public static void main(String[] args)
```

```
    {
        CompletableFuture<String> cf1
            = CompletableFuture.supplyAsync( () -> {
                color1 = "RED"; return null;});
        CompletableFuture<String> cf2
            = CompletableFuture.supplyAsync( () -> {
                color2 = "GREEN"; return null;});

        CompletableFuture<String> cf3
            = CompletableFuture.supplyAsync( () -> {
                color3 = "BLUE"; return null;});

        CompletableFuture
            .allOf(cf1,cf2,cf3)   // CompletableFuture<Void>
            .join();              // Void

        System.out.println(color1 + "," + color2 + "," + color3);
    }
}
```

OUTPUT:

```
RED,GREEN,BLUE
```

The same results could have been obtained using the thenCombine method, which combines the results of two CompletionStages using a BiFunction.

```
<U,V> CompletionStage<V> thenCombine(
  CompletionStage<? extends U> oher,
  BiFunction<? super T, ? super U, ? extends V> fn);
```

The following example defines a BiFunction that adds a comma between the results of the two futures. This function combines the result of a computation with the previous computation in comma-delimited string. Note that fields color1, color2, and color3 are not necessary to store the separate calculations, since the results are being propagated by the method chain.

```
CompletableFuture<String> cf4
    = CompletableFuture.supplyAsync( () -> "RED");
CompletableFuture<String> cf5
```

```
    = CompletableFuture.supplyAsync( () -> "GREEN");
CompletableFuture<String> cf6
    = CompletableFuture.supplyAsync( () -> "BLUE");

BiFunction<String,String,String> bi = (x,y) -> x + "," + y;

System.out.println(cf4.thenCombine(cf5, bi)
                      .thenCombine(cf6, bi)
                      .join());
```

OUTPUT:

RED,GREEN,BLUE

The static anyof method accepts a variable-length list of CompletableFutures and returns the first CompletableFuture to complete. In the following example, the anyOf method executes futures cf1, cf2, and cf3 in parallel. Since future cf1 is the first to complete, "RED" is displayed.

```
CompletableFuture<String> cf1
    = CompletableFuture.supplyAsync( () -> "RED");
CompletableFuture<String> cf2
    = CompletableFuture.supplyAsync( () -> "GREEN");
CompletableFuture<String> cf3
    = CompletableFuture.supplyAsync( () -> "BLUE");

CompletableFuture<Object> result =
        CompletableFuture.anyOf(cf1, cf2, cf3);
System.out.println(result.join());
```

OUTPUT:

RED

Suppose a program needs to concatenate the words entered by a user into a sentence using two parallel, independent threads. The allOf method could be used to run the threads in parallel, but then separate fields are required to store the results since allOf returns a CompletableFuture<Void>. If the thenCombine method were used instead, the words could be concatenated internally and returned by the second thread.

The scanning thread prompts the users to enter a word. A semaphore could be used to inform the other thread that a new word is available. The thread finishes when the user enters a period.

```
Supplier<String> keyboard = () -> {
    Scanner scan = new Scanner(System.in);
    while (!word.equals("."))
    {
        System.out.print("Enter a word (or . when finished):");
        word = scan.nextLine();
        sem.release();
    }
    return null;
};
```

The concatenating thread wakes up when a word is available and then adds the word to the sentence.

```
Supplier<String> concatenator = () -> {
    String sentence = "";
    while (!word.equals("."))
    {
        try {
            sem.acquire();
        } catch (InterruptedException e) {}
        if (!word.equals(".") && sentence.length() > 0)
            sentence += " ";
        sentence += word;
    }
    return sentence;
};
```

The threads can be hosted by futures and run in parallel using the thenCombine method. A BiFunction can select the result of the second thread (the sentence).

```
CompletableFuture<String> keyboardFuture
    = CompletableFuture.supplyAsync(keyboard);
CompletableFuture<String> concatFuture
```

```
           = CompletableFuture.supplyAsync(concatenator);

BiFunction<String,String,String> bi = (x,y) -> y;

System.out.println(keyboardFuture
                   .thenCombine(concatFuture, bi)
                   .join());
```

The complete program is shown as follows. After the user enters the word
"Functional", keyboardFuture releases the semaphore causing concatFuture to
concatenate "Functional" to the sentences. This process happens again for the words
"interfaces" and "rock".

When the user enters a period, keyboardFuture returns a null result and
concatFuture returns the sentence. The BiFunction selects the sentence, and the result
of the combined future is obtained using the join method.

Listing 13-3. MySentence.java

```
import java.util.concurrent.*;
import java.util.function.*;
import java.util.Scanner;
class MySentence
{
    private static Semaphore sem = new Semaphore(0);
    private static String word = "";
    public static void main(String[] args)
    {
        Supplier<String> keyboard = () -> {
            Scanner scan = new Scanner(System.in);
            while (!word.equals("."))
            {
                System.out.print(
                        "Enter a word (or . when finished):");
                word = scan.nextLine();
                sem.release();
            }
            return null;
        };
```

```
        Supplier<String> concatenator = () -> {
            String sentence = "";
            while (!word.equals("."))
            {
                try {
                    sem.acquire();
                } catch (InterruptedException e) {}
                if (!word.equals(".") && sentence.length() > 0)
                    sentence += " ";
                    sentence += word;
            }
            return sentence;
        };

        CompletableFuture<String> keyboardFuture
            = CompletableFuture.supplyAsync(keyboard);
        CompletableFuture<String> concatFuture
            = CompletableFuture.supplyAsync(concatenator);

        BiFunction<String,String,String> bi = (x,y) -> y;

        System.out.println(keyboardFuture
                        .thenCombine(concatFuture, bi)
                        .join());
    }
}
```

PROGRAM OUTPUT (user input in **RED**):

```
Enter a word (or . when finished):
Enter a word (or . when finished): Functional
Enter a word (or . when finished): interfaces
Enter a word (or . when finished): rock
Enter a word (or . when finished): .
Functional interfaces rock
```

PROJECT 13: Sentence Builder

Problem Statement

Write a multithreaded program which prompts the user to enter the words of a sentence one at a time while the program checks for grammatical errors according to four predetermined rules.

When a grammatical error occurs, the program reports which rule is violated and allows the user to replace the offending word. When the user enters a period, the finished grammatically correct sentence is displayed and the program terminates.

The rules of grammar implemented by the program are as follows:

1) Verbs can only follow nouns.

2) Adjectives can only precede nouns.

3) Articles can only precede nouns; however, an adjective may occur between them.

4) Prepositions can only precede nouns; however, an article may occur between them.

Solution

The rules of grammar defined in the preceding list compare as many as three words based on their parts of speech. Therefore, a class which stores the last three words should be written. Each word should also contain its part of speech.

```
enum SPEECH {NOUN,VERB,PREPOSITION,ADJECTIVE,ARTICLE}
class Word
{
    String w;
    SPEECH part;
    public Word(String x, SPEECH p) { w=x; part=p;}
    @Override
    public String toString() { return w; };
}
```

```
class SentenceComponent
{
    Word current;
    Word previous;
    Word second;
    public SentenceComponent(Word c, Word p, Word s)
    {
        current = c;
        previous = p;
        second = s;
    }
    public SentenceComponent()
    {
        current = new Word("" ,null);
        previous = null;
        second = null;
    }
    @Override
    public String toString() { return current.toString(); };
}
```

A thread can be defined that creates a SentenceComponent and provides the component to four additional threads, each of which implements a different rule of grammar. The content of the thread is defined in a supplier which is placed at the beginning of a chain using supplyAsync. The supplier uses a Scanner object to prompt the user to enter a word and its part of speech. Fields can be used to handle the previous and second to last words. The part of speech should be set to null for the period of the sentence. This will inform the remaining threads to avoid validation.

```
Supplier<SentenceComponent> keyboard = () -> {
    Scanner scan = new Scanner(System.in);
    SPEECH part = null;
    System.out.print("Enter a word (or enter .):");
    String w = scan.nextLine();
    if (!w.equals("."))
    {
```

```
        System.out.println("Enter its part of speech");
        System.out.print("0 - NOUN, ");
        System.out.print("1 - VERB, ");
        System.out.print("2 - PREPOSITION, ");
        System.out.print("3 - ADJECTIVE, ");
        System.out.print("4 - ARTICLE:");
        int p = Integer.parseInt(scan.nextLine());
        part = SPEECH.values()[p];
    }
    Word word = new Word(w,part);
    SentenceComponent comp
        = new SentenceComponent(word,previous,second);
    second = previous;
    previous = word;
    return comp;
};
```

Each grammar rule is applied in subsequent links of the future chain, with the result of each rule passed to the next. The CompletionStage output from the thenCompose method can be used to support the chain. A function needs to be defined which takes the SentenceComponent result from one rule and maps it to a CompletionStage<Sentenc eComponent> for the next. If a rule fails, it creates a CompletionStage that contains a null SentenceComponent that is ignored by the next future in the chain. If the component is a period, it is passed through the rules so that it may be written at the end of the sentence.

The following function implements grammar rule 1. If the current word is a verb and the previous word is not a noun, the rule has been violated and a null SentenceComponent is returned. All other combinations pass the SentenceComponent through to the next rule.

```
Function<SentenceComponent,
        CompletionStage<SentenceComponent>> rule1 = x -> {
    CompletableFuture<SentenceComponent> fut
        = new CompletableFuture();
    SentenceComponent comp = null;
    if (x!=null)
    {
```

```java
        if (x.current.part == null)
            comp = x;
        else if (!x.current.part.equals(SPEECH.VERB)
                || (x.previous == null)
                || x.previous.part.equals(SPEECH.NOUN))
            comp = x;
        if (comp == null)
            System.out.println(
                "GRAMMAR RULE 1 ERROR: VERBS CAN ONLY FOLLOW NOUNS.");
    }
    fut.complete(comp);
    return fut;
};
```

The following function implements grammar rule 2. If the current word is a noun and the previous word is not an adjective, the rule has been violated and a null SentenceComponent is returned. All other combinations pass the SentenceComponent through to the next rule.

```java
Function<SentenceComponent,
        CompletionStage<SentenceComponent>> rule2 = x -> {
    CompletableFuture<SentenceComponent> fut
        = new CompletableFuture();
    SentenceComponent comp = null;
    if (x!=null)
    {
        if (x.current.part == null)
            comp = x;
        else if ((x.previous == null)
                || !x.previous.part.equals(SPEECH.ADJECTIVE)
                || x.current.part.equals(SPEECH.NOUN))
            comp = x;
        if (comp == null)
            System.out.println(
        "GRAMMAR RULE 2 ERROR: ADJECTIVES CAN ONLY PRECEDE NOUNS.");
    }
```

```
        fut.complete(comp);
        return fut;
};
```

The following function implements grammar rule 3. If an article is not followed by a noun or an adjective that is followed by a noun, the rule has been violated and a null SentenceComponent is returned. All other combinations pass the SentenceComponent through to the next rule.

```
Function<SentenceComponent,
        CompletionStage<SentenceComponent>> rule3 = x -> {
    CompletableFuture<SentenceComponent> fut
        = new CompletableFuture();
    SentenceComponent comp = null;
    if (x!=null)
    {
        boolean result = true;
        if ((x.current.part != null)
         && (x.previous != null) && (x.second != null))
        {
            if (x.second.part.equals(SPEECH.ARTICLE))
            {
                if (!x.previous.part.equals(SPEECH.ADJECTIVE)
                  || !x.current.part.equals(SPEECH.NOUN))
                    result = false;
            }
            else if ( x.previous.part.equals(SPEECH.ARTICLE)
                    && !x.current.part.equals(SPEECH.NOUN)
                    && !x.current.part.equals(SPEECH.ADJECTIVE))
                result = false;
        }
        if (result == false)
        {
            System.out.println(
            "GRAMMAR RULE 3 ERROR: ARTICLES CAN ONLY PRECEDE NOUNS,");
            System.out.println(
```

```
                        "HOWEVER, AN ADJECTIVE MAY OCCUR BETWEEN THEM.");
        }
        else
            comp = x;
    }
    fut.complete(comp);
    return fut;
};
```

The following function implements grammar rule 4. If a preposition is not followed by a noun or an article that is followed by a noun, the rule has been violated and a null SentenceComponent is returned. All other combinations pass the SentenceComponent through.

```
Function<SentenceComponent,
        CompletionStage<SentenceComponent>> rule4 = x -> {
    CompletableFuture<SentenceComponent> fut
        = new CompletableFuture();
    SentenceComponent comp = null;
    if (x!=null)
    {
        boolean result = true;
        if ((x.current.part != null)
         && (x.previous != null) && (x.second != null))
        {
            if (x.second.part.equals(SPEECH.PREPOSITION))
            {
                if (!x.previous.part.equals(SPEECH.ARTICLE)
                || !x.current.part.equals(SPEECH.NOUN))
                    result = false;
            }
            else if ( x.previous.part.equals(SPEECH.PREPOSITION)
                    && !x.current.part.equals(SPEECH.NOUN)
                    && !x.current.part.equals(SPEECH.ARTICLE))
                        result = false;
        }
```

```
        if (result == false)
        {
            System.out.println(
        "GRAMMAR RULE 4 ERROR: PREPOSITIONS CAN ONLY PRECEDE NOUNS,");
            System.out.println(
                    "HOWEVER, AN ARTICLE MAY OCCUR BETWEEN THEM.");
        }
        else
            comp = x;
    }
    fut.complete(comp);
    return fut;
};
```

The keyboard thread provides the SentenceComponent that is supplied to each rule thread in turn. The resultant SentenceComponent is returned by the join method. This component will be null if any of the grammar rules have been violated.

```
comp = CompletableFuture.supplyAsync(keyboard)
                        .thenCompose(rule1)
                        .thenCompose(rule2)
                        .thenCompose(rule3)
                        .thenCompose(rule4)
                        .join();
```

In the complete program, the chain is placed inside a while loop that runs until the user enters a period. Local variable sentence concatenates the words with a space between them. If the user violates a rule of grammar, the empty SentenceComponent is ignored, and the program attempts to replace the offending word on the next pass of the while loop.

Listing 13-4. SentenceBuilder.java

```
import java.util.concurrent.*;
import java.util.function.*;
import java.util.Scanner;
enum SPEECH {NOUN,VERB,PREPOSITION,ADJECTIVE,ARTICLE}
```

```java
class Word
{
    String w;
    SPEECH part;
    public Word(String x, SPEECH p) { w=x; part=p;}
    @Override
    public String toString() { return w; };
}

class SentenceComponent
{
    Word current;
    Word previous;
    Word second;
    public SentenceComponent(Word c, Word p, Word s)
    {
        current = c;
        previous = p;
        second = s;
    }

    public SentenceComponent()
    {
        current  = new Word("" ,null);
        previous = null;
        second   = null;
    }
    @Override
    public String toString() { return current.toString(); };
}

class SentenceBuilder
{
    static Word previous = null;
    static Word second = null;

    public static void main(String[] args)
```

```
{
    Supplier<SentenceComponent> keyboard = () -> {
        Scanner scan = new Scanner(System.in);
        SPEECH part = null;
        System.out.print("Enter a word (or enter .):");
        String w = scan.nextLine();
        if (!w.equals("."))
        {
            System.out.println("Enter its part of speech");
            System.out.print("0 - NOUN, ");
            System.out.print("1 - VERB, ");
            System.out.print("2 - PREPOSITION, ");
            System.out.print("3 - ADJECTIVE, ");
            System.out.print("4 - ARTICLE:");
            int p = Integer.parseInt(scan.nextLine());
            part = SPEECH.values()[p];
        }
        Word word = new Word(w,part);
        SentenceComponent comp
            = new SentenceComponent(word,previous,second);
        second = previous;
        previous = word;
        return comp;
    };
    Function<SentenceComponent,
            CompletionStage<SentenceComponent>> rule1 = x -> {
        CompletableFuture<SentenceComponent> fut
            = new CompletableFuture();
        SentenceComponent comp = null;
        if (x!=null)
        {
            if (x.current.part == null)
                comp = x;
            else if (!x.current.part.equals(SPEECH.VERB)
                    || (x.previous == null)
                    || x.previous.part.equals(SPEECH.NOUN))
```

321

```java
                comp = x;
            if (comp == null)
                System.out.println(
        "GRAMMAR RULE 1 ERROR: VERBS CAN ONLY FOLLOW NOUNS.");
        }
        fut.complete(comp);
        return fut;
    };

    Function<SentenceComponent,
            CompletionStage<SentenceComponent>> rule2 = x -> {
        CompletableFuture<SentenceComponent> fut
            = new CompletableFuture();
        SentenceComponent comp = null;
        if (x!=null)
        {
            if (x.current.part == null)
                comp = x;
            else if ((x.previous == null)
                    || !x.previous.part.equals(SPEECH.ADJECTIVE)
                    || x.current.part.equals(SPEECH.NOUN))
                comp = x;
            if (comp == null)
                System.out.println(
        "GRAMMAR RULE 2 ERROR: ADJECTIVES CAN ONLY PRECEDE NOUNS.");
        }
        fut.complete(comp);
        return fut;
    };

    Function<SentenceComponent,
            CompletionStage<SentenceComponent>> rule3 = x -> {
        CompletableFuture<SentenceComponent> fut
            = new CompletableFuture();
        SentenceComponent comp = null;
```

```
    if (x!=null)
    {
        boolean result = true;
        if ((x.current.part != null)
         && (x.previous != null) && (x.second != null))
        {
            if (x.second.part.equals(SPEECH.ARTICLE))
            {
                if (!x.previous.part.equals(SPEECH.ADJECTIVE)
                  || !x.current.part.equals(SPEECH.NOUN))
                    result = false;
            }
            else if ( x.previous.part.equals(SPEECH.ARTICLE)
                  && !x.current.part.equals(SPEECH.NOUN)
                  && !x.current.part.equals(SPEECH.ADJECTIVE))
                result = false;
        }
        if (result == false)
        {
            System.out.println(
"GRAMMAR RULE 3 ERROR: ARTICLES CAN ONLY PRECEDE NOUNS,");
            System.out.println(
                "HOWEVER, AN ADJECTIVE MAY OCCUR BETWEEN THEM.");
        }
        else
            comp = x;
    }
    fut.complete(comp);
    return fut;
};

Function<SentenceComponent,
        CompletionStage<SentenceComponent>> rule4 = x -> {
    CompletableFuture<SentenceComponent> fut
        = new CompletableFuture();
```

```
            SentenceComponent comp = null;
            if (x!=null)
            {
                boolean result = true;
                if ((x.current.part != null)
                 && (x.previous != null) && (x.second != null))
                {
                    if (x.second.part.equals(SPEECH.PREPOSITION))
                    {
                        if (!x.previous.part.equals(SPEECH.ARTICLE)
                          || !x.current.part.equals(SPEECH.NOUN))
                            result = false;
                    }
                    else if ( x.previous.part.equals(
                                        SPEECH.PREPOSITION)
                          && !x.current.part.equals(SPEECH.NOUN)
                          && !x.current.part.equals(SPEECH.ARTICLE))
                        result = false;
                }
                if (result == false)
                {
                    System.out.println(
"GRAMMAR RULE 4 ERROR: PREPOSITIONS CAN ONLY PRECEDE NOUNS,");
                    System.out.println(
                        "HOWEVER, AN ARTICLE MAY OCCUR BETWEEN THEM.");
                }
                else
                    comp = x;
            }
            fut.complete(comp);
            return fut;
        };

    SentenceComponent comp = new SentenceComponent();
    String sentence = "";
    while (!comp.current.w.equals("."))
```

```
        {
            comp = CompletableFuture.supplyAsync(keyboard)
                                .thenCompose(rule1)
                                .thenCompose(rule2)
                                .thenCompose(rule3)
                                .thenCompose(rule4)
                                .join();
            if (comp == null)
            {
                comp = new SentenceComponent();
            }
            else
            {
                if (comp.current.w.equals("."))
                 || (sentence.length() == 0))
                    sentence += comp.current;
                else
                    sentence += " " + comp.current;
            }
        }
        System.out.println(sentence);
    }
}
```

If the program is executed with the sentence "The quick fox jumped over the dog" but the user forgets to enter "fox", the program reports on word "jumped" that grammar rule 1 has been violated. The user can then replace "jumped" with "fox" and finish the sentence. After entering the period, the program prints the grammatically correct sentence "The quick fox jumped over the dog."

PROGRAM OUTPUT (user input in **BOLD**):

```
Enter a word (or enter .): The
Enter its part of speech
0 - NOUN, 1 - VERB, 2 - PREPOSITION, 3 - ADJECTIVE, 4 - ARTICLE: 4
Enter a word (or enter .): quick
Enter its part of speech
```

```
0 - NOUN, 1 - VERB, 2 - PREPOSITION, 3 - ADJECTIVE, 4 - ARTICLE: 3
Enter a word (or enter .): jumped
Enter its part of speech
0 - NOUN, 1 - VERB, 2 - PREPOSITION, 3 - ADJECTIVE, 4 - ARTICLE: 1
GRAMMAR RULE 1 ERROR: VERBS CAN ONLY FOLLOW NOUNS.
Enter a word (or enter .): fox
Enter its part of speech
0 - NOUN, 1 - VERB, 2 - PREPOSITION, 3 - ADJECTIVE, 4 - ARTICLE: 0
Enter a word (or enter .): jumped
Enter its part of speech
0 - NOUN, 1 - VERB, 2 - PREPOSITION, 3 - ADJECTIVE, 4 - ARTICLE: 1
Enter a word (or enter .): over
Enter its part of speech
0 - NOUN, 1 - VERB, 2 - PREPOSITION, 3 - ADJECTIVE, 4 - ARTICLE: 2
Enter a word (or enter .): the
Enter its part of speech
0 - NOUN, 1 - VERB, 2 - PREPOSITION, 3 - ADJECTIVE, 4 - ARTICLE: 4
Enter a word (or enter .): dog
Enter its part of speech
0 - NOUN, 1 - VERB, 2 - PREPOSITION, 3 - ADJECTIVE, 4 - ARTICLE: 0
Enter a word (or enter .): .
The quick fox jumped over the dog.
```

Short Problems

1) Write a completable future that creates a list of strings, adds "Hello" and then "Futures" to the list in separate stages, and then prints the list.

2) Write a future chain that generates a null string and then attempts to replace it with the first three characters in the string. If an exception occurs, the chain replaces the string with "Error". Finally, the chain prints the string.

3) Write a future chain that runs three futures in parallel, each of which randomly computes a number between 0 and 99 inclusive and then selects and prints the largest number.

Long Problems

1) Blackjack is a card game that adds the face values of a player's cards. The player attempts to get as close to 21 as possible without going over.

A blackjack dealer at a particular casino is able to deal to five players simultaneously. Use the techniques described in this chapter to deal five blackjack hands simultaneously. A blackjack hand is initially dealt two cards. As long as the sum of the player's cards is less than 13, the player is dealt another card.

The dealer draws a blackjack hand of 17. Any of the 5 players whose hand is greater than 17 without going over 21 has beaten the dealer.

2) Using the techniques described in this chapter, prompt the user to enter a string. If the user has not entered the string within 10 seconds, print a message that indicates that string entry has timed out. Otherwise, print the string entered.

3) It's tax time! Using the techniques described in this chapter, complete your schedule A deductions as follows:

   – Prompt for medical expenses. Deduction is 7.5% of total costs.

   – Prompt for state income tax and real estate taxes. Deduction is 100% of total costs.

   – Prompt for mortgage interest and points. Deduction is 100% of total costs.

   – Prompt for gifts to charity. Deduction is 100% of total costs.

   – Add the result of each component and print your total deduction.

CHAPTER 14

Use in Atomic Calculations

It is unsafe for execution threads to share data without protecting them with locks or some other form of synchronization. In the following program, two parallel threads share an unprotected int variable called num. During an iteration of thread cf2's for loop, the value -1490 was read from num and stored in local variable x. The JVM and the operating system then allow thread cf1 to run for a while, changing the value of num to 8290. When thread cf2 regains control and reads back num, it has the value 8290 instead of -1490 since the value of num has been corrupted by thread cf1.

Listing 14-1. Unsafe.java

```java
import java.util.concurrent.*;
class Unsafe
{
    static int num = 0;
    public static void main(String[] args)
    {
        CompletableFuture<Integer> cf1 =
          CompletableFuture.supplyAsync( () -> {
            for (int i=0; i < 10000; ++i)
            {
                int x = num;
                num += 10;
                if (num != (x+10))
                    System.out.println("cf1 THREAD READ ERROR: x= "
                                    + x +" num= " + num);
```

© Ralph Lecessi 2019
R. Lecessi, *Functional Interfaces in Java*, https://doi.org/10.1007/978-1-4842-4278-0_14

```
        }
        return num;
    });

    CompletableFuture<Integer> cf2 =
        CompletableFuture.supplyAsync( () -> {
        for (int i=0; i < 10000; ++i)
        {
            int x = num;
            num -= 10;
            if (num != (x-10))
                System.out.println("cf2 THREAD READ ERROR: x= "
                                        + x +" num= " + num);
        }
        return num;
    });

    CompletableFuture.allOf(cf1, cf2)
                    .join();
    }
}
```

PROGRAM OUTPUT:

```
cf2 THREAD READ ERROR: x= -1490 num= 8290
```

Section 14.1: Atomic Integers

The classes in the java.util.concurrent.atomic package support atomic operations on variables such that a single read or write operation cannot be interrupted by another thread. The AtomicInteger class protects an underlying int value by providing methods that perform atomic operations on the value.

The addAndGet method performs an atomic operation that adds its argument (a positive integer, negative integer, or zero) to the underlying value and returns the result.

```
int addAndGet(int delta);
```

The previous program can be made thread-safe by replacing the unprotected int variable with an AtomicInteger. The addAndGet operation cannot be interrupted by another thread, so the value assigned to x will not be corrupted. The get method returns the value of the underlying value.

Listing 14-2. Safe.java

```java
import java.util.concurrent.*;
import java.util.concurrent.atomic.*;
class Safe
{
    static AtomicInteger num = new AtomicInteger(0);

    public static void main(String[] args)
    {
        CompletableFuture<Integer> cf1 =
          CompletableFuture.supplyAsync( () -> {
            for (int i=0; i < 10000; ++i)
            {
                int x = num.addAndGet(10);
            }
            return num.get();
        });

        CompletableFuture<Integer> cf2 =
          CompletableFuture.supplyAsync( () -> {
            for (int i=0; i < 10000; ++i)
            {
                int x = num.addAndGet(-10);
            }
            return num.get();
        });

        CompletableFuture.allOf(cf1, cf2)
                    .join();
    }
}
```

Section 14.1.1: Accumulating an Atomic Value

The AtomicInteger class provides the following methods that calculate the value produced by an atomic operation in ways different than simply adding a parameter variable to it:

```
int accumulateAndGet(int i, IntBinaryOperator accumulatorFunction);
int getAndAccumulate(int i, IntBinaryOperator accumulatorFunction);
```

The accumulateAndGet method accepts an IntBinaryOperator that allows us to specify how to calculate the resulting value. The first operand to the IntBinaryOperator is the underlying value of the AtomicInteger, and the second operand to the IntBinaryOperator is the first argument to accumulateAndGet. The result of the calculation is returned from the method.

In the following example, the first call to accumulateAndGet multiplies underlying value 4 by 2, and 8 is displayed. The second call to accumulateAndGet divides 7 by 2 and then adds 3 to underlying value 8, and 11 is displayed.

```
AtomicInteger a1 = new AtomicInteger(4);
System.out.println(a1.accumulateAndGet(2, (x,y) -> x * y));
System.out.println(a1.accumulateAndGet(7, (x,y) -> x + y/2));
```

OUTPUT:

```
8
11
```

The getAndAccumulate method allows you to specify an IntBinaryOperator for the calculation. Unlike the accumulateAndGet method, it returns the value of the underlying value before the calculation is performed.

The following example has the same operators as the previous example but displays different results. The first call to getAndAccumulate returns 4 and then sets the underlying value to 8. The second call returns 8 and then sets the value to 11. An additional call to the get method is needed to display 11.

```
AtomicInteger a2 = new AtomicInteger(4);
System.out.println(a2.getAndAccumulate(2, (x,y) -> x * y));
System.out.println(a2.getAndAccumulate(7, (x,y) -> x + y/2));
System.out.println(a2.get());
```

OUTPUT:

```
4
8
11
```

Section 14.1.2: Updating an Atomic Value

The AtomicInteger class provides the following methods that update an atomic variable without providing a value to be used in the calculation:

```
int updateAndGet(IntUnaryOperator updateFunction);
int getAndUpdate(IntUnaryOperator updateFunction);
```

The updateAndGet method accepts an IntUnaryOperator that specifies how to update the underlying value. The method returns the result of the calculation.

```
AtomicInteger a1 = new AtomicInteger(10);
System.out.println(a1.updateAndGet(x -> x * 2));
System.out.println(a1.updateAndGet(x -> x - 5));
```

OUTPUT:

```
20
15
```

The getAndUpdate method returns the underlying value before the calculation is performed.

```
AtomicInteger a2 = new AtomicInteger(10);
System.out.println(a2.getAndUpdate(x -> x * 2));
System.out.println(a2.getAndUpdate(x -> x - 5));
System.out.println(a2.get());
```

OUTPUT:

```
10
20
15
```

Section 14.1.3: Comparing an Atomic Value

The AtomicInteger class provides the following methods which compare and reset the value of an atomic variable:

```
int compareAndExchange(int expectedValue, int newValue);
int compareAndSet(int exp, int newValue);
```

The compareAndExchange method replaces the underlying value with newValue if the underlying value is equal to expectedValue and returns the result.

The following example adds 10 to an atomic integer and then resets it to 0 when it reaches 50. Due to memory semantics, the get method needs to be called to display 0 on the iteration which resets the value (if the compareAndExchange method were wrapped in a println statement and the get method were not called, 50 would be displayed during the fifth iteration of the loop instead of 0).

```
AtomicInteger a = new AtomicInteger(0);
for (int i=0; i<9; ++i)
{
    a.updateAndGet(x -> x + 10);
    a.compareAndExchange(50,0);
    System.out.println(a.get());
}
```

OUTPUT:

```
10
20
30
40
0
10
20
30
40
```

The compareAndSet method replaces the underlying value with newValue if the underlying value is equal to expectedValue. The compareAndSet method returns true if the exchange was made as opposed to compareAndExchange which returns the witness value.

In the following program, two parallel threads share an atomic integer. Each thread adds 10 to the integer inside a loop. Thread cf1 uses the compareAndSet method to reset the integer back to 0 after comparing it with 100. Thread cf2 resets the integer after comparing it with 80.

Listing 14-3. ShareAnInt.java

```java
import java.util.concurrent.atomic.*;
import java.util.concurrent.*;
class ShareAnInt
{
    public static void main(String[] args)
    {
        AtomicInteger num = new AtomicInteger(0);
        CompletableFuture<Integer> cf1 =
          CompletableFuture.supplyAsync( () -> {
            int x = num.get();
            for (int i=0; i<20; ++i)
            {
                x = num.updateAndGet(z -> z + 10);
                if (num.compareAndSet(100, 0))
                {
                    System.out.println("cf1 resets atomic variable");
                    x = num.get();
                }
                System.out.println("cf1 a = " + x);
            }
            return x;
        });

        CompletableFuture<Integer> cf2 =
          CompletableFuture.supplyAsync( () -> {
            int x = num.get();
            for (int i=0; i<20; ++i)
            {
                x = num.updateAndGet(z -> z + 10);
                if (num.compareAndSet(80, 0))
```

```
            {
                System.out.println("cf2 resets atomic variable");
                x = num.get();
            }
            System.out.println("cf2 a = " + x);
        }
        return x;
    });

    CompletableFuture.allOf(cf1,cf2)
                    .join();
    }
}
```

PROGRAM OUTPUT:

```
cf2 a = 10
cf1 a = 20
cf2 a = 30
cf1 a = 40
cf2 a = 50
cf1 a = 60
cf2 a = 70
cf1 a = 80
cf2 a = 90
cf1 resets atomic variable
cf2 a = 10
cf1 a = 10
cf2 a = 20
cf1 a = 30
cf2 a = 40
cf1 a = 50
cf2 a = 60
cf1 a = 70
cf2 resets atomic variable
cf1 a = 10
cf2 a = 10
```

```
cf1 a = 20
cf2 a = 30
cf1 a = 40
cf2 a = 50
cf1 a = 60
cf1 a = 80
cf1 a = 90
cf1 resets atomic variable
cf1 a = 0
cf1 a = 10
cf1 a = 20
cf1 a = 30
cf1 a = 40
cf1 a = 50
cf2 a = 70
cf2 a = 60
cf2 a = 70
cf2 resets atomic variable
cf2 a = 0
cf2 a = 10
cf2 a = 20
cf2 a = 30
cf2 a = 40
```

Section 14.2: Atomic Longs

The AtomicLong class provides atomic operations for an underlying long variable. It has methods similar to the AtomicInteger class.

The following example calls the accumulateAndGet method to divide 10 by 2, and 5 is displayed. It then uses the compareAndExchange method to reset the underlying long value to 3.

```
AtomicLong l = new AtomicLong(10L);
System.out.println(l.accumulateAndGet(2, (x,y) -> x / y));
l.compareAndExchange(5,3);
System.out.println(l.get());
```

OUTPUT:

5
3

Section 14.3: Atomic Booleans

The AtomicBoolean class provides atomic operations for an underlying boolean variable. It provides get, set, and compareAndExchange methods.

The following example creates an atomic boolean with an underlying value of true. It then uses the compareAndExchange method to reset the value to false. Lastly, it uses the set method to change to underlying value back to true.

```
AtomicBoolean bool = new AtomicBoolean(true);
System.out.println(bool.get());
bool.compareAndExchange(true,false);
System.out.println(bool.get());
bool.set(true);
System.out.println(bool.get());
```

OUTPUT:

```
true
false
true
```

Section 14.4: Atomic Arrays

Using the AtomicIntegerArray and AtomicLongArray classes, arrays of atomic data can be created. Most methods, including accumulateAndGet listed as follows, have an additional first argument which indicates the array element on which to operate.

The following example uses the accumulateAndGet method to add twice the array index to each element of the atomic array.

```
final int ARRAY_SIZE = 4;
AtomicIntegerArray arr = new AtomicIntegerArray(ARRAY_SIZE);
```

```
for (int i=0; i < ARRAY_SIZE; ++i)
{
    System.out.println(i + ": "
                    + arr.accumulateAndGet(i, i,
                                            (x,y) -> x + 2*y));
}
```

OUTPUT:

```
0: 0
1: 2
2: 4
3: 6
```

Section 14.5: Atomic References

The AtomicReference class can be used to make reference variables atomic. This class is generic for the type of the underlying reference.

The following example initializes AtomicReference<String> ref to the string "R" and then inside a loop uses a BinaryOperator<String> to concatenate the loop index to the object referenced by the underlying String.

```
AtomicReference<String> ref = new AtomicReference<>("R");
for (int i=0; i < 5; ++i)
{
    System.out.println(ref.accumulateAndGet(Integer.toString(i),
                                            (x,y) -> x + y));
}
```

OUTPUT:

```
R0
R01
R012
R0123
R01234
```

The previous example was easy to implement, since string concatenation is already defined as a binary operation which results in a new String object. When the AtomicReference type is a user-defined class, both the result of the binary operation and the value passed to the accumulateAndGet method must call the new operator.

Given the following IntAndString class,

```
class IntAndString
{
    int i;
    String s;
    public IntAndString(int x, String y) { i=x; s=y; }
    @Override
    public String toString() { return i + " " + s; }
}
```

an atomic reference to an object of the IntAndString class can be created.

```
AtomicReference<IntAndString> refis =
    new AtomicReference<>(new IntAndString(2,"HI"));
```

The index of a loop can be atomically added to the i field in an IntAndString using the accumulateAndGet method. The first argument to the accumulateAndGet method is a reference to a new IntAndString object whose i field contains the value of the loop counter. The binary operator then creates a new IntAndString object which adds this value to the i field of the existing object and returns a reference to the new object.

```
for (int i=0; i < 5; ++i)
{
    BinaryOperator<IntAndString> bi =
        (x,y) -> new IntAndString(x.i + y.i,null);
    System.out.println(
        refis.accumulateAndGet(new IntAndString(i,null), bi));
}
```

OUTPUT:

```
2 null
3 null
5 null
8 null
12 null
```

PROJECT 14: Bank Account

Problem Statement

Two people open a joint bank account with an initial balance of $500. Over the course of the first week, the first person makes the following transactions:

Deposit, Withdrawal, Deposit, Withdrawal, Withdrawal

Over the course of the first week, the second person makes the following transactions:

Withdrawal, Withdrawal, Withdrawal, Deposit, Withdrawal

The first person makes deposits of $50 and withdrawals of $70.50. The second person makes deposits of $20 and withdrawals of $120.50.

Write a program where the transactions made by both persons on the account during the first week are performed in parallel. Stop executing transactions if the balance is zero or less.

Solution

An atomic variable that contains the account balance can be created. The program can then perform deposits or withdrawals that update the balance concurrently from two different threads. A class which wraps a double balance can be written.

```
class AccountBalance
{
    double balance;
    public AccountBalance(double d) { balance = d; }
    @Override
    public String toString() { return Double.toString(balance); }
}
```

Binary operators for deposits and withdrawals can be defined. These operators will return a reference to a new AccountBalance object that adds or subtracts an amount to the existing balance.

```
BinaryOperator<AccountBalance> deposit = (x,y) ->
    new AccountBalance(x.balance + y.balance);

BinaryOperator<AccountBalance> withdrawal = (x,y) ->
    new AccountBalance(x.balance - y.balance);
```

A BankAccount class with a static AtomicReference<AccountBalance> field can be created. The class should provide an accumulate method that accepts a double value and a binary operator (either deposit or withdrawal). The method calls the accumulateAndGet method of the atomic reference with the binary operator and an AccountBalance constructed from value.

```
class BankAccount
{
    static AtomicReference<AccountBalance> b =
        new AtomicReference(new AccountBalance(500.0));

    static void accumulate(double value, BinaryOperator op)
    {
        b.accumulateAndGet(new AccountBalance(value), op);
    }
}
```

The TRANS enumeration can be provided for the transaction type. A Java array of TRANS can be used by each thread to model the week of activity for each person.

```
enum TRANS { DEP, WITH }
TRANS[] p1Trans =
    {TRANS.DEP, TRANS.WITH, TRANS.DEP, TRANS.WITH, TRANS.WITH};
TRANS[] p2Trans =
    {TRANS.WITH, TRANS.WITH, TRANS.WITH, TRANS.DEP, TRANS.WITH};
```

Threads can be written to execute each person's transactions using the corresponding array of transaction activity. If the transaction type is TRANS.DEP, the deposit BinaryOperator will be passed to the accumulate method. If the transaction type is TRANS.WITH, the withdrawal BinaryOperator will be passed to the accumulate method.

```
CompletableFuture<AccountBalance> p1 =
  CompletableFuture.supplyAsync( () -> {
    for (int i=0; i < p1Trans.length && b.get().balance > 0; ++i)
    {
        if (p1Trans[i] == TRANS.DEP)
            accumulate(50.0, deposit);
        else
```

```
        accumulate(70.50, withdrawal);
        System.out.println("p1: " + b.get().balance);
    }
    return null;
});

CompletableFuture<AccountBalance> p2 =
  CompletableFuture.supplyAsync( () -> {
    for (int i=0; i < p2Trans.length && b.get().balance > 0; ++i)
    {
        if (p2Trans[i] == TRANS.DEP)
            accumulate(20.0, deposit);
        else
            accumulate(120.50, withdrawal);
        System.out.println("p2: " + b.get().balance);
    }
    return null;
});
```

The transactions from both people can then be run in parallel.

```
CompletableFuture.allOf(p1,p2)
                 .join();
```

The complete program is shown in Listing 14-4. In the execution shown as follows, the fifth transaction of thread p2 sets the balance to a negative number, so the fifth transaction of thread p1 does not execute.

Listing 14-4. BankAccount.java

```
import java.util.concurrent.atomic.*;
import java.util.concurrent.*;
import java.util.function.*;
enum TRANS { DEP, WITH }
class AccountBalance
{
    double balance;
    public AccountBalance(double d) { balance = d; }
```

```
    @Override
    public String toString() { return Double.toString(balance); }
}
class BankAccount
{
    static AtomicReference<AccountBalance> b =
        new AtomicReference(new AccountBalance(500.0));
    static void accumulate(double value, BinaryOperator op)
    {
        b.accumulateAndGet(new AccountBalance(value), op);
    }
    public static void main(String[] args)
    {
        TRANS[] p1Trans =
         {TRANS.DEP, TRANS.WITH, TRANS.DEP, TRANS.WITH, TRANS.WITH};
        TRANS[] p2Trans =
         {TRANS.WITH, TRANS.WITH, TRANS.WITH, TRANS.DEP, TRANS.WITH};

        BinaryOperator<AccountBalance> deposit = (x,y) ->
            new AccountBalance(x.balance + y.balance);

        BinaryOperator<AccountBalance> withdrawal = (x,y) ->
            new AccountBalance(x.balance - y.balance);

        CompletableFuture<AccountBalance> p1 =
          CompletableFuture.supplyAsync( () -> {
            for (int i=0; i < p1Trans.length && b.get().balance > 0;
                 ++i)
            {
                if (p1Trans[i] == TRANS.DEP)
                    accumulate(50.0, deposit);
                else
                    accumulate(70.50, withdrawal);
                System.out.println("p1: " + b.get().balance);
            }
            return null;
        });
```

```
CompletableFuture<AccountBalance> p2 =
  CompletableFuture.supplyAsync( () -> {
    for (int i=0; i < p2Trans.length && b.get().balance > 0;
        ++i)
    {
        if (p2Trans[i] == TRANS.DEP)
            accumulate(20.0, deposit);
        else
            accumulate(120.50, withdrawal);
        System.out.println("p2: " + b.get().balance);
    }
    return null;
});

CompletableFuture.allOf(p1,p2)
                 .join();
  }
}
```

PROGRAM OUTPUT:

```
p2: 429.5
p1: 550.0
p2: 309.0
p1: 238.5
p2: 118.0
p1: 168.0
p2: 188.0
p1: 117.5
p2: -3.0
```

Short Problems

1) Using two atomic integers, generate and print the first 10 entries
   in the Fibonacci series (see problem 1 from Chapter 7).

2) Repeat problem 1 using an atomic array of integers.

3) Create an atomic reference variable that stores a whitespace-separated list of names. Write a future chain that runs three futures in parallel, each of which places a different name into the list. Print the list of names after the futures have completed.

Long Problems

1) Write a password generator that prompts the user for his or her last name. The program creates a password consisting of the first three letters of the user's last name concatenated with a random number between 0 and 1000. For security reasons, a new random number is atomically generated (on a separate thread) every .5 seconds. Print the resulting password.

2) A car dealership has a showroom that picks a different car every 10 seconds selected randomly from the cars in stock and displays it. The information for each car consists of its make, model, list price, and quantity in stock. The sales team makes changes to any car's list price or the quantity in stock. It is undesirable for a car to be read from the database for display when a salesperson is making a modification.

   Write a program consisting of a thread that atomically displays a car randomly selected from the database every 10 seconds and another thread that allows a salesperson to select and modify the list price or quantity of any car in the database.

3) A teacher and her grader both work on the grades to her class of 30 students. The grader populates the grades, but the teacher can at any time select and print a grade or apply a curve to all the grades. The curve is a constant multiplier applied to each grade.

   Write a program consisting of a thread for the grader to atomically enter the grades and another thread where the teacher can select and print any grade or apply a curve to all the grades.

CHAPTER 15

Use in JavaFX Applications

In Java 11, JavaFX was removed from the JDK and has been made available as a separate module. In order to run these examples in Java 11, the JavaFX SDK must be installed and added to the module path. The classes and methods have been available since JavaFX 2.0.

Section 15.1: Handling JavaFX Events

JavaFX provides the EventHandler functional interface to handle events. It has functional method handle which accepts an Event.

```
@FunctionalInterface
public interface EventHandler<T extends Event> extends EventListener
{
    void handle(T event);
}
```

The following example implements a handler for an ActionEvent that occurs when a button is pressed. It increments the count field and then prints a message to the display.

```
EventHandler<ActionEvent> handler = x -> {
    count++;
    System.out.println("The button has been clicked "
                    + count + " times");
};
```

The handler is registered with the button using the setOnAction method.

```
Button click = new Button("Click me");
click.setOnAction(handler);
```

© Ralph Lecessi 2019
R. Lecessi, *Functional Interfaces in Java*, https://doi.org/10.1007/978-1-4842-4278-0_15

The complete program is shown as follows. The displayed output is generated by pressing the button twice.

Listing 15-1. TestEventHandler.java

```java
import javafx.application.Application;
import javafx.event.*;
import javafx.scene.Scene;
import javafx.scene.control.Button;
import javafx.scene.layout.StackPane;
import javafx.stage.Stage;

public class TestEventHandler extends Application
{
    int count = 0;
    @Override
    public void start(Stage primaryStage)
    {
        Button click = new Button("Click me");
        EventHandler<ActionEvent> handler = x -> {
            count++;
            System.out.println("The button has been clicked "
                                + count + " times");
        };
        click.setOnAction(handler);

        StackPane root = new StackPane();
        root.getChildren().add(click);

        Scene scene = new Scene(root, 300, 100);

        primaryStage.setTitle("Test Event Handler");
        primaryStage.setScene(scene);
        primaryStage.show();
    }
```

```
public static void main(String[] args)
{
    launch(args);
}
}
```

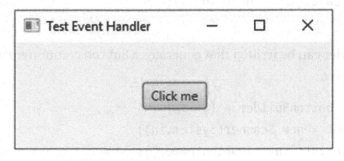

Figure 15-1. *GUI for TestEventHandler.java*

PROGRAM OUTPUT (two button presses):

```
The button has been clicked 1 times
The button has been clicked 2 times
```

Note   The launch method is defined in the Application superclass.

Section 15.2: Building JavaFX UI Components

JavaFX provides the Builder functional interface which is useful for generating UI components.

```
@FunctionalInterface
public interface Builder<T>
{
    T build();
}
```

A label builder can be written that generates a `Label` component whose label is provided by the user.

```
Builder<Label> labelBuilder = () -> {
    Scanner input = new Scanner(System.in);
    System.out.print("Enter label name:");
    return new Label(input.nextLine());
};
```

A button builder can be written that generates a `Button` component whose name is provided by the user.

```
Builder<Button> buttonBuilder = () -> {
    Scanner input = new Scanner(System.in);
    System.out.print("Enter button name:");
    return new Button(input.nextLine());
};
```

The build method of these builders can then be called to add components to the layout.

```
VBox box = new VBox();
box.getChildren().addAll(labelBuilder.build(),
                         buttonBuilder.build());
```

The complete program is shown as follows. If the user enters "label1" and "button1" when prompted, then a label entitled "label1" appears above a button entitled "button1" on the GUI.

Listing 15-2. TestBuilder.java

```
import javafx.application.Application;
import javafx.scene.Scene;
import javafx.scene.control.*;
import javafx.scene.layout.*;
import javafx.stage.Stage;
import javafx.util.Builder;
import java.util.Scanner;
```

```java
public class TestBuilder extends Application
{
    @Override
    public void start(Stage primaryStage)
    {
        Builder<Label> labelBuilder = () -> {
            Scanner input = new Scanner(System.in);
            System.out.print("Enter label name:");
            return new Label(input.nextLine());
        };

        Builder<Button> buttonBuilder = () -> {
            Scanner input = new Scanner(System.in);
            System.out.print("Enter button name:");
            return new Button(input.nextLine());
        };

        VBox box = new VBox();
        box.getChildren().addAll(labelBuilder.build(),
                                buttonBuilder.build());
        StackPane root = new StackPane();
        root.getChildren().add(box);

        Scene scene = new Scene(root, 250, 100);

        primaryStage.setTitle("Test Builder");
        primaryStage.setScene(scene);
        primaryStage.show();
    }

    public static void main(String[] args)
    {
        launch(args);
    }
}
```

Figure 15-2. GUI for TestBuilder.java

Section 15.3: JavaFX Builder Factories

Factories that generate JavaFX builders can be written using the BuilderFactory
functional interface. Its functional method getBuilder accepts the class of the
component to be built.

```
@FunctionalInterface
public interface BuilderFactory
{
    Builder<?> getBuilder(Class<?> type);
}
```

In the following example, the getBuilder method uses a BuilderFactory to
retrieve the Builder corresponding to the component passed by name to the method.
It determines the class of the component, or null if the component is not supported.

```
Builder<?> getBuilder(String className)
{
    Class c = null;
    if (className.equals("Label"))
        c = new Label().getClass();
    if (className.equals("Button"))
        c = new Button().getClass();
```

The BuilderFactory then returns the Builder corresponding to the class of the component, or null if the component is not supported.

```
BuilderFactory factory = x -> {
    if (x == Label.class)
        return labelBuilder;
    else if (x == Button.class)
        return buttonBuilder;
    return null;
};

return factory.getBuilder(c);
}
```

The complete program is shown as follows. The user is prompted to select a component or enter "Quit" when finished. If the Builder returned by the BuilderFactory is non-null, it is used to generate a component which is added to the list field. The finished list is converted to an array which is added to the VBox.

Listing 15-3. TestBuilderFactory.java

```
import javafx.application.Application;
import javafx.scene.*;
import javafx.scene.control.*;
import javafx.scene.layout.*;
import javafx.stage.Stage;
import javafx.util.*;
import java.util.*;

public class TestBuilderFactory extends Application
{
    ArrayList<Node> list;
    Builder<?> getBuilder(String className)
    {
        Builder<Label> labelBuilder = () -> {
            Scanner input = new Scanner(System.in);
            System.out.print("Enter label name:");
            return new Label(input.nextLine());
        };
```

```
        Builder<Button> buttonBuilder = () -> {
            Scanner input = new Scanner(System.in);
            System.out.print("Enter button name:");
            return new Button(input.nextLine());
        };

        Class c = null;
        if (className.equals("Label"))
            c = new Label().getClass();
        if (className.equals("Button"))
            c = new Button().getClass();

        BuilderFactory factory = x -> {
            if (x == Label.class)
                return labelBuilder;
            else if (x == Button.class)
                return buttonBuilder;
            return null;
        };

        return factory.getBuilder(c);
    }

    void addComponent(String name)
    {
        Builder<?> builder = getBuilder(name);
        if (builder != null)
            list.add((Node)builder.build());
    }

    @Override
    public void start(Stage primaryStage)
    {
        list = new ArrayList<>();
        VBox box = new VBox();
```

```
        Scanner keyboard = new Scanner(System.in);
        String name = "";
        while (!name.equals("Quit"))
        {
            System.out.print(
                "Enter component name(Enter Quit when finished):");
            name = keyboard.nextLine();
            if (!name.equals("Quit"))
                addComponent(name);
        }

        Node[] nodes = new Node[list.size()];
        list.toArray(nodes);
        box.getChildren().addAll(nodes);

        StackPane root = new StackPane();
        root.getChildren().add(box);

        Scene scene = new Scene(root, 250, 100);

        primaryStage.setTitle("Test Builder");
        primaryStage.setScene(scene);
        primaryStage.show();
    }

    public static void main(String[] args) {
        launch(args);
    }
}
```

The program is demonstrated as follows. A layout containing a label named "label1" and a button named "button1" directly beneath it is generated. Since the builder factory does not support checkboxes, no corresponding component is generated.

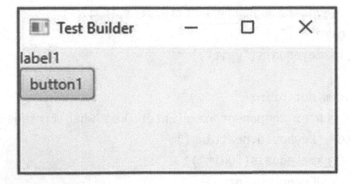

Figure 15-3. *GUI for TestBuilderFactory.java*

PROGRAM OUTPUT (user input shown in **BOLD**):

```
Enter component name(Enter Quit when finished): Label
Enter label name: label1
Enter component name(Enter Quit when finished): Button
Enter button name: button1
Enter component name(Enter Quit when finished): CheckBox
Enter component name(Enter Quit when finished): Quit
```

Section 15.4: Monitoring Changes in Collections

It is possible to create observable collections in JavaFX. Then listeners can be attached which are invoked when the collections change.

Section 15.4.1: Monitoring List Changes

JavaFX provides functional interface ListChangeListener which is used to monitor changes in an observable list. Its functional method onChanged accepts a reference to a ListChangeListener.Change object, which is generated when the list changes.

Nested class `ListChangeListener.Change` has many useful methods. Those that are demonstrated in this section are listed as follows.

Table 15-1. *Some Useful ListChangeListener.Change Methods*

next()	Retrieves the next change to the observable list
wasAdded()	Returns true when an element is added to the observable list
wasRemoved()	Returns true when an element is removed to the observable list
wasReplaced()	Returns true when the value in an element in an observable list is replaced by another value
getAddedSubList()	Returns the elements that were just added to an observable list
getRemoved()	Returns the elements that were just removed from an observable list
getFrom()	Returns the index of the first element that was changed in an observable list
getTo()	Returns the index of the last element that was changed in an observable list
getList()	Returns the observable list

In the following example, the static `observableArrayList` method of the `FXCollections` class creates an empty `ObservableList<String>` object. A `ListChangeListener` is then defined which loops through each change to the observable list and then prints notifications if the list was added to, removed from, or an element was replaced. The list is displayed after all the changes have been processed. The listener is then registered with `ObservableList` `list` in order to monitor changes to the list.

```
ObservableList<String> list = FXCollections.observableArrayList();

ListChangeListener listener = x -> {
    while (x.next())
    {
        System.out.print("list event from " + x.getFrom()
                    + " TO " + x.getTo() + ":");
        if (x.wasAdded())
        {
```

```
            System.out.print(" ADD " + x.getAddedSubList());
        }
        if (x.wasRemoved())
        {
            System.out.print(" RMV " + x.getRemoved());
        }
        if (x.wasReplaced())
        {
            System.out.print(" RPL from " + x.getFrom()
                            + " TO " + x.getTo());
        }
    }

    System.out.println("\nNew list:");
    x.getList().forEach( y -> System.out.println(y));
};

list.addListener(listener);
```

The list is used to back TextFields value and index and Buttons add and rmv.
When the user clicks the add button, value is added to the end of the list if index is equal
to the size of the list. If index is less than the size of the list, value replaces the element
at index. If index is greater than the size of the list, the request is ignored. When the user
clicks the rmv button, the element at index is removed from the list if index is less than
the size of the list. If index is greater than or equal to the size of the list, the request is
ignored.

This logic is performed with two implementations of EventHander<ActionEvent>,
which are registered using the Button class's setOnAction method. Whenever an event
handler changed the list, the ListChangeListener is triggered.

```
TextField value = new TextField();
TextField index = new TextField();
Button add = new Button("add");
Button rmv = new Button("remove");

add.setOnAction(x -> {
    int i = Integer.parseInt(index.getText());
    if (list.size() == i)
```

```
            list.add(value.getText());
        else if (list.size() > i)
            list.set(i,value.getText());
});

rmv.setOnAction(x -> {
    int i = Integer.parseInt(index.getText());
    if (list.size() > i)
        list.remove(i);
});
```

The complete program is shown as follows.

Listing 15-4. TestListChangeListener.java

```
import javafx.application.Application;
import javafx.collections.*;
import javafx.event.*;
import javafx.scene.Scene;
import javafx.scene.control.*;
import javafx.scene.layout.*;
import javafx.stage.Stage;

public class TestListChangeListener extends Application {

    @Override
    public void start(Stage primaryStage)
    {
        ObservableList<String> list
            = FXCollections.observableArrayList();
        ListChangeListener listener = x -> {
            while (x.next())
            {
                System.out.print("list event from " + x.getFrom()
                            + " TO " + x.getTo() + ":");
                if (x.wasAdded())
                {
                    System.out.print(" ADD " + x.getAddedSubList());
```

```
            }
            if (x.wasRemoved())
            {
                System.out.print(" RMV " + x.getRemoved());
            }
            if (x.wasReplaced())
            {                                      .
                System.out.print(" RPL from " + x.getFrom()
                             + " TO " + x.getTo());
            }
        }
        System.out.println("\nNew list:");
        x.getList().forEach( y -> System.out.println(y));
    };
    list.addListener(listener);

    TextField value = new TextField();
    TextField index = new TextField();
    Button add = new Button("add");
    Button rmv = new Button("remove");
    add.setOnAction(x -> {
        int i = Integer.parseInt(index.getText());
        if (list.size() == i)
            list.add(value.getText());
        else if (list.size() > i)
            list.set(i,value.getText());
    });

    rmv.setOnAction(x -> {
        int i = Integer.parseInt(index.getText;
        if (list.size() > i)
            list.remove(i);
    });

    HBox hBox = new HBox();
    hBox.getChildren().addAll(value, index, add, rmv);
```

```
        StackPane root = new StackPane();
        root.getChildren().add(hBox);
        Scene scene = new Scene(root);

        primaryStage.setTitle("List Change Listener");
        primaryStage.setScene(scene);
        primaryStage.show();
    }

    public static void main(String[] args) {
        launch(args);
    }
}
```

The program is demonstrated as follows. When "RED" is added at index 0, the
ListChangeListener is triggered and wasAdded returns true. When "GREEN" is added
at index 1, the ListChangeListener is triggered and wasAdded returns true. When
"BLUE" is added at index 0, the ListChangeListener is triggered and wasAdded,
wasRemoved, and wasReplaced return true. When "BLUE" is removed from index 0, the
ListChangeListener is triggered and wasRemoved returns true.

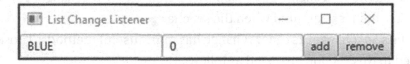

Figure 15-4. *GUI for TestListChangeListener.java*

PROGRAM OUTPUT (events shown in **BOLD** and parentheses):

(type RED in value TextField)
(type 0 in index TextField)
(press add)
list event from 0 TO 1: ADD [RED]
New list:
RED
(type GREEN in value TextField)
(type 1 in index TextField)
(press add)

361

```
list event from 1 TO 2: ADD [GREEN]
New list:
RED
GREEN
```
(type BLUE in value TextField)
(type 0 in index TextField)
(press add)
```
list event from 0 TO 1: ADD [BLUE] RMV [RED] RPL from 0 TO 1
New list:
BLUE
GREEN
```
(press rmv)
```
list event from 0 TO 0: RMV [BLUE]
New list:
GREEN
```

Section 15.4.2: Monitoring Set Changes

Functional interface SetChangeListener is used to monitor changes in an observable set. Its functional method onChanged accepts a reference to a SetChangeListener. Change object, which is generated when the set changes.

Nested class SetChangeListener.Change has many useful methods. Those that are demonstrated in this section are listed as follows.

Table 15-2. *Useful SetChangeListener.Change Methods*

wasAdded()	Returns true when an element is added to the observable set
wasRemoved()	Returns true when an element is removed to the observable set
getElementAdded()	Returns the element that was just added to the observable set
getElementRemoved()	Returns the element that was just removed from the observable set
getSet()	Returns the observable set

In the following example, the static observableSet method of the FXCollections class creates an empty ObservableSet<String> object. A SetChangeListener is then defined which prints notifications if the set was added to or removed from. The set is displayed after all the changes have been processed. The listener is then registered with ObservableSet set in order to monitor changes to the set.

```
set = FXCollections.observableSet();

SetChangeListener listener = x -> {
    System.out.print("set event:");
    if (x.wasAdded())
    {
        System.out.print(" ADD " + x.getElementAdded());
    }
    if (x.wasRemoved())
    {
        System.out.print(" RMV " + x.getElementRemoved());
    }
    System.out.println("\nNew set:");
    x.getSet().forEach( y -> System.out.println(y));
};
set.addListener(listener);
```

The set backs TextField element and Buttons add and rmv. Since sets are unordered, TextField index is not provided. When the user clicks the add button, element is added to the set if it doesn't already exist. If element already exists, the request is ignored. When the user clicks the rmv button, the element is removed if it exists. If index doesn't exist, the request is ignored.

This logic is performed with event handlers which are registered using the Button class's setOnAction method. Whenever an event handler changed the set, the SetChangeListener is triggered.

```
TextField element = new TextField();
Button add = new Button("add");
Button rmv = new Button("remove");

add.setOnAction(x -> set.add(element.getText()));
rmv.setOnAction(x -> set.remove(element.getText()));
```

The complete program is shown as follows.

Listing 15-5. TestSetChangeListener.java

```java
import javafx.application.Application;
import javafx.collections.*;
import javafx.event.*;
import javafx.scene.Scene;
import javafx.scene.control.*;
import javafx.scene.layout.*;
import javafx.stage.Stage;

public class TestSetChangeListener extends Application {
    ObservableSet<String> set;
    @Override
    public void start(Stage primaryStage)
    {
        set = FXCollections.observableSet();
        SetChangeListener listener = x -> {
            System.out.print("set event:");
            if (x.wasAdded())
            {
                System.out.print(" ADD " + x.getElementAdded());
            }
            if (x.wasRemoved())
            {
                System.out.print(" RMV " + x.getElementRemoved());
            }
            System.out.println("\nNew set:");
            x.getSet().forEach( y -> System.out.println(y));
        };
        set.addListener(listener);

        TextField element = new TextField();
        Button add = new Button("add");
        Button rmv = new Button("remove");
```

```
        add.setOnAction(x -> set.add(element.getText()));
        rmv.setOnAction(x -> set.remove(element.getText()));

        HBox hBox = new HBox();
        hBox.getChildren().addAll(element, add, rmv);

        StackPane root = new StackPane();
        root.getChildren().add(hBox);

        Scene scene = new Scene(root);

        primaryStage.setTitle("Test Set Change Listener");
        primaryStage.setScene(scene);
        primaryStage.show();
    }

    public static void main(String[] args) {
        launch(args);
    }
}
```

The program is demonstrated as follows. When "RED" is added, the SetChangeListener is triggered and wasAdded returns true. When the add button is pressed again, nothing happens because "RED" is already in the set. When the "GREEN" is added at index 1, the SetChangeListener is triggered and wasAdded returns true. When "RED" is removed, the SetChangeListener is triggered and wasRemoved returns true.

Figure 15-5. *GUI for TestSetChangeListener.java*

PROGRAM OUTPUT (events shown in **BOLD** and parentheses):

(type RED in element TextField)
(press add)
set event: ADD RED
New set:
RED

(type RED in element TextField)
(type GREEN in element TextField)
(press add)
set event: ADD GREEN
New set:
RED
GREEN
(type RED in element TextField)
(press remove)
set event: RMV RED
New set:
GREEN

Section 15.4.3: Monitoring Map Changes

Functional interface MapChangeListener monitors changes in an observable map. Its functional method onChanged accepts a reference to a MapChangeListener.Change object, which is generated when the map changes.

Nested class MapChangeListener.Change has many useful methods. Those that are demonstrated in this section are listed as follows.

Table 15-3. *Useful MapChangeListener.Change Methods*

wasAdded()	Returns true when an element is added to the observable list
wasRemoved()	Returns true when an element is removed to the observable list
getKey()	Returns the key of the map entry that was changed
getValueAdded()	Returns the value that was just added to an observable map
getValueRemoved()	Returns the value that was just removed from an observable map
getMap()	Returns the observable map

In the following example, the static observableHashMap method of the FXCollections class creates an empty ObservableMap<String, Integer> object. A MapChangeListener is then defined which prints notifications if the map was added to or removed from. The map is displayed after all the changes have been processed. The listener is then registered with ObservableMap map in order to monitor changes to the map.

```
map = FXCollections.observableHashMap();

MapChangeListener listener = x -> {
    System.out.print("map event:");
    if (x.wasAdded())
    {
        System.out.print(" ADD " + x.getKey() + ","
                        + x.getValueAdded());
    }
    if (x.wasRemoved())
    {
        System.out.print(" RMV " + x.getKey() + ","
                        + x.getValueRemoved());
    }
    System.out.println("\nNew map:");
    x.getMap().forEach( (y,z) -> System.out.println(y + "," + z));
};

map.addListener(listener);
```

The map is used to back TextFields key and value. Instead of buttons, the text in key and value is processed when the user hits Enter while the cursor is positioned in value. This results in a call to the map's put method with value and key. Whenever an event handler changed the map, the MapChangeListener is triggered.

```
TextField key   = new TextField();
TextField value = new TextField();

value.setOnAction(x ->
    map.put(key.getText(),Integer.parseInt(value.getText())));
```

The complete program is shown as follows.

Listing 15-6. TestMapChangeListener.java

```java
import javafx.application.Application;
import javafx.collections.*;
import javafx.event.*;
import javafx.scene.Scene;
import javafx.scene.control.*;
import javafx.scene.layout.*;
import javafx.stage.Stage;

public class TestMapChangeListener extends Application {
    int count = 0;
    ObservableMap<String,Integer> map;

    @Override
    public void start(Stage primaryStage)
    {
        map = FXCollections.observableHashMap();
        MapChangeListener listener = x -> {
            System.out.print("map event:");
            if (x.wasAdded())
            {
                System.out.print(" ADD " + x.getKey() + ","
                                + x.getValueAdded());
            }
            if (x.wasRemoved())
            {
                System.out.print(" RMV " + x.getKey() + ","
                                + x.getValueRemoved());
            }
            System.out.println("\nNew map:");
            x.getMap().forEach( (y,z) -> System.out.println(y + ","
                                                + z));
        };
        map.addListener(listener);
```

```
    TextField key   = new TextField();
    TextField value = new TextField();

    value.setOnAction(x ->
        map.put(key.getText(),Integer.parseInt(value.getText())));

    HBox hBox = new HBox();
    hBox.getChildren().addAll(key, value);

    StackPane root = new StackPane();
    root.getChildren().add(hBox);

    Scene scene = new Scene(root);


    primaryStage.setTitle("Test Map Change Listener");
    primaryStage.setScene(scene);
    primaryStage.show();
    }

    public static void main(String[] args) {
        launch(args);
    }
}
```

The program is demonstrated as follows. When RED, 1 is entered, the
MapChangeListener is triggered and wasAdded returns true. If RED, 1 is entered again,
nothing happens, because the map has not changed. When GREEN, 2 is entered, the
MapChangeListener is triggered and wasAdded returns true. When RED, 1 is entered, the
ListChangeListener is triggered and both wasAdded and wasRemoved return true.

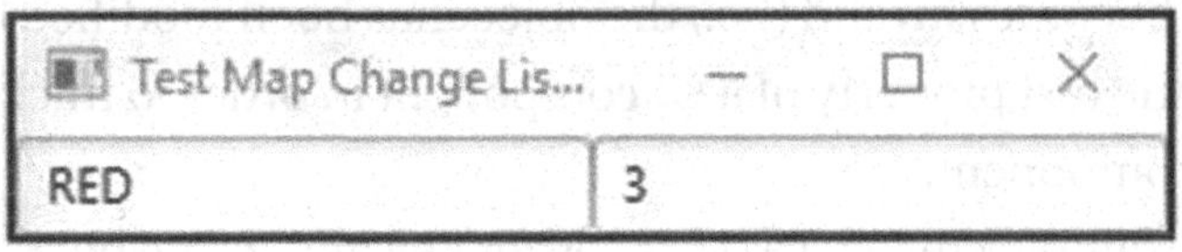

Figure 15-6. *GUI for TestMapChangeListener.java*

PROGRAM OUTPUT (events shown in **BOLD** and parentheses):

(type RED in key TextField)
(type 1 in value TextField)
(hit Enter)
map event: ADD RED,1
New map:
RED,1
(hit Enter)
(type GREEN in key TextField)
(type 2 in value TextField)
(hit Enter)
map event: ADD GREEN,2
New map:
RED,1
GREEN,2
(type RED in key TextField)
(type 3 in value TextField)
(hit Enter)
map event: ADD RED,3 RMV RED,1
New map:
RED,3
GREEN,2

Section 15.5: Invalidating an Observable Object

JavaFX provides functional interface InvalidationListener that is invoked when an Observable object becomes invalid (i.e., the object has been modified). The listener can be registered with the text property of a UI component in order to track when the user interacts with the component.

The following example creates TextFields for key and value backed by an ObservableMap. A MapChangeListener prints the map whenever it changes.

```
map = FXCollections.observableHashMap();
TextField key = new TextField();
TextField value = new TextField();
```

```
MapChangeListener listener = x -> {
    x.getMap().forEach( (y,z) -> System.out.println(y + "," + z));
};
map.addListener(listener);
```

The functional method of InvalidationListener accepts the Observable object that was invalidated. The program can check if key corresponds to an entry in the map, and put value if so. This will trigger the MapChangeListener if the map has changed.

```
InvalidationListener inv = x -> {
    String text = key.getText();
    if (map.containsKey(text))
    {
        int oldValue = map.get(text);
        map.put(text,Integer.parseInt(value.getText()));
        System.out.println("REPLACE " + text + "," + oldValue
                            + " with " + text + "," + value.getText());
    }
};
```

If the InvalidationListener is registered with the text property of the key TextField, the listener will be triggered whenever the user enters text. An event handler is also needed in the value TextField to put new entries into the map.

```
key.textProperty().addListener(inv);
value.setOnAction(x ->
    map.put(key.getText(),Integer.parseInt(value.getText()))
);
```

The complete program is shown as follows.

Listing 15-7. TestInvalidation.java

```
import javafx.application.Application;
import javafx.collections.*;
import javafx.event.*;
import javafx.scene.Scene;
import javafx.scene.control.*;
import javafx.scene.layout.*;
```

371

```
import javafx.stage.Stage;
import javafx.beans.*;
public class TestInvalidation extends Application {
    ObservableMap<String,Integer> map;

    @Override
    public void start(Stage primaryStage)
    {
        map = FXCollections.observableHashMap();
        TextField key = new TextField();
        TextField value = new TextField();
        MapChangeListener listener = x -> {
            x.getMap().forEach( (y,z) -> System.out.println(y + ","
                                                        + z));
        };
        map.addListener(listener);

        InvalidationListener inv = x -> {
            String text = key.getText();
            if (map.containsKey(text))
            {
                int oldValue = map.get(text);
                map.put(text,Integer.parseInt(value.getText()));
                System.out.println("REPLACE " + text + "," + oldValue
                            + " with " + text + ","
                            + value.getText());
            }
        };

        key.textProperty().addListener(inv);
        value.setOnAction(x ->
            map.put(key.getText(),Integer.parseInt(value.getText()))
        );

        HBox hBox = new HBox();
        hBox.getChildren().addAll(key, value);

        StackPane root = new StackPane();
```

```
        root.getChildren().add(hBox);

        Scene scene = new Scene(root);

        primaryStage.setTitle("Invalidation");
        primaryStage.setScene(scene);
        primaryStage.show();
    }

    public static void main(String[] args) {
        launch(args);
    }
}
```

The program is demonstrated as follows. When RED,1 is entered, the EventHandler puts the entry into the map and the MapChangeListener displays "RED,1". When backspace is hit in the key TextField, nothing happens because "RE" does not correspond to any entries in the map. When we type "D" in the key TextField, the InvalidationListener puts "RED,2" in the map and the MapChangeListener displays "RED,2".

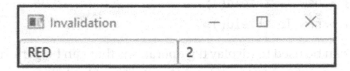

Figure 15-7. *GUI for TestInvalidation.java*

PROGRAM OUTPUT (events shown in **BOLD** and parentheses):

(type RED in key TextField)
(type 1 in value TextField)
(hit Enter)
RED,1
(hit backspace in value TextField)
(type 2 in value TextField)
(hit backspace in key TextField)
(type D in key TextField)
RED,2
REPLACE RED,1 with RED,2

PROJECT 15: DMV GUI

Problem Statement

Add a JavaFX GUI to the Department of Motor Vehicles program from Chapter 9.

Solution

Four combinations of text fields and labels can be used to prompt the user for input. Since program should initially prompt the user to add a driver, the labels should initially display license id, year, month, and day.

```
Label label1 = new Label("licenseId:");
Label label2 = new Label("Year:       ");
Label label3 = new Label("Month:     ");
Label label4 = new Label("Day:        ");

TextField text1 = new TextField();
TextField text2 = new TextField();
TextField text3 = new TextField();
TextField text4 = new TextField();
```

A choice box can be used to display the operations that can be performed on a license. The first choice, "Add Driver", should be displayed initially.

```
ChoiceBox box = new ChoiceBox();
box.getItems().addAll("Add Driver",
                      "Remove Driver",
                      "Change Insurance",
                      "Suspend License",
                      "Renew License",
                      "Add Vehicle",
                      "Remove Vehicle",
                      "Quit");
box.getSelectionModel().selectFirst();
```

Label/TextField combination 1 will always be used to input license id. The data input using the other three combinations will vary based on the selected operation. An event handler can be registered with the choice box that generates the correct text for

374

labels 2 through 4 for each selection. The handler should also clear text fields 2 through 4 and shuts down the application when the user selects "Quit".

```
box.setOnAction( x -> {
    text2.setText("");
    text3.setText("");
    text4.setText("");
    switch (box.getSelectionModel().getSelectedIndex())
    {
        case 0:
        case 4: label2.setText("Year:   ");
                label3.setText("Month: ");
                label4.setText("Day:    ");
                break;
        case 1:
        case 3: label2.setText("              ");
                label3.setText("              ");
                label4.setText("              ");
                break;
        case 2: label2.setText("Insurance:");
                label3.setText("              ");
                label4.setText("              ");
                break;
        case 5:
        case 6: label2.setText("Make:     ");
                label3.setText("Model:    ");
                label4.setText("Year:     ");
                break;
        default: Platform.exit();
    }
});
```

The expDate and vehicle suppliers from Chapter 9 can be rewritten to retrieve input values from the text fields.

```
Supplier<LocalDate> expDate = () -> {
    int year = Integer.parseInt(text2.getText());
    Month month = Month.valueOf(text3.getText());
```

375

```
        int day = Integer.parseInt(text4.getText());
        return LocalDate.of(year, month, day);
};

Supplier<Vehicle> vehicle = () -> {
        String make = text2.getText();
        String model = text3.getText();
        int year = Integer.parseInt(text4.getText());
        return new Vehicle(make, model, year);
};
```

An ObservableMap can be used to store the data input in the text fields. The MapChangeListener from the example in Section 4.c can be used to show the user that the operation was processed successfully.

```
d = FXCollections.observableHashMap();

MapChangeListener listener = x -> {
        System.out.print("map event:");
        if (x.wasAdded())
        {
                System.out.print(" ADD " + x.getKey() + ","
                                + x.getValueAdded());
        }
        if (x.wasRemoved())
        {
                System.out.print(" RMV " + x.getKey() + ","
                                + x.getValueRemoved());
        }
        System.out.println("\nNew map:");
        x.getMap().forEach( (y,z) -> System.out.println(y + "," + z));
};
d.addListener(listener);
```

Since the HashMap which backs the ObservableMap implements the merge and computeIfPresent methods, the switch statement from the Chapter 9 solution can be modified to work with the GUI. The switch statement should be placed inside the event handler of a button. When the handler modifies the map, its change listener is triggered and output is displayed.

376

```java
Button submit = new Button("submit");
submit.setOnAction( x -> {
    switch (box.getSelectionModel().getSelectedIndex())
    {
        case 0: // Add Driver
                BiFunction<License,License,License> addDriver
                    = (ov,nv) -> ov;
                d.merge(text1.getText(),
                        new License(expDate.get(), null),
                        addDriver);
                break;

        case 1: // Remove Driver
                BiFunction<String,License,License> remove
                    = (k,v) -> null;
                d.computeIfPresent(text1.getText(),remove);
                break;

        case 2: // Change Insurance
                BiFunction<License,License,License> changeInsurance
                    = (ov,nv) -> new License(ov.expDate, nv.insurance,
                                             ov.status, ov.vehicles);
                d.merge(text1.getText(),
                        new License(null, text2.getText()),
                        changeInsurance);
                break;

        case 3: // Suspend License
                BiFunction<String,License,License> suspend
                    = (k,v) -> new License(v.expDate, v.insurance,
                                           STATUS.SUSPENDED,
                                           v.vehicles);
                d.computeIfPresent(text1.getText(),suspend);
                break;

        case 4: // Renew License
                BiFunction<License,License,License> renew
```

```
                  = (ov,nv) -> new License(nv.expDate, ov.insurance,
                                           STATUS.ACTIVE,
                                           ov.vehicles);
            d.merge(text1.getText(),
                    new License(expDate.get(), null),
                    renew);
            break;

      case 5: // Add Vehicle
            BiFunction<License,License,License> addVehicle
                = (ov,nv) -> {
                    License temp = new License(ov);
                    temp.vehicles.add(nv.vehicles.get(0));
                    return temp;
            };
            d.merge(text1.getText(),
                    new License(null, null,vehicle.get()),
                    addVehicle);
            break;

      case 6: // Remove Vehicle
            BiFunction<License,License,License> removeVehicle
                = (ov,nv) -> {
                    License temp = new License(ov);
                    Vehicle r = nv.vehicles.get(0);
                    temp.vehicles.removeIf(z ->
                                    z.make.equals(r.make)
                                && z.model.equals(r.model)
                                && z.year == r.year);
                    return temp;
            };
            d.merge(text1.getText(),
                    new License(null, null,vehicle.get()),
                    removeVehicle);
    }
});
```

The complete program is shown as follows.

Listing 15-8. DMVGUI.java

```java
import javafx.application.*;
import javafx.scene.Scene;
import javafx.stage.Stage;
import javafx.scene.layout.*;
import javafx.scene.control.*;
import java.util.function.*;
import java.util.*;
import java.time.*;
import javafx.collections.*;
enum STATUS {ACTIVE, SUSPENDED}
class Vehicle
{
    String make;
    String model;
    int year;
    public Vehicle(String ma, String mo, int y)
    {
        make = ma;
        model = mo;
        year = y;
    }
    public String toString()
    {
        return year + " " + make + " " + model;
    }
}
class License
{
    LocalDate expDate;
    String insurance;
    STATUS status;
    ArrayList<Vehicle> vehicles;
```

```java
    public License(LocalDate e, String i, Vehicle... v)
    {
        expDate = e;
        insurance = i;
        status = STATUS.ACTIVE;
        vehicles = new ArrayList<>();
        for (Vehicle r : v)
            vehicles.add(r);
    }
    public License(LocalDate e, String i, STATUS s,
                   ArrayList<Vehicle> vs)
    {
        expDate = e;
        insurance = i;
        status = s;
        vehicles = new ArrayList<>(vs);
    }
    public License(License l)
    {
        expDate = l.expDate;
        insurance = l.insurance;
        status = l.status;
        vehicles = new ArrayList<>(l.vehicles);
    }
    public String toString()
    {
        return expDate + " " + insurance + " " + status + " "
            + vehicles;
    }
}
public class DMVGUI extends Application {
    ObservableMap<String,License> d;

    @Override
    public void start(Stage primaryStage) {
```

```
d = FXCollections.observableHashMap();
MapChangeListener listener = x -> {
    System.out.print("map event:");
    if (x.wasAdded())
    {
        System.out.print(" ADD " + x.getKey() + ","
                        + x.getValueAdded());
    }
    if (x.wasRemoved())
    {
        System.out.print(" RMV " + x.getKey() + ","
                        + x.getValueRemoved());
    }
    System.out.println("\nNew map:");
    x.getMap().forEach( (y,z) -> System.out.println(y + ","
                                + z));
};
d.addListener(listener);

GridPane gridPane = new GridPane();

Label label1 = new Label("licenseId:");
Label label2 = new Label("Year: ");
Label label3 = new Label("Month: ");
Label label4 = new Label("Day: ");

TextField text1 = new TextField();
TextField text2 = new TextField();
TextField text3 = new TextField();
TextField text4 = new TextField();

ChoiceBox box = new ChoiceBox();
box.getItems().addAll("Add Driver",
                      "Remove Driver",
                      "Change Insurance",
                      "Suspend License",
                      "Renew License",
```

```
                        "Add Vehicle",
                        "Remove Vehicle",
                        "Quit");
    box.getSelectionModel().selectFirst();
    box.setOnAction( x -> {
        text2.setText("");
        text3.setText("");
        text4.setText("");
        switch (box.getSelectionModel().getSelectedIndex())
        {
            case 0:
            case 4: label2.setText("Year:       ");
                    label3.setText("Month:      ");
                    label4.setText("Day:        ");
                    break;
            case 1:
            case 3: label2.setText("            ");
                    label3.setText("            ");
                    label4.setText("            ");
                    break;
            case 2: label2.setText("Insurance:");
                    label3.setText("            ");
                    label4.setText("            ");
                    break;
            case 5:
            case 6: label2.setText("Make:       ");
                    label3.setText("Model:      ");
                    label4.setText("Year:       ");
                    break;
            default: Platform.exit();
        }
    });

    Supplier<LocalDate> expDate = () -> {
        int year = Integer.parseInt(text2.getText());
        Month month = Month.valueOf(text3.getText());
```

```java
    int day = Integer.parseInt(text4.getText());
    return LocalDate.of(year, month, day);
};

Supplier<Vehicle> vehicle = () -> {
    String make = text2.getText();
    String model = text3.getText();
    int year = Integer.parseInt(text4.getText());
    return new Vehicle(make, model, year);
};

Button submit = new Button("submit");
submit.setOnAction( x -> {
    switch (box.getSelectionModel().getSelectedIndex())
    {
        case 0: // Add Driver
                BiFunction<License,License,License>
                    addDriver = (ov,nv) -> ov;
                d.merge(text1.getText(),
                    new License(expDate.get(), null),
                    addDriver);
                break;

        case 1: // Remove Driver
                BiFunction<String,License,License>
                    remove = (k,v) -> null;
                d.computeIfPresent(text1.getText(),remove);
                break;

        case 2: // Change Insurance
                BiFunction<License,License,License>
                  changeInsurance = (ov,nv) ->
                    new License(ov.expDate, nv.insurance,
                            ov.status, ov.vehicles);
                d.merge(text1.getText(),
                        new License(null, text2.getText()),
                        changeInsurance);
                break;
```

```
case 3: // Suspend License
        BiFunction<String,License,License>
          suspend = (k,v) ->
          new License(v.expDate, v.insurance,
                      STATUS.SUSPENDED, v.vehicles);
        d.computeIfPresent(text1.getText(),suspend);
        break;

case 4: // Renew License
        BiFunction<License,License,License>
          renew = (ov,nv) ->
            new License(nv.expDate, ov.insurance,
                        STATUS.ACTIVE, ov.vehicles);
        d.merge(text1.getText(),
            new License(expDate.get(), null),
            renew);
        break;

case 5: // Add Vehicle
        BiFunction<License,License,License>
          addVehicle = (ov,nv) -> {
            License temp = new License(ov);
            temp.vehicles.add(nv.vehicles.get(0));
            return temp;
        };
        d.merge(text1.getText(),
                new License(null, null,
                            vehicle.get()),
                addVehicle);
        break;

case 6: // Remove Vehicle
        BiFunction<License,License,License>
          removeVehicle = (ov,nv) -> {
            License temp = new License(ov);
            Vehicle r = nv.vehicles.get(0);
```

```java
                        temp.vehicles.removeIf(z ->
                                    z.make.equals(r.make)
                            && z.model.equals(r.model)
                            && z.year == r.year);
                    return temp;
                };

                d.merge(text1.getText(),
                        new License(null,
                                    null,vehicle.get()),
                        removeVehicle);
            }
        });

        gridPane.add(label1,0,0);
        gridPane.add(text1 ,1,0);
        gridPane.add(label2,0,1);
        gridPane.add(text2 ,1,1);
        gridPane.add(label3,0,2);
        gridPane.add(text3 ,1,2);
        gridPane.add(label4,0,3);
        gridPane.add(text4 ,1,3);
        gridPane.add(box ,1,4);
        gridPane.add(submit,1,5);

        Scene scene = new Scene(gridPane, 300, 250);

        primaryStage.setTitle("DMV");
        primaryStage.setScene(scene);
        primaryStage.show();
    }

    public static void main(String[] args) {
        launch(args);
    }
}
```

The program is demonstrated as follows. When driver 123 with expiration date May 7, 2022, is added, an add to map event is triggered and the new entry is displayed. When driver 123's insurance policy is changed to INS22, add to map and remove from map events are triggered and the new map entry containing the insurance policy is displayed. When the driver's privilege is suspended, add to map and remove from map events are triggered and the new map entry showing the SUSPENDED status is displayed. When driver 123's license is renewed, add to map and remove from map events are triggered and the new map entry showing the ACTIVE status and expiration date June 11, 2022, is displayed. When a 2017 Honda Accord is added to the driver's license, add to map and remove from map events are triggered and the new map entry showing the Accord is displayed. When the Accord is removed from the license, add to map and remove from map events are triggered and the new map entry with no vehicles is displayed. When driver 123 is removed from the database, a remove from map event is triggered and the map is now empty. The user then quits, and the program terminates.

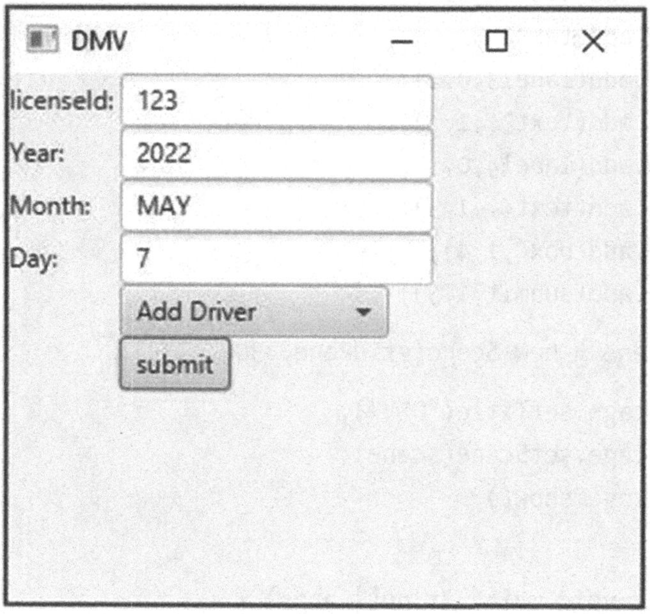

Figure 15-8. *GUI for DMVGUI.java*

PROGRAM OUTPUT (events shown in **BOLD** and parentheses):

(type "123" in textfield labeled "licenseId:")
(type "2022" in textfield labeled "Year:")
(type "MAY" in textfield labeled "Month:")
(type "7" in textfield labeled "Month:")
(press submit button)
map event: ADD 123,2022-05-07 null ACTIVE []
New map:
123,2022-05-07 null ACTIVE []
(select Change Insurance)
(type "INS22"in textfield labeled "Insurance:")
(press submit button)
map event: ADD 123,2022-05-07 INS22 ACTIVE [] RMV 123,2022-05-07 null ACTIVE []
New map:
123,2022-05-07 INS22 ACTIVE []
(select Suspend License)
(press submit button)
map event: ADD 123,2022-05-07 INS22 SUSPENDED [] RMV 123,2022-05-07 INS22
ACTIVE []
New map:
123,2022-05-07 INS22 SUSPENDED []
(select Renew License)
(type "2022" in textfield labeled "Year:")
(type "JUNE" in textfield labeled "Month:")
(type "11" in textfield labeled "Month:")
(press submit button)
map event: ADD 123,2022-06-11 INS22 ACTIVE [] RMV 123,2022-05-07 INS22 SUSPENDED []
New map:
123,2022-06-11 INS22 ACTIVE []
(select Add Vehicle)
(type "Honda" in textfield labeled "Make:")
(type "Accord" in textfield labeled "Model:")
(type "2017" in textfield labeled "Year:")
(press submit button)

map event: ADD 123,2022-06-11 INS22 ACTIVE [2017 Honda Accord] RMV
123,2022-06-11 INS22
ACTIVE []
New map:
123,2022-06-11 INS22 ACTIVE [2017 Honda Accord]
(select Remove Vehicle)
(type "Honda" in textfield labeled "Make:")
(type "Accord" in textfield labeled "Model:")
(type "2017" in textfield labeled "Year:")
(press submit button)
map event: ADD 123,2022-06-11 INS22 ACTIVE [] RMV 123,2022-06-11 INS22
ACTIVE [2017 Honda Accord]
New map:
123,2022-06-11 INS22 ACTIVE []
(select Remove Driver)
(press submit button)
map event: RMV 123,2022-06-11 INS22 ACTIVE []
New map:
(select Quit)

Short Problems

1) Write a JavaFX builder factory that prompts the user to enter the
   name of a text field. The factory will generate the text field and a
   label displaying the name of the text field. The label and the text
   field should be displayed on the same row with the label on the
   left and the text field on the right. Allow the user to enter names
   for various text fields until he or she enters "Quit".

   Demonstrate and display in a JavaFX GUI program.

2) Back the text fields in the program you wrote for problem 1 with an observable list of String objects. The program should write a message to the display whenever an element in the list is added, removed, or replaced. The message should describe the contents of the modification and on which element in the list the modification was performed.

3) Write a JavaFX program with a text field named `index` and a second text field named `value`. The text fields are backed by an observable list of Integer objects. The observable list's listener prints list modifications to the display. The `value` text field's listener is responsible for adding new entries to the list. Attach an invalidation listener to the text property of the `index` text field. When the index of an existing list entry is typed in the `index` text field, the invalidation listener will update the corresponding entry in the list and write a message to the display indicating the change that was made.

Long Problems

1) It's tax time, again! Write a program with a JavaFX GUI with the following text fields and a label for each field:

   – Wages

   – Taxable refunds

   – Adjusted gross income (wages + taxable refunds)

   – Deductions

   – Taxable income (adjusted gross income – deductions)

   – Tax due (taxable income * 0.20)

   – Tax withheld

   – Refund (tax withheld – tax due)

Back the text fields with an observable list so that all calculations update when the user enters data in the wages, taxable refunds, deductions, or tax withheld text fields.

2)   Write a JavaFX GUI for the poker game from homework problem
     1 in Chapter 9. The player is initially dealt five random cards,
     whose face values occupy the first column in five rows of text
     fields and whose suites occupy the second column. Include a
     remove button to the right of each suite. If the player clicks a
     remove button, the corresponding card is replaced with another
     card drawn at random and the row of text fields is updated. The
     player can replace any three cards. After the third card has been
     replaced, the hand is evaluated, and if it contains a straight, a
     flush, or a full house, the player wins. Otherwise, the dealer wins.
     The winner is displayed in a text field beneath the other five rows.

3)   Write a program with a JavaFX GUI that uses an observable map
     to maintain a customer database with fields for name, address,
     telephone number, and email. The GUI also has insert, select,
     update, and delete buttons. When the insert button is pressed,
     the program attempts to add an entry with the name field value
     as its key to the map. When the select button is pressed, then the
     program looks up the entry whose key matches the name field,
     and the program populates the other fields. When the update
     button is pressed, the program updates the record using the
     data in the text fields. When the delete button is pressed, the
     corresponding entry is removed from the database.

APPENDIX

Method References

In Java 8, method references were introduced. They are an alternative to lambda expressions as a means to represent functional interfaces. Method references offer a simple syntax, but usually at the cost of defining an additional method.

Section A.1: Using References to Static Methods to Represent Functional Interfaces

A method reference is created by specifying the name of the class in which the method exists followed by "::" followed by the name of the method. The name of the method is not followed by parentheses. The basic form for a reference to a static method is as follows:

```
ClassName::methodName
```

In Section 2 of Chapter 3, a `Predicate<Integer>` was represented using the lambda expression x -> x > 7. This was used to verify that the number 9 was greater than 7.

```
Predicate<Integer> p1 = x -> x > 7;
if (p1.test(9))
    System.out.println("Predicate x > 7 is true for x==9.");
```

OUTPUT:

```
Predicate x > 7 is true for x==9.
```

Recall that the `Predicate<T>` functional interface has functional method `test` which evaluates a condition using argument T and returns `true` if the condition is true. A static method that takes an argument of type T and returns a `boolean` can be written. Method `myTest` in class `PredicateMR` as follows performs the greater than 7 test.

391

© Ralph Lecessi 2019
R. Lecessi, *Functional Interfaces in Java*, https://doi.org/10.1007/978-1-4842-4278-0

```
public class PredicateMR
{
    public static boolean myTest(Integer x)
       { return (x > 7)? true : false; }
    ...
}
```

A Predicate<Integer> can then be represented by a reference to method myTest.

```
Predicate<Integer> p2 = PredicateMR::myTest;
```

A call to Predicate p2's test method will then invoke the myTest method.

```
if (p2.test(9))
    System.out.println("Predicate x > 7 is true for x==9.");
```

The complete program is shown and demonstrated as follows. It verifies that 9 is greater than 7 using predicates represented by both a lambda expression and a method reference.

Listing A-1. PredicateMR.java

```
import java.util.function.Predicate;
public class PredicateMR
{
    public static boolean myTest(Integer x)
        { return (x > 7)? true : false; }

    public static void main(String[] args)
    {
        Predicate<Integer> p1 = x -> x > 7;
        if (p1.test(9))
            System.out.println("Predicate x > 7 is true for x==9.");

        Predicate<Integer> p2 = PredicateMR::myTest;
        if (p2.test(9))
            System.out.println("Predicate x > 7 is true " +
                               "for x==9.") ;
    }
}
```

PROGRAM OUTPUT:

```
Predicate x > 7 is true for x==9.
Predicate x > 7 is true for x==9.
```

Section A.2: References to Instance Methods

The program in Listing A-1 contains a reference to a static method. The inline lambda expressions provided in the chapter portion of this book are consistent with static methods, since no objects are created for the lambdas.

A reference to an instance method of a particular object can be created by specifying a reference to the object followed by "::" followed by the instance method name. The basic form for a reference to an instance method is as follows:

```
InstanceReference::methodName
```

The program in Listing A-2 defines classes P1 and P2, both of which provide instance methods with the same signature as Predicate.test. The main method creates instances of P1 and P2. Predicate pred1 is represented by method reference p1::greaterThan7. Predicate pred2 is represented by method reference p2::isOdd. When the test method of Predicate p1 is invoked, the greaterThan7 method of the P1 object is executed, resulting in true. When the test method of Predicate p2 is invoked, the isOdd method of the P2 object is executed, resulting in false.

Listing A-2. TestInstanceMethodReference.java

```java
import java.util.function.Predicate;
class P1
{
    public boolean greaterThan7(Integer x)
        { return (x > 7)? true : false; }
}
class P2
{
    public boolean isOdd(Integer x)
        { return (x%2==1)? true : false; }
}
```

```
class TestInstanceMethodReference
{
    public static void main(String[] args)
    {
        P1 p1 = new P1();
        P2 p2 = new P2();
        Predicate<Integer> pred1 = p1::greaterThan7;
        Predicate<Integer> pred2 = p2::isOdd;
        System.out.println(pred1.test(8));
        System.out.println(pred2.test(8));
    }
}
```

PROGRAM OUTPUT:

```
true
false
```

Section A.3: References to Constructors

A reference to the constructor method of a class is created by specifying the class name
followed by "::" followed by new. Note that a constructor reference can only be used
to call the class's no-argument constructor. Constructor references are often used to
represent suppliers, which are responsible for generating objects.

The program in Listing A-3 defines class X which counts the number of its instances.
The main method uses a reference to the X class's no-argument constructor to represent
Supplier getX. The get method of the supplier is then called ten times, and ten X
objects are created.

Listing A-3. TestConstructorReference.java

```
import java.util.function.Supplier;
class X
{
    static int count=0;
    public X() { count++;}
    @Override public String toString() { return "" + count; }
}
```

```
public class TestConstructorReference
{
    public static void main(String[] args)
    {
        Supplier<X> getX = X::new;
        X x = null;
        for (int i = 0; i < 10; i++)
            x = getX.get();
        System.out.println(x) ;
    }
}
```

PROGRAM OUTPUT:

10

Section A.4: Passing Method References as Arguments

A method reference can be passed to a method parameter whose type is a functional interface.

The program in Listing 3-2 contained a method named `result` that defined `Predicate<Integer>` and `Integer` parameters. The method called the `test` method of the predicate using the `Integer` and printed a message indicating true or false.

This program can be rewritten using method references by defining method `myTest` to represent the predicate and then passing in as the first argument to the `result` method using a method reference.

Listing A-4. PredicateMethodsMR.java

```
import java.util.function.*;
class PredicateMethodsMR
{
    public static boolean myTest(Integer x)
        { return (x > 7)? true : false; }
```

```java
    public static void result(Predicate<Integer> p, Integer arg)
    {
        if (p.test(arg))
            System.out.println("The Predicate is true for " + arg);
        else
            System.out.println("The Predicate is false for " + arg);
    }
    public static void main(String[] args)
    {
        result(PredicateMethodsMR::myTest,5);
    }
}
```

PROGRAM OUTPUT:

```
The Predicate is false for 5
```

The `PredicateHelper` class in Listing 3-3 defined the static `result` method that used a generic predicate to test a value. The `TestPredicateHelper` program from Listing 3-4 which demonstrates it can be rewritten using method references. Overloaded versions of method `myTest` are defined to host the logic previously contained in lambda expressions. The compiler is able to invoke the correct version of `myTest` based on the type of the second argument to the `result` method. In the first call, the integer literal 6 causes `myTest(Integer)` to be invoked. In the second call, the string literal "Hello" causes `myTest(String)` to be invoked.

Listing A-5. TestPredicateHelperMR.java

```java
class TestPredicateHelperMR
{
    public static boolean myTest(Integer x)
    {
        return (x > 2)? true : false;
    }
    public static boolean myTest(String s)
    {
        return (s.charAt(0) == 'H')? true : false;
    }
```

```
    public static void main(String[] args)
    {
        result(TestPredicateHelperMR::myTest, 6);
        result(TestPredicateHelperMR::myTest, "Hello");
    }
}
```

PROGRAM OUTPUT:

```
The Predicate is true for 6
The Predicate is true for Hello
```

Section A.5: Representing Functions with Method References

Method references can represent functional interfaces whenever a method matches the signature of the functional method, and the method can be called without modification of its inputs. If any such special processing is needed, such as the input needs to be multiplied by a scale factor before being passed to the method, then lambda expressions must be used. If a method that matches the needed functionality exists, then it is convenient to use method references.

Functions can be represented by method references if a simple mapping from one type to another is all that is required. Furthermore, many methods that perform mappings have already been defined by the wrapper classes in the java.lang package and elsewhere in the Java API.

The NumberParser program from Listing 4-2 can be rewritten by replacing the lambda expressions with references to the parse methods of the numeric wrapper classes.

Listing A-6. NumberParserMR.java

```
import java.util.function.Function;
import java.util.ArrayList;
class NumberParserMR
```

```java
{
    private static <R extends Number> R parse(String x,
                                              Function<String, R> f)
    {
        return f.apply(x);
    }
    public static void main(String[] args)
    {
        ArrayList< Function<String,? extends Number> > list
            = new ArrayList<>();
        list.add(Byte::parseByte);
        list.add(Short::parseShort);
        list.add(Integer::parseInt);
        list.add(Long::parseLong);
        list.add(Float::parseFloat);
        list.add(Double::parseDouble);

        String[] numbers = {"10", "20", "30", "40", "50", "60"};
        Number[] results = new Number[numbers.length];

        for (int i=0; i < numbers.length; ++i)
        {
            results[i] = parse(numbers[i], list.get(i));
            System.out.println(results[i]);
        }
    }
}
```

PROGRAM OUTPUT:

```
10
20
30
40
50.0
60.0
```

Section A.6: Using Method References with Comparators

The static comparing method of the Comparator<T> interface uses a Function as a key extractor. If the key extraction is a simple mapping accomplished by a method, a method reference can be used.

Adding accessor methods to the Student class from Listing 10-1 creates several mapping methods.

Listing A-7. Student.java

```
class Student
{
    String name;
    Integer id;
    Double gpa;
    public Student(String n, int i, double g)
    {
        name = n;
        id   = i;
        gpa  = g;
    }
    @Override
    public String toString() { return name + " " + id + " " + gpa; }

    public String getName()  { return name; }
    public Integer getId()   { return id;   }
    public Double getGpa()   { return gpa;  }
}
```

A method reference to each of these methods can be used to create a difference comparator.

```
Comparator<Student> byName = Comparator.comparing(Student::getName);
Comparator<Student> byId   = Comparator.comparing(Student::getId);
Comparator<Student> byGpa  = Comparator.comparing(Student::getGpa);
```

399

Students can then be compared by name, id, or GPA. Note that the by GPA comparison outputs 1 since 3.82 is greater than 3.76 as specified by the `compareTo` method of the `Double` class. If 0.06 is the desired result, then a lambda expression which performs the subtraction must be used.

```
Student s1 = new Student("Larry", 1000, 3.82);
Student s2 = new Student("Libby", 1001, 3.76);

System.out.println(byName.compare(s1,s2));
System.out.println(byId.compare(s1,s2));
System.out.println(byGpa.compare(s1,s2));
```

OUTPUT:

```
-8
-1
1
```

Section A.7: Using Method References with Streams

Method references are frequently used with streams. The `Stream` class's `map` and `flatmap` methods accept mapping functions which can usually be represented using method references. Suppose an accessor for the `students` field were added to class `Class` from Section 7 of Chapter 12.

```
class Class
{
    String subject;
    Collection<Student> students;
    public Class(String su, Student... st)
    {
        subject = su;
        students = Arrays.asList(st);
    }
    Collection<Student> getStudents() { return students; }
}
```

The second example in Section 7 of Chapter 12 can be rewritten using method references. A reference to the getStudents method maps each element of type Class in the stream to a list of students.

```
Stream.of(
    new Class("Biology",
        new Student("Joe" ,1001,3.81),
        new Student("Mary",1002,3.91)),
    new Class("Physics",
        new Student("Kalpana",1003,3.61),
        new Student("Javier" ,1004,3.71))) // Stream<Class>
        .map(Class::getStudents)           // Stream<List<Student>>
        .forEach(x -> System.out.println(x));
    }
}
```

OUTPUT:

```
[Joe 1001 3.81, Mary 1002 3.91]
[Kalpana 1003 3.61, Javier 1004 3.71]
```

The Stream class's collect method accepts methods to create and accumulate stream elements. These methods are often already available in the element, so method references are common.

The StringBuilder example from Section 9 in Chapter 12 can be rewritten to utilize method references. The supplier, combiner, and finishers are simply references to the StringBuilder class's new, append, and toString methods, respectively. A reference to the StringBuilder class's constructor (StringBuilder::new) is used as the supplier, since the supplier is responsible for generating a StringBuilder object. Since the accumulator does more than simply call the StringBuilder's append method, a lambda expression must be used.

```
BiConsumer<StringBuilder,String> accs = (x,y) ->
  x.append(y.replaceAll("[aeiou]",""));

String s = Stream.of("Joe","Kalpana","Christopher")
                .collect(Collector.of(
                            StringBuilder::new,
```

```
                        accs,
                        StringBuilder::append,
                        StringBuilder::toString));
    System.out.println(s);
```

OUTPUT:

JKlpnChrstphr

Since the Collectors class's groupingBy and mapping methods accept functions, these arguments are frequently represented by method references. Suppose accessors were added to the Car class from Section 9a in Chapter 12.

```java
class Car
{
    String manu;
    String model;
    int mpg;
    public Car(String ma, String mo, int mp)
    {
        manu = ma;
        model = mo;
        mpg = mp;
    }
    public String toString()
    {
        return manu + " " + model + " gets " + mpg + " mpg";
    }
    public String getManu()  { return manu; }
    public String getModel() { return model; }
    public int    getMpg()   { return mpg; }
}
```

The following example uses a reference to the Car class's getManu method to group cars by manufacturer. A reference to the Car class's getMpg method is then used to extract a car's mpg, which is then collected into a list of integers.

```
Stream.of(new Car("Buick" ,"Regal" ,25),
        new Car("Hyundai","Elantra",27),
        new Car("Buick" ,"Skylark",26),
        new Car("Hyundai","Accent" ,30))
    .collect(Collectors.groupingBy(
        Car::getManu,
        Collectors.mapping(Car::getMpg,
                            Collectors.toList())))
    .forEach( (x,y) ->
            System.out.println(x + ": " +y ));
```

OUTPUT:

```
Buick: [25, 26]
Hyundai: [27, 30]
```

Index

A

ActionListener interface, 40
AllOf.java, 307–308
andThen method, 73, 97, 111, 118, 121
applyAsDouble method, 97, 101
ArrayIndexOutOfBounds exception, 37
Array populate, 182–183
ArraySpliterator .java, 162–164
AtomicBoolean class, 338
Atomic calculations
    accumulating value, 332
    atomicInteger class, 330, 331
    bank account, project, 341–345
    comparing value, 334–335
    problems, 345–346
    Unsafe.java program, 329–330
    update variable, 333
AtomicIntegerArray class, 338
AtomicInteger class, comparing value,
    334–336
AtomicLong class, 337
AtomicLongArray class, 338
AtomicReference class, 339–340

B

BankTransactions.java, 122–127
BiConsumer functional interface, 114–115
BiFunction, 78, 84, 184

BinaryOperator interface, 98–99
BiPredicate interface, 59
BuilderFactory functional interface, 352

C

Calculator.java, 103–106
Car.java, 151–152
Chained filter methods, 261
collectingAndThen method, 271
Collection object
    motor vehicle department, 191–197
    remove elements, 181
Comparator chain components,
    specializations, 221–222
Comparator comparing methods, 212–216
Comparator comparing methods,
    specializations, 217–218
Comparator interface, 209–210
Comparator methods, 211–212
Comparators
    BinaryOperators, 228–229
    building chains, 218–221
    map interface, 227–228
    sort Java arrays, 224–226
    sort lists, 222–224
compareTo method, 213
comparingInt method, 217
Comparing objects, real estate broker,
    229–239

© Ralph Lecessi 2019
R. Lecessi, *Functional Interfaces in Java*, https://doi.org/10.1007/978-1-4842-4278-0

U, V, W, X, Y, Z

Printed in the United States
By Bookmasters